刘浩然 著

中国公办与民办学校教师专业身份认同比较研究

A Comparative Study of Teachers' Professional Identities in State and Private Primary Schools in China

厦门大学出版社 国家一级出版社
全国百佳图书出版单位

图书在版编目（CIP）数据

中国公办与民办学校教师专业身份认同比较研究 ＝ A Comparative Study of Teachers' Professional Identities in State and Private Primary Schools in China：英文 / 刘浩然著． -- 厦门：厦门大学出版社，2024.5
　　ISBN 978-7-5615-9343-1

　　Ⅰ．①中… Ⅱ．①刘… Ⅲ．①教师-师资培养-研究-中国 Ⅳ．①G525.1

　　中国国家版本馆CIP数据核字(2024)第067740号

责任编辑	王扬帆
责任校对	白　虹
美术编辑	蒋卓群
技术编辑	许克华

出版发行	厦门大学出版社
社　　址	厦门市软件园二期望海路39号
邮政编码	361008
总　　机	0592-2181111　0592-2181406(传真)
营销中心	0592-2184458　0592-2181365
网　　址	http：//www.xmupress.com
邮　　箱	xmup@xmupress.com
印　　刷	厦门市明亮彩印有限公司

开本　720 mm×1 020 mm　1/16
印张　16
插页　3
字数　368 千字
版次　2024 年 5 月第 1 版
印次　2024 年 5 月第 1 次印刷
定价　79.00 元

本书如有印装质量问题请直接寄承印厂调换

厦门大学出版社
微信二维码

厦门大学出版社
微博二维码

Preface

Teachers' professional identities (TPIs) need to be considered as crucial to link teachers' personal experiences with the social and professional changes needed for improved learning and developmental skills in schools. In the context of China's social transformation and educational reform, private schools have become increasingly popular among parents who seek educational opportunities for their children to improve their developments and life chances. The private sector has grown significantly with five times increase in numbers of students enrolled in private primary schools between 1996 to 2003 (Shanghai Education Science Research Institute, 2004: 3). Despite policy changes, the Chinese government began to improve its regulations on establishing private schools by providing policy support for non-profit private schools, prohibiting profit-led private schools and controlling foreign entities that provide China's nine-year compulsory education (Ministry of Justice of the People's Republic of China, 2018). Against this background, a growing number of college graduates and qualified teachers work in the non-state sectors[①]. Due to the limited knowledge of the nature and diversity of private schools, evidences of the roles and impacts of private schools in developing countries remain insufficient (Ashley et al., 2014). Similarly, teachers'

[①] In this study, I use the term "non-state", which applies generally to providers across the formal and informal education, for-profit and non-profit providers. Otherwise, I will specify the particular type of providers the study relates to (private international schools, charity schools, private tutoring institutes, etc.).

learning and professional experiences in private schools have been a long-neglected topic in the field of teacher education and professionalism.

In this research project, I aim to compare the ways teachers construct their identities to strategically negotiate the meaning of their work in both private and state schools in Nanqi (a pseudonym) County in China. I began this research project with a broad view of identity as a process through which a person understands his or her values, relationship with the world and possibilities for the future. I gradually develop the research aims by comparing the ways state school teachers and private school teachers draw on multiple personal, professional and cultural resources in forming their narratives to provide the distinctive and common features of their educational values and experiences. In particular, I focus on the notion of teachers' agency—their strategic capacity to question and negotiate dominant discourses in teaching.

A constructivist perspective had guided the choice of a qualitative approach to inquiry in this study. From February to August 2016, I visited four schools (two state schools and two private) to conduct interviews with 16 teachers and 4 school managers in Nanqi. Employing the research strategy of narrative inquiry and comparative analysis in the tradition of grounded theory, I suggested a two-dimensional matrix that demonstrates the common features among the 16 participant teachers and identified different types and orientations of teachers' identities and commonalities across teacher cases in four different state and private schools in this research context: (1) transcendence; (2) determination; (3) enhancement; and (4) control. This research study found fewer differences in teachers' narratives between the four school cases; there were more differences among the 16 teachers in interpreting and reacting to changing school contexts in China. Meanwhile, ambiguities, tensions as well as culturally specific references coexisted in TPIs and individual teachers' pursuit of integrity and purpose at work.

This study's unique contributions lie in its innovative design in investigating teachers in both state schools and private schools, and in embedding TPIs in different school contexts in China. The comparative typology from the matrix of TPIs could serve as a means to help teachers further identify, articulate and, if necessary, justify the sense of their professional identities. This study also provides some critical reflections on the issues of language and culture, as well as the researcher's identity in conducting an empirical study to better understand teachers' experiences and the formation of their professional identities in different school contexts in China.

Acknowledgments

I would like to express my deep gratitude to my supervisors, Professor Pam Sammons and Professor Ian Menter, for their enthusiastic encouragement, valuable and constructive guidance, and great care of my well-being during the planning and development of this book.

I would also like to extend my thanks to my colleagues, friends and the staffs from the Department of Education, the Social Science Division, Green Templeton College and Bodleian Library in Oxford University. This research study would not be possible without the participant teachers and principals who shared their experiences, passions, hopes and dreams with me. Their stories, generosity and contributions to this research have been very much appreciated.

My very special thanks to my grandparents, Mrs. Chen Jirong and Mr. Liu Changrong, and my parents, Mrs. Xu Meihua and Mr. Liu Jin. Their unconditional love, patience and encouragements throughout the process had made the journey unforgettable.

Abbreviations

AIS	Ash International School
AS	Aspen School
AST	advanced skill teacher
BA	Bachelor of Arts
BoE	Bureau of Education
BoS	Bureau of Statistics
CoP	community of practice
CPD	continuing professional development
CUREC	Central University Research Ethics Committee
MoE	Ministry of Education in China
MSc	Master of Science
NCR	national curriculum reform
PE	physical education
PST	private school teacher
PTI	Private Tutoring Institute
RCS	Redwood Charity School
RO	research objective
RQ	research question
SST	state school teacher
SPED	Shandong Provincial Education Department
TPI	teachers' professional identity
WS	Willow School

Contents

Chapter 1 Introduction and Research Background ········· 001
  1.1 Origin of This Study ········· 001
  1.2 Research Aims and Objectives ········· 003
  1.3 Research Questions ········· 005

Chapter 2 Primary School Teachers in China: Diversification and Structural Complexity ········· 007
  2.1 Teacher Education and the Global Question on Professional Identity ········· 007
  2.2 The Context of Primary Education and Teacher Education in China ········· 009
  2.3 Ongoing Debate on the "Public" and the "Private" in Education ········· 017
  2.4 The Role of Public and Private Sectors in China's Education System ········· 019
  2.5 The Status Quo of Private School Teachers in China ········· 024

Chapter 3 Literature Review ········· 030
  3.1 Introduction ········· 030
  3.2 Defining Identity ········· 031
  3.3 How Does Professional Identity Affect Teachers' Practices? ········· 042
  3.4 What Develops and Affects TPIs? ········· 043
  3.5 Developing a Conceptual Framework ········· 057

3.6　Summary ·· 061

Chapter 4　Research Design and Methodology ·· 065
4.1　Origin of the Study ·· 065
4.2　RQs and Research Strategy ··· 067
4.3　The Pilot Study ·· 073
4.4　The Sampling Scheme ·· 076
4.5　The Use of Interviews ·· 084
4.6　Data Analysis ·· 086
4.7　Strategies of Comparative Analysis ··· 090
4.8　Ensuring the Rigour and Quality of Qualitative Research ······· 091
4.9　Research Ethics and Limitations ·· 095
4.10　Summary ·· 097

Chapter 5　Characteristics of TPIs in Willow School and Aspen School (State Schools) ·· 098
5.1　Introduction ·· 098
5.2　Introducing Willow School (State School) ··· 100
5.3　Example Teacher Case: Ruolan ·· 106
5.4　Introducing Aspen School ·· 111
5.5　Example Teacher Case: Xinxin ·· 113

Chapter 6　Comparing State School TPIs ·· 120
6.1　Narrative of a Lack of Career Choice ··· 122
6.2　Addressing Challenges to Support Students' Learning ············ 126
6.3　Summary ·· 131

Chapter 7　The Ash International School and the Redwood Charity School (Private Schools) ··· 133
7.1　Introducing the Ash International School (AIS) ················· 133
7.2　Example Teacher Case: Baihe ··· 139

7.3 Introducing the Redwood Charity School (RCS) ········ 144
7.4 Example Teacher Case: Ting ········ 146
7.5 Summary ········ 150

Chapter 8 Comparing Private School TPIs ········ 152
8.1 Narratives of Students' Learning and Development ········ 153
8.2 Narratives of the Curriculum ········ 158
8.3 Narrative of Job Involvement and Professional Image ········ 162
8.4 Narratives of Spirituality and Tangible Satisfaction ········ 168
8.5 Summary ········ 175

Chapter 9 Comparative Analysis: Exploring the Significance of Contexts ········ 177
9.1 The Four Orientations of TPI Narratives ········ 177
9.2 Towards a Typology of Situated TPIs ········ 181
9.3 Summary ········ 205

Chapter 10 Discussion and Conclusion ········ 206
10.1 Teacher Training and Education ········ 206
10.2 Professionalism and Policy Demands ········ 208
10.3 Community and Collaborations ········ 209
10.4 Sense of Vocation and Personal Values ········ 209
10.5 Revisiting the Concepts of "State" Versus "Private" Schools ········ 210
10.6 Reflections on Trustworthiness and Quality in Narrative Studies ········ 211
10.7 Summary of the Contribution to Knowledge, Strengths, Limitations and Recommendations for Further Studies ········ 213

References ········ 215

Chapter 1
Introduction and Research Background

1.1 Origin of This Study

This study seeks to explore the notion of professional identity against the background of recent educational reforms in China. The origin of this research stems from my personal experiences in teaching English to primary school students in a private tutoring school in Shandong province. In this role, I became aware of the significance of teachers in shaping the quality of students' learning. I witnessed teachers' efforts to support student learning. However, private school teachers (PSTs) often perceive themselves as being "outside the state system"[①] and lacking professional status and development due to a significant gap in their career infrastructure, qualifications, rights and welfare benefits, in contrast with those of state school teachers (SSTs) (Figure 1). While an increasing number of parents are paying fees to send their children to private schools for various reasons (e.g., different and more suitable learning environments and educational outcomes), little is known about teachers' experiences and how these may shape their sense of professional identities in private and state schools in China. I believe that policies aimed at improving the quality of education in both private and state schools should take TPIs and their sense of belongingness in both sectors into consideration.

In my earlier research project, *Teaching in the Shadow: An Exploration*

---

① 体制外

into Teachers' Professional Identities in Private Tutoring Institutions in China, my interviews with ten private tutoring school teachers revealed that teachers had developed a "temporary worker" identity and often lacked a sense of belongingness. A metaphor employed by one teacher in the MSc study offered a powerful expression of her uncertainties about the basis of her career in teaching:

> You might love this field from your heart. However, if the base was not set up, it will collapse out of the blue and break into pieces regardless of how fancy it is above the ground. (Xiaoxue, teaching six months, kindergarten English)

Xiaoxue (a pseudonym) was a graduate from a local teacher education institute and a qualified teacher, who had worked in a private tutoring school for six months at the time of the interview. Although the feeling of a lack of belonging in Xiaoxue's story cannot be generalised as a common feature of PSTs' identities from my small-scale MSc study, other research has demonstrated that PSTs often lack a sense of belonging, job security and a stable professional identity (Mei, 2007; Zhou and Tan, 2010). In this supposedly diversified "educational market", where a wide range of formal and informal learning activities take place against the background of a proliferation of educational entrepreneurs and learning technologies and digital tools, (the no longer exists and work union[①] system that kept teaching jobs in one system.) How do teachers know where to work and belong as a profession? How do teachers construct their identities among their different commitments and roles? In this sense, PSTs' experiences as "temporary workers" in China raise essential questions about teachers' identity, agency and resistance within unique social and educational contexts.

My previous study focused on a small number of teachers in one type of private educational/training institute. This larger-scale research project builds on and extends my previous small-scale enquiry through more extensive fieldwork

---

① 单位

and adds a comparative perspective through semi-structured narrative interviews with a larger sample of teachers working in different school contexts. The present study explores teachers' experiences in both private and state primary schools. It seeks not only to provide evidence of the influences of teachers' personal experiences and particular school contexts, but also to illustrate some of the broader social and educational transformations in contemporary Chinese society that may influence the development of TPIs.

1.2 Research Aims and Objectives

The main research aims of this DPhil study are: (1) to explore the processes and factors influencing professional identity construction in different primary school contexts; (2) to compare the characteristics of TPIs across individual and school cases in both state and private schools; and (3) to investigate teachers' strategies to reconcile tensions and uncertainties in these processes. This section further explains these aims and research objectives to facilitate the achievement of these aims:

Research aim 1: To explore how teachers construct their professional identities in different primary schools (two state schools and two private schools).

I argue that individual teachers' identity formation needs to be examined in both state schools and private schools as a part of the development and challenges facing educators in the Chinese society. Therefore, this research approaches teachers as individuals who are capable of actively engaging with dominant discourses as well as of trying to make sense of their personal experiences; as such, the critical analytical considerations lie in exploring teachers' stories within the specific school as well as the broader social and cultural contexts. The following research objectives (RO) seek to facilitate the achievement of this aim.

RO 1: Identifying the perceived factors impacting the changes and development of individual teachers' sense of identity at work.

RO 2: Assessing teachers' perceptions and experiences of their engagements with others in their particular school contexts and how this might influence teachers' professional self-efficacy and sense of belongingness at work.

Research aim 2: To compare the characteristics of TPIs between two state schools and two private schools to identify the shared features and the differences.

Drawing on insights from theories of teacher identities (see Chapter 2 for a literature review), this exploratory study also aims to compare and contrast teachers inside and outside private schools to include insights into teachers' different experiences and responses to changes arising from different school settings. An earlier comparative study demonstrated that it is not possible to fully understand either the private sector or the state sector of education in isolation from each other (Walford, 1989: 5). However, there is still a lack of a research focus on the formation of teachers' identities in private and state schools; this might be due to the highly systematic and structured research designs that focus exclusively on either SSTs or PSTs as the research interest groups. This limitation of previous studies might also be the outcome of restrictions faced by researchers in accessing multiple schools and different groups of teachers. To achieve the second aim in this study, I address the following ROs:

RO 3: Identifying the differences and similarities of school contexts that are relevant to TPIs.

RO 4: Identifying the characteristics of individual TPI constructions and comparing these characteristics within and across four school cases.

Research aim 3: To investigate the strategies that teachers employ to reconcile tensions and uncertainties at work in state and private primary schools in Nanqi.[①]

---

① More information on the geographical and educational situations of Nanqi is given in Chapter 4.

This study views TPIs as a part of the broader processes of human development, which might involve confusions about one's roles, tensions in managing multiple demands and expectations, as well as changes in one's personality. To gain a deeper understanding of the relationship between teachers' agency, career choices and experiences in schools, the investigation into tensions and uncertainties in the changing educational landscape in China is of vital importance. The following ROs seek to facilitate the achievement of this research aim:

RO 5: Identifying the tensions that teachers experienced in constructing their professional identities, and their perceived conditions and strategies to address those tensions.

RO 6: Further recording and theorising teachers' narratives of the processes of reacting to these perceived tensions and uncertainties, which may or may not further influence teachers' sense of their professional identities.

1.3 Research Questions

As outlined earlier, this study investigates the formation and characteristics of TPIs in private and state schools in one county in Shandong province in China. Embedded in the general inquiry are the following specific research questions (RQs):

RQ 1: What characterises teachers' sense of their professional identities in the four different primary schools (two state schools and two private schools) in Nanqi in China?

Sub-question 1: How do teachers within each school construct their professional identities?

Sub-question 2: How do teachers experience and reconcile tensions in their identity construction?

Sub-question 3: What are the other characteristics of TPIs?

RQ 2: What personal and social factors do teachers consider important in shaping their professional identities?

RQ 3: What are the differences and similarities in the TPIs in the two state schools and two private schools in Nanqi?

To achieve the main purpose of the enquiry, I chose to explore the similar and different characteristics of TPIs by using an interpretive approach and by employing in-depth narrative interviews to collect empirical data about 16 individual teachers' narratives in four different school contexts. Thus, the first RQ identifies the characteristics of teachers' work experiences in state and private schools on multiple professional, social and personal levels. The second RQ investigates the perceived factors that influence their sense of self as teachers; it also attempts to explore how individual teachers respond to multiple structural restrictions and opportunities in their professional lives. This question also allows for an exploration of other factors that may shape teachers' experiences beyond the school context. The third question further examines the similarities and differences of TPIs across the two sectors and the four schools to illuminate the role of these contextual features.

Chapter 2
Primary School Teachers in China: Diversification and Structural Complexity

2.1 Teacher Education and the Global Question on Professional Identity

What characterises a good teacher? Many of us have memories of teachers who played crucial roles in our lives; however, defining a good teacher is difficult, and knowing how to support someone to become a good teacher has been a subject of much debate. The shortage of well-trained teachers is a global problem. As the UNESCO Institute for Statistics estimates, there is a need for 69 million teachers to be recruited worldwide to reach the objectives of universal primary and secondary education by 2030. In the Incheon Declaration, UNESCO specifically called for the Member States to "ensure that teachers and educators are empowered, adequately recruited, well-trained, professionally qualified, motivated and supported within well-resourced, efficient and effectively governed systems". Authors worldwide from different academic fields have commented on the changing environment of school education and teachers' professional lives in the context of a globalised world. The American economist Peter F. Drucker (1993) defined the "knowledge society" as a modern society where land, labour and capital are no longer the most important resources; instead, knowledge has become the only meaningful resource. Drucker defined knowledge as the capacity to produce and effectively apply knowledge, which is complex, flexible and unpredictable. As he claimed, the role of school education has shifted from social transformation to the cultivation of lifelong learning by individuals. These ideas have raised a series of questions about the purpose of teaching, teacher-student relationships and the roles of teachers worldwide.

In *Teaching in the Knowledge Society: Education in the Age of Insecurity* (2003), Andy Hargreaves analysed and discussed the challenges of school education, teaching and teachers' professional development, particularly the problem of teachers' identity. He cited Richard Sennett's *The Corrosion of Character* (1998) and pointed to the demanding challenges facing teachers in terms of their personal development and emotions. Sennett (1998) argued that personal characteristics are eroded in the context of neo-capitalism. In the past, according to the author, one's work was often carried out in one workplace alongside other people. One could cultivate positive experiences by engaging with others over a long period. However, it has become increasingly difficult for employees to find lifelong careers in ever-changing societies. Flexible work times and changes to workplaces and jobs have led to alienated and superficial relationships among colleagues. As a result, employees have become anxious and uncertain; individuals lack a sense of security and become depressed and challenged in their personalities. In many countries, researchers have argued that the increasing marketisation of education has brought about complex changes and fostered new relationships in the education sector; as a result, the teaching profession faces new challenges, not just in terms of how it performs its professional role to meet diverse demands, but also fundamental questions about teachers' values and sense of identity (Ball, 1994; Whitty et al., 1998; Mok, 1997; Whitty and Power, 2000). It is particularly important for educational researchers to address the roles of teachers' beliefs and values in interpreting, adapting to and resisting such changes.

Nevertheless, the vagueness of the notion of identity could be a barrier to teachers' professional and personal development (Hargreaves, 2003: 63). Having said that, it is essential to be aware that the formation of TPIs is complex and variable, and open to influences from many sources. For example, the impact of broader changes, including educational policies on the actors involved, may differ considerably as a result of the particular cultural context within which they are situated. Elements such as national education culture, school culture and teacher culture could all play important roles, leading to different interpretations of teachers' work and identities.

2.2 The Context of Primary Education and Teacher Education in China

This section discusses the context in which primary school teachers have worked in the Chinese context over recent years. In this section, I develop the argument that to understand better the development of primary school TPIs, we need to understand the particular social and historical contexts of teachers' work and roles. I first review the historical status of primary school teachers and teacher education in contemporary China. I then identify recent trends and the characteristics of the broader social and cultural contexts of primary education and teacher education in China.

Over the last 40 years, Chinese society has been engaged in a complicated process of development and transformation that has influenced people's daily lives, work and experiences. This process, at the same time, has also created unprecedented challenges, such as environmental degradation, an ageing society and corruption. In 2006, China initiated a 15-year Medium and Long-Term Plan for the Development of Science and Technology (2006-2020). The plan sets out a blueprint to transform the Chinese economy by 2020 into one that will derive 60% of GDP growth from innovation and spend 2.5% of its GDP on research and development. The Chinese government aims to build a knowledge society, one in which its citizens' educational levels and capacity for innovation and enterprises become the key to its social and economic development.

Primary education in China has witnessed significant changes and development over the last 40 years. The 99.8% net enrolment rate for primary school children in 2011 signified the early achievement of the 2015 goal for universal access to primary education in China. The expansion of primary education in China has also had a significant impact on poverty reduction, especially in urban areas (Song, 2012: 105; Lee and Song, 2018:96). However, the disparities in terms of the quality of primary education remain wide between rural and urban areas and across different regions (ibid.). Table 2-1 demonstrates the number of schools, students and teachers in China by educational level. It also showed the average student-teacher ratios at different school levels. The government statistics may have painted a positive and simplified picture of what actually happens in the classroom; as Yang has pointed out, oversized classes are still common in China (Yang, 2014). Moreover, the teaching force remains undersupplied, with high turnover rates, particularly in disadvantaged rural schools in China (An, 2018) and in particular subjects (i.e. physical education, English and the arts).

Table 2-1 Number of schools, students and teachers in China by educational level in 2016

	Schools	Students	Full-time teachers	Student-teacher ratio
Primary education	177,600	99,130,100	5,789,100	17.12:1
Junior secondary education	52,100	43,293,700	3,487,100	12.41:1
Senior secondary education	13,400	23,666,500	1,733,500	13.65:1
Specialised schools	2,080	491,700	53,200	—

Source: MoE, 2017

In 2005, the Ministry of Education (MoE) released *Several Opinions on Further Promoting the Balanced Development of Compulsory Education*[①]. It was the first time the balanced development of compulsory education became the focus of educational reform in China. As the 2006 Compulsory Education Law stated: "The State Council and local people's governments at or above the county level shall rationally allocate educational resources to promote the balanced development of compulsory education", the "balanced development" was

---

① 《教育部关于进一步推进义务教育均衡发展的若干意见》(http://www.moe.gov.cn/srcsite/A06/s3321/200505/t20050525_81809.html)

further promoted as a legal responsibility of the local governments. Offering equal and quality primary education to every child became the new goal of primary schools in China.

Meanwhile, policy makers and educators in China have been reflecting upon the drawbacks of an exam-oriented education and their educational values. The issue of the *Decision on Deepening of Educational Reform and Full Promotion of Quality-oriented Education*[①] in 1999 symbolised the start of the new curriculum reform (Cui and Zhu, 2014). The curriculum reform was expected to transform the school system and "liberate" students from the exam-oriented learning culture. As Cui and Zhu (2014) pointed out, the national curriculum reform (NCR) touched upon the entire education system from educational aims, system, to methods and contents. Guo (2012:90) summarised the six objectives of the Basic Education Curriculum Reform Outline (on trial) promulgated in 2001 as follows:

1. Changing the function of curriculum from knowledge transmission to cultivation of active lifelong learners.
2. Changing from the subject-specific curriculum to an integrated curriculum structure with optional courses to meet students' diverse learning needs.
3. Highlighting the relevance of the curriculum to students' everyday lives.
4. Promoting constructivist learning and changing the rote learning to active learning based on students' overall abilities to process information, acquire knowledge, solve problems and collaborate.
5. Changing the curriculum assessment from its selective purpose to the supportive purpose in improving teaching and learning.
6. Decentralising the curriculum administration and enhancing its relevance to local contexts by joint efforts of the central government, local government and schools.

---

① 《中共中央、国务院关于深化教育改革,全面推进素质教育的决定》(http://old.moe.gov.cn/publicfiles/business/htmlfiles/moe/moe_177/200407/2478.html)[Retrived on 5th. May, 2018]

This approach is very different from previous curriculum reforms, as more choices and space for self-development are encouraged in education. Cultivating students' creative abilities and practical skills have been placed as the core of the reform. The process of implementing NCR, however, has not been smooth. Liu and Kang (2011) have summarised the five distinct stages of the curriculum reform: (1) curriculum ideology and planning (1996-1998); (2) the design, dissemination and experimental phase of the curriculum documents (1999-2001); (3) the compulsory education curriculum pilot and finalisation of the senior high school curriculum program (2001-2004); (4) the finalisation of compulsory educational curriculum, nationwide implementation and the new senior high school curriculum pilot (2004-2007); and (5) reflection, reinterpretation and further implementation (2007-present). Although there was initial resistance among many in the education system, empirical studies have identified a general accepting attitude towards the new curriculum and have described positive changes in local schools (Guan and Meng, 2007; Liu and Kang, 2011). Guan and Meng (2007) reviewed the eight changes in practice:

1. the beginning of the three-level curriculum management mechanism;
2. more flexibility in school management;
3. diverse curriculum structure (e.g., required course, elective course and integrated practice activities);
4. more learning opportunities to improve teachers' competences so they are aligned with the curriculum reform;
5. the gradual adoption of a student-centred approach;
6. the adoption of developmental evaluation to cater to learners' diversity;
7. the broader use of technology in teaching; and
8. the enhancement of skills to help students master more life or work-related skills.

Other scholars found little evidence of change in real classroom practices. For example, Sargent (2011) analysis of videos of demonstration lessons in Nanjing led to their conclusion that forms of student participation remained highly limited. Both progression and barriers in the curriculum reform were identified (Li and Ni, 2011). Despite the different results, both scholars and practitioners advocated that bringing changes to teachers' pedagogical and conceptual understanding and classroom practice would be the key to the successful implementation of the NCR in China. Table 2-2 summarises studies on the impact of curriculum reform on teachers in China. I have included studies in secondary school contexts for their reference value to clarify the broader impact of curriculum reform in the area of compulsory education in China. The literature showed that NCR has brought both professional development opportunities and psychological struggles to teachers at various school levels. These studies have also reported that the curriculum was largely welcomed by teachers, despite their struggles with the structural restrictions and the beliefs in traditional teaching and learning within the Chinese cultural tradition.

Table 2-2 Summary of studies on the impacts of the NCR on teachers in China

Authors	Research design and methods	Study population	Findings/arguments
Zhong (2006)	Reflection on policy implementation		Teachers' "curriculum inertia" as a challenge for changes in subject and teaching materials; the risks of a conflictual way of thinking that leads to misunderstanding and a rejection of the curriculum reform.
Lee et al. (2011)	Survey	1646 teachers from six provinces	Teachers are positive in terms of their receptivity to the reform outcomes, and negative in terms of their participation in the decision-making process. Female teachers felt more empowered and receptive than male teachers.
Sargent (2012)	Classroom observations and in-depth interviews	Teachers in rural primary schools in Gansu province	Rural school teachers who have more familiarity and positive attitudes about the NCR have more "progressive" beliefs about teaching based on the constructivist conception of knowledge. For the "traditional teachers", success in teaching is still measured by content mastery and examination results.

Continued

Authors	Research design and methods	Study population	Findings/arguments
Yin, Lee and Law (2012)	Qualitative case study	Interviews with 18 teachers in Guangzhou province	Teachers' emotional experiences vary according to the different teacher-trainer interactions during the curriculum reform. The mixed feelings could be the result of interplay between professional orientations, power relationships and moral purposes. Teachers tended to have more positive feelings when the trainer was an expert teacher.
Qian and Walker (2013)	In-depth interviews	Principals from three "ordinary"[6] urban schools in Shanghai	Commonalities in principals' teacher development strategies across the three schools included data-informed decision making, adaptations of strategies to school contexts, emphasis on the collaborative culture and the use of action research. Potential issues and gaps included principals' lack of confidence in teachers' capacity and commitment, the top-down manner in implementing teacher development activities, a lack of focus on teachers' creativity and a lack of informal and spontaneous learning opportunities for teachers to become "comprehensive change agents" in the curriculum reform.
Yan (2015)	Interviews	Secondary English teachers from three schools in central China	A gap between the new curriculum and teachers' classroom practices and the interrelated contextual restrictions, which included psychological challenges for teachers, students' resistance, lack of school support, physical constraints and the "backwash effect" of the examination culture in China.
Li and Ni (2012)	Reflections of debates on China's new Basic Education Curriculum Reform and observations of challenges facing teachers in implementing the NCR		Lack of clear guidance in implementation, which led to a formulaic and simplified understanding of the concepts in the curriculum reform. There was also a tendency to adapt a simple "old or new method" divide in teacher appraisal standards. How to cope with the changing contents for teaching and keep a balance between students' inquiry-based learning and teacher guidance became urgent problems for further investigation and improvement.

Continued

Authors	Research design and methods	Study population	Findings/arguments
Fu and Clarke (2018)	Qualitative study (interviews, observations, teachers' reflective journals and associated fieldnotes)	Eight physics teachers in one high school	The collaborative culture and openness in learning the subject of physics contributed to the teachers' sense of safety and mutual support in sharing their thoughts and offering critical feedback to each other. Concrete examples during the collective curriculum development process enabled teachers' sense of agency within their group, which may surpass other factors (i.e. government policies, textbooks and government-run professional development programmes) in empowering teachers due to the consistency of these interactions in a local educational structure.

It is worth noting that there have been active attempts to improve teachers' competency and professional development to facilitate the process of educational reform in China. In terms of formal teacher education, China has three major types of teacher training institution: (1) secondary teachers' schools; (2) normal colleges; and (3) normal universities. Other institutions, such as comprehensive universities, have been permitted to run teacher training courses. The Teacher Qualification Certificate is open for individuals to apply for without a teacher education degree. In terms of teachers' on-the-job training, studies have identified the emphasis on subject matter knowledge and professional communities as the merits of teacher education programmes that benefited students' academic achievement in international tests (Han and Paine, 2010; Paine and Ma, 1993). At the same time, reviews and empirical studies have found other enduring issues in teacher education programmes and professional development in China (Gu, 2006; Zhou, 2014). One of the criticisms is the lack of evidence about the effectiveness of connecting educational theories with classroom practices (Zhou, 2014).

Formal in-service teacher education in China is mostly focusing on implementation of the NCR. The government has adopted the cascade approach[①] to teachers' professional development (Zhou, 2014). However, empirical studies have revealed problems in the top-down mandated training for in-service teachers (Feng, 2003; Zhu, 2005; Lai, 2010). Listening to government policy analysis and experts' speeches on theories of the NCR are the main activities in these formal training. Teachers, however, found it difficult to understand and implement these separate and abstract ideas in their classroom teaching (Zhu, 2005). Some of the teachers also felt that their expertise was ignored in the experts' discourses (Zhou, 2014).

In addition, schools have been allowed to adopt more innovative approaches (i.e., school networks, peer support and teachers' reflective writing) to tackle problems in the structures and processes of the educational reform. Educators, school leaders and scholars have been encouraged to take advantage of university-school collaborations, lesson study-based action research, school visits, adoption of digital technology and private-public partnerships to support teachers' reflection and professional development. Chinese culture holds teachers in high regard. Teachers enjoy occupational prestige and society is considered highly accountable for students' learning. In a comparative study that set out to investigate the perceived qualities of effective teachers in China and the United States, Yin and Lee (2012) found that teachers' ethics constitute the shared standard for effective teaching among different stakeholders (teacher, students and parents). The teachers also considered that teachers' professional skills and professional development were the other two elements of being an effective teacher. In addition to these three aspects, parents' high expectations of students' academic achievement constituted another important evaluative standard for good teachers in China. While the standard for effective Chinese teachers shared similarities with those identified in Western

---

[①] A cascade model of professional development presents a particular way of promoting the professional knowledge by passing from originators of the programme to local trainers and then to the target teachers. Despite its cost efficiency in bringing large-scale changes, this approach is believed to have the risks of distortion and dilution of knowledge in the process (Soloman and Tresman, 1999; Kennedy, 2005).

countries, the authors argued that differences in cultures and educational systems could diversify the conditions and influencing factors (Yin and Lee, 2012). Gu's investigation of the perceptions and experiences of a cross-cultural professional development programme among Chinese English-as-a-Foreign-Language (EFL) teachers and British teacher educators has also revealed the significant differences in attitudes and perceived changes in teachers' professional knowledge (Gu, 2007). Several lines of evidence have suggested that the system of teaching and the cultural roles of teachers, rather than individual teachers' beliefs and behaviours, are the underlying basis of differences between countries in students' academic performances (Hiebert et al., 2005; LeTendre et al., 2001). To date, the development of primary school teachers' sense of identity in the contexts of major education reform and cultural influences has still not yet been carefully investigated in China.

2.3 Ongoing Debate on the "Public" and the "Private" in Education

Education has been considered a public good (i.e., a good to be provided by the state) in global public policy at least since 1945 (Daviet, 2016: 1-2). However, such claims are called into question when we witness the increasing involvement of non-state actors in education (Daviet, 2016). The fact is that private contributions—from civil societies, the business sectors and families—have long been relevant to the public education system. The distinction between the public and the private is not always clear. One the one hand, there is a general understanding of the private sector as any educational organisations and activities that are apart from the state. On the other hand, the discipline of economics tends to contrast the "state" with the "market" in determining the role and comparative efficacy of the private and public sectors in education. The situation is even more complicated in the context of the emerging global knowledge economy, where education is considered a private good for individual competitiveness as well as a public good that provides national rather than the global benefits (Robertson et al., 2012).

While the claimed merit of private schools is that they offer parents greater "choices", there is an increasing concern that private schools undermine social cohesion and threaten equality. Not all parents can afford private schooling, and this can create a two-tier system in features such as class size and education resources. Those who oppose private schools argue that private actors have no reason to consider its impact on the broader educational landscape, including issues such as social stratification. The concern is particularly severe when private schools' selection of the top performers seems to have left only average or struggling students in public or state schools. Besides, more school autonomy may not guarantee that private schools will base their teaching on core social values.

Figure 2-1 presents the distribution of state-funded, hybrid (or private) school and special schools in the United Kingdom, the United States of America, the Chinese Mainland and Singapore. This figure was generated from government data sources to present up-to-date comparative scales of state-funded and private/hybrid schools in these four places. As it is demonstrated in the chart, although the number of private schools in China (focused on Chinese Mainland) (16,076 private schools) exceeds the United Kington and Singapore in the three other countries, its proportion remains the smallest in the education system in comparison with that in the other three countries.

In their discussion on the rise of public-private partnerships in education, Robertson et al. (2012:3) pointed out that the definition of "public education" (and perhaps private education) is still in dispute at various levels of national and international policies and negotiations. For instance, although the World Bank has considered countries such as Canada and the Netherlands as benefiting from large state-aided private education systems, the OECD (Organization for Economic Co-operation and Development, OECD) has reported that these countries have close-to-100% enrolment in public (or state) schools (2010). The distinction between the public and the private, therefore, is not fixed. Instead, the public-private distinction evolves in specific exchange relationships of particular social and cultural contexts and is therefore deserving careful investigations and interrogation (Robertson et al., 2012).

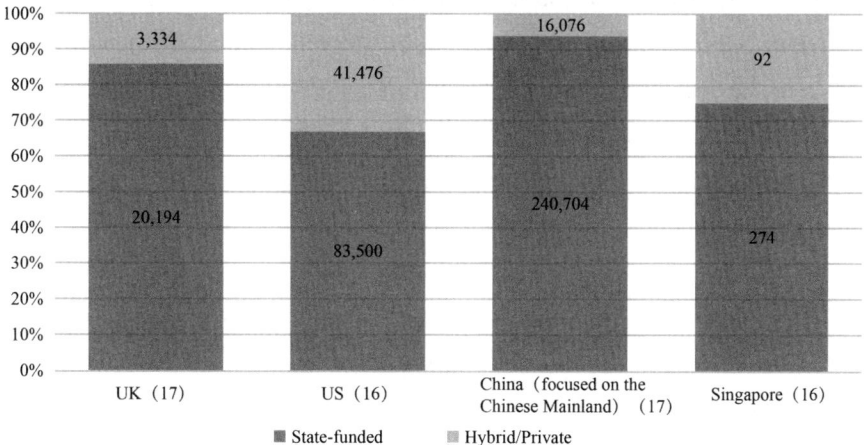

Figure 2-1 Distribution of state-funded, hybrid/private schools and special schools in four countries (2016-2017)

* (16) indicates data collected in 2016; (17) indicates data collected in 2017.

* Sources:

https://nces.ed.gov/surveys

http://www.moe.edu.cn

https://www.gov.uk/government/statistics

https://www.moe.gov.sg

2.4 The Role of Public and Private Sectors in China's Education System

State schools remain the primary provider of formal schooling in the Chinese Mainland. The finance and delivery of formal learning in Chinese schools, however, come from both state and private sectors. Government spending on education has grown, yet it represents less than 5% of GDP. The numbers of private schools are limited in China, but parents' demands for and expenditure on educational resources are significant. The widespread use of private tutors has become a substitute method for formal private schools. Despite the policy changes, the Chinese government has been slowly relaxing restrictions on private and foreign investment in education.

Private education has played an important role throughout Chinese history since the Spring-Autumn period (Chunqiu Shidai, 770-476 BC). The development of the private sector is a reflection of changing Chinese society. During the era under Chairman Mao, all for-profit enterprises were officially forbidden due to restrictions on capitalist entrepreneurship. Private organisations were called "minban (people-run)/private unions" and those private schools were funded by individuals, households and local communities in villages and rural mountainous areas; they were mostly closed down or integrated into state schools in towns until the reform era began in 1978. Private education—from short-term supplementary classes organised in schools and colleges to prepare students for the College Entrance Examination to specialised vocational skill tests—re-emerged in the 1980s.

When China's economic growth became the top priority for the country's development in 1992, private schools experienced a long period of expansion (Chan and Wang, 2009; Yan and Lin, 2004; Wang, 2013). The devolution of financial responsibility from central to local governments has brought about complex institutional changes and fostered new relationships between the public and private sectors (Chan and Wang, 2009; Cheng, 1994). Local governments in China take increasingly proactive roles in improving the provision of educational services and encourage investments from enterprises and individuals alike. Following the 1993 Outline for Education Reform and Development in China, the government recognised the legal status of private schools and specified the regulations for private school establishment and management. Different forms of private involvement in education were encouraged, and schools with various financial and management forms were created (Yan and Lin, 2004).

Under state ownership, state schools are allowed to convert to state-owned-and-people-managed (gongyou minban/private) or people-managed-and-state-sponsored (minban/private gongzhu). Different forms of state-to-minban/private conversions started to take place, including key school[①] conversion, weak school conversion, community school conversion, key school and weak school alliance conversion and more (Wen, 2009). Schools are divided into four groups concerning funding, ownership, organisational structures, student admissions and teacher employment conditions. On the whole, two main types of private schools can be defined: (1) schools established by social or private capital or (2) schools converted from state schools into private schools (Chan and Wang, 2009). In spite of regional differences, the converted private schools comprise the primary type of private education available in China today (Xu and Ge, 2003).

Despite the policy changes, the Chinese government has been slowly relaxing restrictions on private and foreign investments in education. In 2003, the Law on Promoting Private Education developed the government's legal framework for regulating private schools and educational institutions. This law stated that corporations, public enterprises, social organisations, social groups, and individuals drawing on non-fiscal institutional funds together constitute the types of private educational contributors. Regulations include methods of establishment, organisation and activities, teachers' working conditions and students' benefits, capital and finance management, educational quality evaluations, government supports and rewards, as well as organisational change and termination. The release of the Law on Promoting Private Education was a milestone for minban/private education development. China's focus on economic efficiency, the enforcement of local initiatives, the highly competitive College Entrance Examination[②] system and the encouragement of individual efforts in their educational provision and achievement have led to a more vocationally oriented school curricula and a growing number of private educational institutes in higher education (Mok, 2009: 264). According to the 2013 Government Report on Education Development, there were 149,000 private schools, colleges and other educational institutes in China, with an

---

① 重点学校
② 高考

increase of 9,057 from the previous year (MoE, 2013). The increase of 444,900 students enrolled in the private education sector became a strong indicator of the further expansion of private education.

Yan and Lin (2004) summarise the three developmental stages of private schools based on their analysis of local government policies since 1978: (1) the recovery and development stage (1978-1992), (2) the rapid development stage (1992-1997) and (3) the normalisation stage (1997-2004). Wang's (2013) theory is based on the observation of the deceleration in growth of private secondary schools in China since 2003. He extends Yan and Lin's (2004) framework by offering a five-model development frame, which includes (1) disruption (1949-1977), (2) re-emergence (1978-1991), (3) development (1992-1996), (4) normalisation (1997-2001) and (5) legalised regression (2002 onwards).

Wu's (2012) analysis of the national statistics also reveals the increasing number of students enrolled in private schools at the level of pre-school, vocational and higher education. On top of this, several problems with the expansion of private education need to be discussed. The existence of education corruption, school bankruptcy and incidences of organisers absconding have been reported in social media. The dramatic decrease in the number of private primary and secondary schools has been published in empirical studies (Wu, 2012; Wang, 2013). There are multiple policies and social issues involved in the changes. Basing their research on private education in 14 provinces in China, Yan and Lin (2004:78-85) identified four critical issues in the development of private schools in China:

> 1. Relationships between state schools and private schools are dialectic, namely they are both competitive and complementary. The blurred boundaries between state and private schools, especially the converted schools, are accompanied by the authoritative role of local governments in managing educational resources and inspecting education quality among schools. In this sense, private education seems to have fewer advantages in comparison with their counterparts in the state system.

Chapter 2 Primary School Teachers in China: Diversification and Structural Complexity

2. Chinese regulations treat education as a public good, which has led to the controversy of using enterprises to defend private education. In China, private schools are categorised as private yet non-enterprise unities, which often holds back the autonomy of private schools in deciding their financial income and sustainability, educational administration and management processes.

3. The dominant influence of the state in the ownership of private schools has significant implications for the internal governance structures in the schools.

4. The unclear role of the school board in decision making and policy implementation might lead to the relatively casual and unstable allocation of resources in private schools. Blurred responsibilities and authorities might lead to chaotic situations in school management and limit the capacities of private schools to adjust to changing social and political environments, improve the education qualities, and to meet their social responsibilities and accountabilities.

In 2005, the *Several Opinions on Further Promoting the Balanced Development of Compulsory Education*[①] was published by the MoE, aiming to address contrasting educational qualities and outcomes among schools and the issue of school choices. As part of China's political reform in "constructing incorrupt government", the *Opinions on Governing the Education Arbitrary Charge* was published in 2006, marking a major policy change in converted private schools. The government began to rectify and regulate state-to-private school conversion, which produced resistance from local governments and schools. The "four independence" principles, i.e., independent legal personnel, a separate campus, a separate accounting system and an independent school management, were set up to evaluate which state schools could be converted to private. Those that did not meet the requirements were transferred to state schools or closed. Fee-charging institutes inside state schools, such as international programmes, were also required to be dissolved.

In response to critics of current private education policies, the Opinions

---

① 《教育部关于进一步推进义务教育均衡发展的若干意见》(http://www.moe.gov.cn/srcsite/A06/s3321/200505/t20050525_81809.html)

on Further Promoting the Private Education Development released in 2011 claimed to provide private schools with more autonomy by allowing schools to be for-profit legal organisations. In the amendment, a category of minban/private enterprise schools has been created: the management and funding of private schools will depend on whether the school is registered as minban/private non-enterprise organisation or enterprise organisation. For-profit educational enterprises, be it formal schools, vocational training institutes or private tutoring institutes, could register with the local Bureau of Commerce and establish governing structures and accounting systems according to the Enterprise Law. Schools are encouraged to attract a wide range of non-governmental capital for their establishment and operations. The state government also helps further adjustments concerning human resources, government fiscal supports, and other financial property and social welfare policies in its support of private education. Formal withdrawal mechanisms are required for schools to be established as private schools. According to the draft amendment, school boards will be given more autonomy in their decisions on tuition fees, curriculum design and teachers' welfare and working conditions. Although the policy changes have come to be widely recognised, the complexities and changes of China's educational and socio-economic contexts seem to pose further challenges and raise uncertainties for stakeholders. When and how they will be implemented, and what influences they will exert on private schools and educational institutions more broadly, remain to be seen.

2.5 The Status Quo of Private School Teachers in China

Historically, the term minban/private (people-managed) teacher is most commonly used to describe teachers who taught in village-funded schools in deprived rural areas in the early stages of communist China. The term minban/private, and its translation as "people-managed", is explained by the fact that these teachers are not employed by the government and hence are excluded from the state system. In Mao's era, all private schools were abandoned or re-registered as state schools, yet PSTs nonetheless retained their place as the major teaching force in rural schools. In 1977, there were approximately 3.4 million PSTs in rural primary schools, numbering 65% of the total number of teachers in primary schools in China (Ma and Long, 1999). From the 1970s to the 1990s, rural PSTs were paid by local communities or schools to teach primary school students from villages and they often worked simultaneously as farmers to add to their low incomes. Most of the PSTs were graduates from local secondary schools without having received professional teacher training. The differences among state and private primary school teachers' general backgrounds and work conditions in China are summarised in Table 2-3.

In China, bianzhi, which refers to membership of the government personnel system, is the key institution in distinguishing the social status and welfare benefits of state teachers and PSTs. Bianzhi can be directly translated as the "enrolment system" and it usually refers to administrative posts in the government with a state payroll in China. People who have bianzhi are mostly working in the public sectors and are often described as state employees who "eat imperial grain"[①]. PSTs who do not have the bianzhi status are often perceived as a marginalised occupational group in China's education system. The reconstruction of the education sector since the 1980s has had numerous different effects on the teacher education system (Paine and Fang, 2007:29) and on the lives of PSTs. All primary school teachers are required to obtain a degree from the teacher education colleges and a series of policies have been released to differentiate teachers' pay in order to transfer PSTs to state teachers through a series of evaluations and inspections of teachers' professional diplomas and certificates (Wang, 2005).

---

① 吃皇粮

Table 2-3　Different groups of teachers and focus of this study

	Primary school teachers		
	State school teachers (SSTs)	Private school teachers (PSTs)	Minban teachers/Daike (substitute) teachers
Definition	Teachers who are employed by the local government, most of whom work in state schools.	Teachers who work in private/minban schools. The teacher may or may not be state employed.	Teachers who are not employed by the local government, who only work temporarily in state schools.
Bianzhi	Yes	Yes / No	No
Employment	Government employee	Contract-based / government employee	No contract / temporary contract
Recruited by	Local government	Local government / the school	The school
Qualifications	National teacher qualification	Diverse educational backgrounds. Teacher qualification is required, preferably with teacher education backgrounds and teaching experiences	Local graduates / normal college graduates. Some teachers (will) become SSTs
Actors in teachers' in-service education	State and local governments, universities, teacher training agencies, schools and school networks.	Depending on different types of private schools, teachers' in-service education may involve teacher training agencies, publishing companies, schools and school networks. There might be less involvement of governments and universities.	Given limited resources, minban teachers / substitute teachers are mostly trained on their job in schools.
Curriculum	State curriculum and/or school-based curriculum	State curriculum and/or alternative curriculum	State curriculum

The 1992 *Work Opinions on Further Improving and Strengthening Issues of Private School Teachers*① identified a five-character plan in eliminating numbers of private school teachers, namely, stopping recruitment, selection, transfer to other occupations, dismissal and retirement② of private school teachers. Ma and Long (1999) have summarised four characteristics of PSTs in the context of rural education in China:

1. PSTs are acknowledged by the state and teach in rural schools.

2. PSTs are not state employees and do not possess the state bianzhi. They are paid by local communities and schools and may receive certain government subsidies. PSTs have rural residences with rural hukou.

3. The existence of PSTs temporarily solved the problem of teacher shortages in rural schools and played an important role in the development of China's modern education system.

4. The PST is a "historical phenomenon" in the development of education in China's rural areas.

The implementation of minban/private-to-state teacher conversion policies and the increasing number of well-educated teachers in rural state schools largely solved the problem of PSTs.

Several empirical research studies of private teachers aiming at revealing policy processes that were intended to transform rural private teachers' status have been conducted. Le and Lao (2004) use a questionnaire survey to investigate teacher qualifications, income and social status, and the effectiveness of teacher training programmes in learning and communication technology for PSTs in six provinces in China. In his PhD study, *Government, Local Community and Rural Teachers*, Li (1996) takes an "education system-social structure" perspective in order to understand the inclusion of PSTs in the state management system from the end of the Qing dynasty. The author identifies

---

① 《关于进一步改善和加强民办教师工作若干问题的意见》
② 关,招,转,辞,退

the characteristics of PSTs in terms of their relationships with the state, communities and schools in one county. In contrast with state teachers, the research found, PSTs were marginalised in terms of their occupational behaviour and sense of belongingness in the process of status conversion. Yan (2006) adopts state-society theories in his PhD thesis, which investigates state and rural PST identity formation in an extreme example of the private-to-state teacher conversion process in a particular urban location ("G town"). The author discusses the reconstruction of PST policy discourse by local governments and how it resulted in petitions advanced by the PST group.

Regarding teachers in urban private schools in China, Wu's (2011) ethnographic study is worth mentioning here. Wu uses critical discourse analysis to study the discursive construction of teachers' identities from teachers' stories in a minban/private high school in a small town in southern China. In this study, the discourse of "dagong" (migrant labour) is defined as a language game that constructs the reality of teachers' lives and the way teachers come to self-identify with the private school. Although these studies are not specifically focused on the impact of educational policies, they nonetheless shed light on those teachers' day-to-day interactions in the school contexts that shape their experiences.

With the exception of Wu's research, existing studies on non-state/bianzhi teachers have been conducted primarily in rural schools, involving rural communities and local governments; these are insightful yet may potentially limit our understanding of other types of minban teachers/PSTs and their work in different social and cultural contexts. For instance, PSTs are perceived differently in urban schools in China. First of all, the notion of private school covers a very wide range of purposes, student groups, leadership styles and organisational structures in China; it includes elite and international schools, schools for migrant children, charity schools and private tutoring institutions. Teachers in private schools can also be differentiated in terms of their educational and training backgrounds, teaching experiences, working environments and daily practices.

According to the Several Opinions on Encouraging Social Forces in Education and Promoting the Healthy Development of Minban Education[①] in 2017(The State Council, 2017), PSTs are as entitled as state teachers to equal access for qualifications, professional title appraisal, in-service training and education, research project application and international exchange. On the other hand, teacher policies also tend to encourage local authorities to replace the permanent state employee status[②] with short-term contracts and periodic reviews of teacher qualifications. Local government policies on promoting teacher exchanges and collaboration programmes also aim to promote teachers' learning and professional development in order to ensure a high-quality education for all students. In spite of the difference between schools and the changes in policy, many PSTs still identify themselves as "lower-level citizens" in the state education system. I would argue that teachers and teaching in private schools require further attention by researchers. Questions of how the expansion of private primary education might influence teacher qualities in terms of the development of TPIs currently remain unaddressed by scholars.

---

① 《国务院关于鼓励社会力量兴办教育促进民办教育健康发展的若干意见》(http://www.gov.cn/zhengce/content/2017-01/18/content_5160828.htm)[Retrived on 5th. May, 2018]

② 编制

Chapter 3
Literature Review

The purpose of this literature review is to clarify the concept of TPIs better and to review the empirical research studies on how TPIs are developed. In this chapter, I will discuss the relevant literature on the three major aspects that have informed this research study: (1) the definition and significance of professional identities; (2) relating concepts and influences on teacher identities; and (3) the construction of a conceptual framework to guide my study. The review of existing research aims to define gaps in the literature and serves as a basis for comparison and consensus in the choice of research design and methodology to study TPIs. On the basis of the review, I will summarise the key messages and discuss the focus of this study, which leads on to the next chapter, on the research design and methodology.

3.1 Introduction

Recent years have witnessed intense interest in questions concerning identity in a remarkable array of social sciences and humanities disciplines. Within cultural studies, for example, identity is often connected with socially constructed labels based on a person's race, gender, class and education. In political sciences, many studies have focused on the "identity politics" of race, gender and sexuality. Identity is also a central concept in works on multiculturalism and ethical conflicts in education. Initially, scholars used the term "identity" as a way to describe how one person positions himself/herself with relation to others' perceptions of his or her positions; it is as a process of "subject formation over one's life experiences" (Urrieta and Noblit, 2018: 4). One can find definitions of identity in many places. Table 3-1 gives some examples, which are mainly used in the literature of educational research studies. The primary purpose of this section is to understand the definition of TPI and to situate the concept in the broader field of teacher education. The review will also seek to understand how TPIs influence teacher practices.

3.2 Defining Identity

The traditional psychological frames of identity treat individuals as fixed, and in earlier literature (e.g. Cooley, 1902; Erikson, 1968) the concept of identity tended to focus on the unity and continuity of the concept of self. As Day et al. (2007: 602) noted, earlier perspectives on self tend to focus on "the inner world of the individual and to position the self as a singular, stable essence that was little affected by context". In contrast, from a poststructuralist perspective, identity is considered multiple and dynamic, and individuals actively construct their identity on an ongoing basis. Educational research has drawn on a number of theoretical positions in investigating teachers' lives and professional identities, including symbolic interactionism (e.g. Nias, 1989; Czerniawski, 2011), sociocultural perspectives (e.g. Lasky, 2005; Tsui, 2007) and poststructuralist perspectives (e.g. Kelchtermans and Vandenberghe, 1994; Morgan, 2004).

Scholars have linked education and identity. Some have focused on how characteristics of group identities might shape students' (or teachers') academic engagement (e.g. Oyserman, Bybee and Terry, 2003; Steele, 1997). Other scholars have focused on how a particular learning context exert influences on students' identities (e.g. Davidson, 1996; Delpit, 1995). As shown in Table 3-1, there are multiple linkages between identity and educational research studies. Different RQs and approaches have evolved somewhat different conventions regarding the term.

Researchers might also have different intentions in using the term in their specific arguments. For instance, in their study on effective mentoring practices for research students, Griffiths, Thompson and Hryniewicz (2010) focused on the effectiveness of the programme; the definition of researcher identity was somewhat ambiguous, as it might only be used to indicate a "feeling" of being a researcher. In contrast, the auto-ethnographic study by Mertkan and Bayrakli (2018) specifically employed the poststructuralist perspective to identity in exploring the interrelations between the process of "becoming" a qualitative researcher with contextual influences. Different disciplines have different focuses when it comes to the use of "identity" in studies. As Orde (2016:6) summarised, there is a wide range of variations of RQs on identity: psychology has addressed the importance of self-concepts; educational theory links the learning process and highlights the developmental aspect of identity; sociology tends to reconstruct the social prerequisites for identity concepts; and cultural studies and media studies focus on analysing the symbolic or power-related context of identity patterns. Adding to the complexity is a range of related concepts often mixed with identity, such as identification, role identities, self-concept, self-image and personhood. Therefore, it is crucial to give the concept a more precise definition within its theoretical traditions before moving on to the context of teachers' education and professional lives. In the following sections, I will present a brief review of identity from the perspectives of three theoretical traditions: (1) symbolic interactionism; (2) sociocultural theory; and (3) poststructuralism.

Table 3-1 Examples of difinitions of identity in educational research literature

Group	Authors	Nature of the study	Definitions of identity
Student/ learner identity	Lawson (2014) (UK)	A small-scaled mixed-method research on the connections between business students' learner identities, social-economic backgrounds and subject choice.	"A 'learner identity' can be broadly defined as how an individual feel about herself/himself as a learner and the extent to which he/she describes himself/herself as a 'learner'"(2014:343).
	Turner and Tobbell (2018) (UK)	An ethnographic study of first-year undergraduate students' academic participation and its links with identity transition.	"[…] learners' identities as trajectory, the reconciliation and negotiation of which exert influences on the transition process"(2018:708).

Continued

Group	Authors	Nature of the study	Definitions of identity
Teacher identity	Kayi Aydar (2017) (USA)	A narrative case study of a bilingual teacher's invested agency in developing professional identities in various contexts.	"identities [...] as teachers' selves as professionals, including personal and institutional aspects of being a teacher (Moate and Rouhotie-Lyhty, 2014).
	Menter (2010) (England)	A literature review that considers the implications of historical and political changes in teacher education on teacher identities.	"[...] how teacher see themselves and their work [...] shaped in large measure by the social settings in which any individual teacher finds her/himself, be that at national, local or school level" (2010:29).
Researcher identity	McEachern and Horton (2016) (USA)	Two teachers' reflections on their own practices that support researcher identity development.	"Identity is not a stagnant property, but rather an entity that changes with time, often going through stages, and is continuously modified based on the surrounding environment (Brownell and Tanner, 2012:341).
	Mertkan and Bayrakli (2018) (Turkey)	An auto-ethnographic study of contextual influences on becoming a qualitative researcher.	"[...] identity is multiple, always-in-the-making, 'a becoming not a being' (Frith, 1996:109), socially constructed and negotiated across time through discourse (Gee, 2008) in inequitable relations of power (Peirce, 1995: 12) in social, cultural and political contexts (Varghese et al, 2005)".

Continued

Group	Authors	Nature of the study	Definitions of identity
Teacher educator identity	Griffiths, Thompson and Hryniewicz (2010) (England)	A qualitative study to identify effective mentoring practices, forms of support and barriers or problems in developing research profiles and identities.	Not clearly defined.
	Skerrett (2008) (USA)	An autobiographical study of how the teacher educators' biography and identity influence the lived experiences of teaching and stance in research.	"teacher role identity […] (as) the way in which individuals think about themselves as teachers—the image they have of self-as-teacher" (Knowles,1992:99).

3.2.1 Symbolic Interactionism

We can trace the modernist approaches to identity in sociology to symbolic interactionism, which originally derives from the work of the pragmatic philosophers Charles Sanders Peirce, John Dewey, William James and George Herbert Mead (Crotty, 2003:73-75). Symbolic interactionism examines how individuals interact, and the creation of personal identities through interactions, with others. Blumer first coined the term "symbolic interactionism". This theory includes three core principles: meaning, language and thought. Humans act towards each other and things on the basis of the meaning they attribute to people or things. Humans also use language or symbols as tools to negotiate these meanings. Human thoughts then modify the interpretation of these symbols, when language is used in conversations. On the basis of symbolic interactionism, Holland et al. (1998) summarised:

> People tell others who they are, but even more importantly, they tell themselves who they are and then try to act as though they are who they say they are. These self-understandings are what we refer to as identities. (1998:3)

Holland and Lachicotte (2007:103) further suggested that Mead's conception of the "I-me" dynamic grounds the formation of self in the social coordination of activity and highlights the significance of the relation between "self" and the "linguistically recognized social positions and roles" to the conduct of social activities. The "Me" (as I respond to the world), other than the "I" (as I present myself to the world), plays a central role in the process of social construction, implying the self as constructed via the "generalized other" (Crotty, 1998:62).

Within this frame, the focus is on the subjective experiences of individuals as the basis for understanding the systems of a society, such as the education system. From this perspective, one could draw insights into TPIs through an understanding of how teachers view themselves as well as how they believe others perceive them. Teachers interact socially and could adjust their behaviours in response to others' actions. As such, teachers socialise with each other as social actors and engage actively as they construct their social world. An example would be Nias' (1989) exploration of the "me" of the teachers' selves that are situated in the teachers' working lives in the study in primary school teachers' selves in England in the 1980s. She distinguished the personal and professional elements of teachers' identities and found that teachers incorporated the social identity as "a teacher" into an individual's self-image over time. In this sense, the process of socialisation at one's workplace become significant in the creation of TPIs. A teacher may share similar attitudes and norms of behaviour that the other peers have in the same organisation, as a result of the process of learning from others, which gradually becomes a part of one's "self". The symbolic interactionist notion of social identity implies that individuals view the world from others' standpoints; by taking the role of the other, one can imagine alternative and evaluate these alternatives on the basis of the likely reactions of others.

3.2.2 The Sociocultural Perspective

Vygotsky (1978) examined the social origin of mental functioning, which is historically and institutionally situated. He developed the concept of the zone of proximal development, which serves as a model to explain the interactions through which individuals construct knowledge. In the words of Rio and Álvarez (2007), the zone of proximal development is a "frontier territory" which consists of the "situated-embodied mind and the cognitive mind, the individual mind and the social mind, the development already attained and the development to be attained" (2007:301). From the Vygotskian perspective, identity is a higher-order psychological function that "organises sentiments, understandings, and embodied knowledge relevant to culturally imagined, personally valued social position[s]" (Holland and Lachicotte, 2007: 113). As a higher-order psychological function, identity is formed in sociocultural practices. Unlike Mead's focus on the resulting linkages formed between the self and society, the stress in Vygotsky's work is on the development of mind and further expands the theorisation of not only symbolic, but also material artefacts in social and cultural structures.

Like Vygotsky, Wenger (1998) highlights the profound connections between learning, identity development and sociocultural contexts. Learners become involved in a community of practice (CoP), which is a group of individuals interacting with each other and engaging in common interests (Lave and Wenger, 1991). In this sense, CoP encompasses characteristics of all social relations that are contained within a community who share similar activities and identities (Wenger, 1998). Wenger further defines five characterisations of the identity in the community:

1. Identity as a collection of self-images as well as the lived experience of participation in specific communities (negotiated experience).

2. Identity as a display of competence, which relates to a world with "a mix of the familiar and the foreign, the obvious and the mysterious, the transparent and the opaque" (community membership).

3. Identity negotiation in the present context *incorporates the past and future* (learning trajectory).

4. Identity is more than a single trajectory. The multiple paths interact and influence each other through the work of reconciliation in maintaining an

integrated sense of identity across boundaries (nexus of multi-membership).

5. People experience broader categories and institutions. Individuals define who they are by "negotiating local ways of belonging to broader constellations and manifesting broader styles and discourses" (the relation between the local and the global). (1998:149)

As mentioned before, a sociocultural perspective places the emphasis on the "participatory aspects" of learning (Morgan, 2004:174). As Varghese et al. commented, under the theoretical framework of CoP, the focus of research would be placed on the "structure of group practice in which identities are constructed" (2005:30). We could understand professional identity as a development process concerning social and cultural contexts as well as the practice of the individual's working contexts. Lasky (2005) drew upon earlier works and summarised the conceptualisation of TPI as follows:

Teacher professional identity is how teachers defined themselves to themselves and others. It is a construction of personal self and evolves over career stage [...] and can be shaped by school, reform and political contexts. (2005: 901)

In summary, from a sociocultural perspective, identity is developed in the ongoing interaction between the personal and the professional, between agency and social structure. Beauchamp and Thomas summarised the sociocultural perspective towards TPIs as "both product (a result of influences on the teacher) and process (a form of ongoing interaction within teacher development)" (2009: 177). From a sociocultural perspective, institutional settings are emphasiszed in the formation of professional identity, which I regard as of referential value to enriching the understanding of this research study.

3.2.3 Poststructuralist Perspectives

From the poststructuralist perspective, Zembylas (2003: 221) noted that "identity is formed in this shifting space where narratives of subjectivity meet the narratives of culture", or putting it another way, identity is formed "in the space between the 'structure' (of the relations between power and status) and 'agency' (in the influence which we and others can have); and it is the interaction between these which influences how teachers see themselves, i.e. their personal and professional identities" (Day et al., 2007: 613). Scholars (Zembylas, 2003; Morgan, 2004; Day et al, 2007) have pointed out that the poststructuralists challenge the notion of the unified "self": identity is conceived as unstable, dynamic, relative and multiple. Wenger (1998:145) also described identity as a "constant becoming", which is constructed within the rich and complex set of relations of practice.

Roberts conceptualised that "a teaching identity develops through exchange between our personal theories and self-concept on one hand, and the demands of our social and occupational context on the other" (2000:22). In the exploration of the contextual factors that differentiate teachers' professional identities, Cooper and Olson (1996) viewed professional identity as a multi-dimensional, multi-layered and dynamic process. They demonstrated how historical, sociological, psychological and cultural aspects shape the construction of teacher identity and how the influences create tensions between systems and individuals. In line with this, Coldron and Smith (1999) also claimed that "being a teacher is a matter of the teacher being seen as a teacher by himself or herself and by others; it is a matter of acquiring and then redefining an identity that is socially legitimated" (1999:712). The authors pointed to the tension between the personal and the "socially given" dimension of teaching. They described the professional identity of teachers as a process of taking a position in social space by a particular person within the "professionally pertinent array of possibilities" (1999:714). Here, the authors described the "possibilities" as conveyed by the pedagogic traditions that teachers variously embody through their practice in the various professional communities to which they belong, and through external practice brought into critical relation to teaching. The wider social/pedagogic traditions of the craft, the moral, the artistic and the scientific were addressed as significant in teachers' educational practices. Gee (2001) placed the emphasis on the multifaceted nature of identity. He suggested that while one might have a "core identity", there are multiple forms of this identity as one operates across different contexts (2001:99). He came up with four ways to perceive identity:

1. the natural identity that stems from one's natural state;

2. the institutional identity that is derived from a position recognised by authority;

3. the discursive identity resulting from the discourse of others about oneself; and

4. the affinitive identity that is determined by one's practices in relation to external groups. (2001: 99)

According to Gee (2001), these four perspectives are interrelated and closely linked to connected historical, institutional and sociocultural forces. Each perspective provides an "interpretive system underwriting the recognition of identity by others" (Gee, 2001:108). In summary, the poststructuralist perspective tends to view identity as inherently unstable, fluid and fragmented, and as constantly changing over time and across contexts (Cooper and Olson, 1996); it is considered inextricably linked to emotion and values (Zembylas, 2003).

So far, I have reviewed the three major theoretical approaches and their different focuses in defining identity. Mead's notion of identity (1934) focused on the process of socialisation and the impact on self-formation in socially coordinated activities through symbolic communications and the negotiation of meaning through daily interactions. The emphasis is on the means by which individuals develop in their relations to roles and status and how these identities, in turn, exert effects on motivations, actions and agency. Vygotsky (1978) noted the continuous development of mind and facilitating of technical, material and symbolic tools as important to identity development. The poststructuralist approach focused on the unstable and fragmented nature of identity and the dynamics and tensions as it is connected with not only cognitive but also emotional meaning in teachers' everyday lives. So far, I have reviewed different definitions and characteristics of TPIs in research based on various theoretical perspectives. Each approach to identity has different focuses, yet they shared the common ground that identity is changing and developing under the influences of the social contexts in which an individual evolves.

3.2.4 The Personal and Social Identity

Despite the disciplinary and theoretical differences, the concept of identity often encompasses two interrelated aspects: social identity and personal identity. On the one hand, identity could be used by a group of people who assign specific labels to themselves or/and others. On the other hand, identity could be a set of attributes, beliefs, expectations and principles of actions that a person thinks distinguish him or her from others that gives him or her pride, orient his or her behaviours, restrict his or her actions and forms the basis for his or her dignity and self-respect (Cameron, 1999: 181). In the language analysis of the daily use of identity, James (Fearon, 1999) referred identity to the distinct yet significant functions: 1) social categories; and 2) the source of an individual's self-respect or dignity. He argued against the simplified idea of identity as a "social category" because such claim often missed the process of social categories that "enter into" people's sense of selves as individuals in complex ways (ibid.). That is to say, one's social identity is often intertwined with one's personal identity. In educational studies, much of the interest in identities also comes from the implicit interaction of the social and personal aspects of identities (Menter, 2010:5). In the discipline of psychology, we can also find a general distinction between personal identity and social identity.

Scholars have defined identity as a unitary and continuous awareness of who one is (Baumeister, 1998; Ellemers et al., 2002). That is to say, we consider ourselves and others as continuing entities, which can be affirmed and reinforced through social interactions; most importantly, the continuity of our personal identities is framed in our own memories and the memories of others. In this sense, part of our sense of identity is independent of our group affliation and social categories. This aspect of our identity is more personal than social. Besides this need for the continuity and unity of our personal identities, we also have to take into account the social and cultural contexts with our personal identities to have a full picture of identity. The psychological phenomena of identity are also influenced by macro-level factors such as social institutions, artefacts, social images and collective cultural beliefs. Therefore, social identities might encompass two major parts: 1) the relational/communal sense of self as belonging to groups; and 2) the symbolic categories that define how one acts according to different situations and demands.

The personal and social identities are essentially intertwined, and different scholars have focused on various cognitive and linguistic phenomena in connecting the two. For instance, Yeager et al. (2012) investigated adolescents' career development. In their mixed-method research, the authors found that students' occupation and vocational pursuits have been the central domain in their identity formation. According to the researchers, students' sense of purposes go beyond their interests and involve the promotion of the welfare of others. The researchers identified three identity types among a diverse group of middle- and high-school students in the San Francisco Bay Area. Germeijs et al.'s (2012) study of students' decision-making on college majors used Marcia's (1993) identity status paradigm as a framework that focuses on the adaptive nature of decision-making process. Such a decision-making process is found to correspond to identity characteristics, including identity achievement, identity foreclosure, identity moratorium and identity diffusion.

Figure 3-1 represents the interactions of personal and social identities as a key issue in identity research. In what follows, I focus on the discussion of the significance of identity and its implications in teachers' practices. I will then review influences on teachers' identities with reflection upon the use of the concepts in specific research contexts. These discussions help me to construct a framework to better capture teachers' sense of "identity" in this research project (See Section 4.4). Researchers (e.g. Day et al., 2007;

Menter, 2008) recognised the complex contexts and noted the importance of drawing upon a wide range of works to obtain a richer understanding of the process and contexts of teachers' identity that represent "structure and agency, creativity and constraint" (Menter, 2008:61). In the following section, I will review recent empirical studies on how TPIs may influence teachers' practices and the influencing factors to the formation of TPIs in different social and cultural contexts.

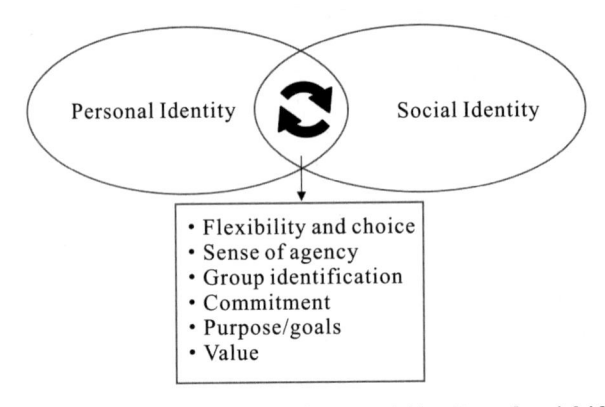

```
         ╭─────────╮   ╭─────────╮
        ╱           ╲ ╱           ╲
       │ Personal    ⟳   Social    │
       │ Identity   ╱ ╲   Identity │
        ╲           ╳           ╱
         ╰─────────╯   ╰─────────╯
                   │
                   ▼
         ┌─────────────────────────┐
         │ • Flexibility and choice│
         │ • Sense of agency       │
         │ • Group identification  │
         │ • Commitment            │
         │ • Purpose/goals         │
         │ • Value                 │
         └─────────────────────────┘
```

Figure 3-1 **Proposed interactions of personal identity and social identity**

3.3 How Does Professional Identity Affect Teachers' Practices?

There are indications that professional identities can have positive influences on teachers' practices and performances. Linking TPIs to teachers' willingness to implement innovation in teaching within a changing professional environment, Beijaard et al. (2000) argued that a teacher's professional identity guides his/her thinking, actions and interactions with the students. Meanwhile, Burn (2007) argued for a professional identity that can act as a tool enabling student teachers and teacher educators to take different approaches to develop their pedagogical knowledge concerning the secondary school history curriculum in England. Taylor (2017) investigated the subject knowledge and examined how an instructor could use personal narratives to support teacher researchers' identity construction in teacher research contexts.

Relatedly, Day et al. (2005) pointed out that the failure to recognise TPIs often leads to the tension and crisis that diminish teachers' capacity in sustaining their commitment to teaching. In this sense, if teachers and policy makers could identify what is distinct about their profession, there is a chance that teachers will develop a stronger sense of belongingness and commitment to teaching in the long term. This idea is echoed in Izadinia's (2015) research, which identified the impact of positive mentoring relationships on TPIs and teachers' sense of confidence. The author also observed that negative social relationships often lead to a lack of perceived progress at work. Meanwhile, a stronger sense of professional identity may be a factor that enables integration in teaching and teachers' adaptation to changing educational contexts. Another study reported on how two vocational teachers critically reflected on and negotiated ethical dimensions of their professional identities in response to the flow of international students and the commercialisation of vocational education (Thi Tran and Thi Nguyen, 2013). This study identified the extension of teachers' professional responsibilities from the facilitation of students' development of vocational skills and knowledge to students' provision of pastoral care, as well as their sense of social justices for international students. In the light of these links between TPIs and the quality of teaching, it is worth reviewing in more detail how different aspects of being and becoming teachers in the state and private primary schools can be developed and fostered.

3.4 What Develops and Affects TPIs?

In this section, I highlight different factors that have been identified in the literature as affecting the formation and development of TPIs.

3.4.1 Teacher Training and Education

A growing number of scholars in the field of teacher education have argued for a paradigm shift to integrate the transposition of teachers' knowledge and skills with strategies to enable teachers to navigate the complex process of teaching and learning to develop and consolidate their professional identities. Drawing upon theories and studies that frame TPI as socially situated cognition, Dotger and Smith (2009:162) state that teaching is a "social profession" that relies on the formative intentions between students and teachers. These authors highlighted that the professional self occurs "at the intersection of their professional training, their own experiences as students, the teachers whom they hope to model, and their tacit images of the classroom teacher". In an era of constant change and diversification of the teacher and student groups, TPI became a significant aspect of the scholarly debate concerning how to prepare teachers to meet the needs of diverse learners and staff development for innovating TPIs. Against this background, teacher education no longer serves the sole purpose of communicating a set of professional skills, but a process of developing the new teachers' awareness about the centrality of their self-transformation and role as agents of adaptation and change.

Researchers investigated teacher identity formation in a wide range of formal teacher learning activities and programmes. Earlier studies used questionnaire surveys to examine the impact of teachers' learning and classroom practices on TPIs. For example, Lamote and Engels (2010) focused on student teachers' perceptions of their TPIs by comparing the focuses of teaching among groups of teachers who were respectively with and without classroom practice experiences in a three-year course. The questionnaire included four aspects of TPIs: 1) commitment to teaching; 2) professional orientation; 3) task orientation; and 4) self-efficacy. Although the finding reflected certain differences between these two groups of student teachers, it is important to note that the finding of TPIs was not based on understandings of teachers' experiences; therefore, teachers' ideas and the complexity in their development remain unarticulated in this research.

Researchers also employed qualitative research methods in investigating the development of TPIs in small-scale studies. Dikilitas and Yayl (2018), for example, investigated the promotion of action research in a Turkish university and its impact on TPIs for language teachers. They found that teachers constructed four main types of identities within the action research context: 1) sensitive teacher; 2) active seeker of informed practices; 3) self-reflector; and 4) empathy builder and collaborator. These authors argued that a teacher's ability to "observe" themselves, their teaching and their relationships with colleagues during the research serves as an important factor to contribute to TPI development. They further pointed out that the opportunities provided for increased self-awareness and self-reflection are considered efficient methods for the construction of TPI.

Teachers' reflective activities are important tools to employ in educational programmes to develop TPIs (e.g. Beauchamp and Thomas, 2009: 182). Korthagen and Vasalos' "onion model" (2005) revealed six levels on which reflection can take place: mission; identity; beliefs; competencies; behaviour; and environment. It is argued that the inner levels of this frame, such as mission and identity, shape the outer levels of reflection, and vice versa. For this research study to better understand TPIs, it is essential to incorporate questions that invite teachers to reflect upon the critical incidence of positive and negative experiences of their roles as teachers in their personal and professional lives.

In another study that investigated teachers' participation in an online discussion forum, Sutherland and Markauskaite (2012) used the teacher reflection literature to explore the role of authentic online learning experiences in transforming student teachers into professionals. These researchers identified five levels of engagement in teachers' reflections: (1) professional analysis; (2) linking analysis; (3) theoretical, critical analysis; (4) theoretical analysis; and (5) theoretical identifying. In an interpretative case study on novice mathematics teachers, Losanom et al. (2018) identified the tensions and contradictions experienced by first-year mathematical teachers in schools. These novice teachers were found to confront a significant contrast between their understanding of mathematical teaching and the social and cultural complexities and restrictions in the school context. Pescarmona (2017) explored how experimenting with the *Complex Instruction* for a group of in-service teachers can develop teachers' understanding of the classroom as a complex social and cultural system. This researcher identified disorientation in teachers' experiences and sense of uncertainty, which, according to the researcher, strengthened teachers' ability to raise questions about their practices and awareness of their roles in facilitating equal participation in class. In the context of this research study, teachers recognised others as resources for solving problems and the development of professional skills and developed a sense of flexibility and openness in their careers and the ability to connect the recognition of their learning abilities with the diversity of students.

Dvir and Avissar (2014) focused on the development of "critical professional identities" among teacher candidates in a service-learning programme that incorporated post-structural pre-service and a critical pedagogy approach to learning. These authors examined the process that teachers underwent to cope with various conflicts to enhance their understanding and relationships with the contexts: (1) deconstructing stereotypes through engagement with the "other"; (2) coping with difficulties, dilemmas or conflicts that arise from dialogues with the "other"; and (3) shifting from a hegemonic professional perception to a dialogic one. Scholars have also investigated teachers' practical and reflective arts experiences (Kenny et al., 2015) and use of language in classroom interactions, in which teachers' strong agency against discouragement was considered key for teachers to develop a sense of their professional identities.

While looking at formal education contexts is useful to identify changes in teachers' identities, other researchers reconsidered the importance of many other areas and formats that extended the influencing factors from formal teacher education curriculum to informal interactions and exchanges in the daily and hybrid settings. In Taiwan, Wang (2018) explored how a teacher readers' club helped to support an expert EFL teacher's reader identity and its impact on her pedagogical decisions. Employing the method of narrative inquiry, the researcher recorded how the teacher developed a better understanding of herself through her reflection in the readers' club and found the reader (teacher)-text-reader (student) interaction to be the main contributing feature of the readers' club. Luehmann (2008) conducted a case study that explored the affordance of weblog offered to an urban middle school science teacher in developing her TPI. In this research study, the researcher found that not only did the writing but also the teachers' use of the digital platform provided opportunities for the science teacher to become a self-directed, reflective and interacting thinker who critically engaged with her work.

3.4.2 Teacher Professionalism and Policy Demands

As a way to understand the condition of teachers' work, teacher professionalism can help to illuminate the challenges as well as opportunities that teachers face in their daily lives. The notion of teachers as professionals, as asserted by Nixon et al. (1997), has the widest popular support in recent teacher education policies and practices. Policy makers, educational researchers and practitioners are all engaged with the question of what being a "professional teacher" means.

With regards to the changing nature of teaching and teachers' work in response to socioeconomic development, the literature on teacher professionalism provides a focused framework for the context-teacher connection. Furlong (2001) engaged with this question through a broader discussion of teacher professionalism and identified three dimensions that characterise the concept: (1) the dimension of professional knowledge that refers to the system of knowledge used in teaching and learning; (2) the responsibility and authority of teachers' work over their students' learning experiences; and (3) and teachers' autonomy in managing and planning their work in schools. This understanding of teacher professionalism is often perceived as the fixed standard and ethical core of teaching guaranteeing an equal and efficient education system (ibid.). The nature and extent of teacher professionalism vary across systems (OECD, 2016). The OECD's publication *Supporting Teacher Professionalism: Insights from TALIS* 2013 proposed the framework based on Wang, Lai and Lo's (2014) classification of domains of teacher professionalism (Figure 3-2). These three domains are teachers' knowledge base, their autonomy and their peer networks. Based on the analysis of cross-country survey results, the report identified five models of teacher professionalism (OECD, 2016):

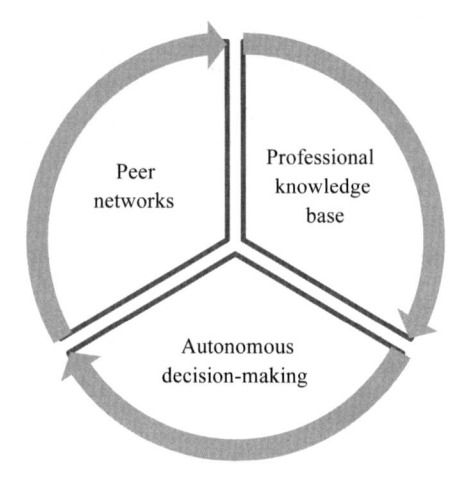

Figure 3-2 Three major domains of teacher professionalism (Wang, Lai and Lo, 2014)

1. the high peer networks and low autonomy model [Malaysia, Shanghai (China), South Korea];
2. the high autonomy model (Italy, Denmark and Czech Republic);
3. the knowledge emphasis model [France, the Netherlands, Flanders (Belgium)];
4. balanced domains and high overall professionalism [Poland, England (the UK) and New Zealand]; and
5. balanced domains, low professionalism (Portugal, Brazil and Mexico).

In many countries, issues in teachers' social roles and status, professional competence and autonomous judgements in current neo-liberal educational reforms are revealed as primary concerns on teacher professionalism. Ball (2003) summarised the three major policy technologies to improve education quality: educational devolution, quasi-market and performance management. As a result of these changes, accountability has become an important rationale for policy changes (Wang, Lai and Lo, 2014). As Wang, Lai and Lo (2014) summarised, scholars identified the shift from the traditional approach of professional accountability, namely the accountability to one's peers through a professional organisation, to forms of market accountability, performance accountability and contractual accountability to policy makers, funders and parents (Perryman, 2006; Ranson, 2007). The authors further indicated that, as such, teachers and schools are accountable for their own performances, often monitored by other stakeholders of school education (ibid.).

In addition to the theoretical discussions of teacher professionalism, scholars have drawn on their observations of teachers' actual practices in schoolwork in order to contextualise the concept of teacher professionalism. Hoyle (1980), for example, identified the phenomenon of "restricted professionalism" as teachers' tendency to rely on intuitive, classroom-focused and experience-centred teaching approaches. Nias (1989) used the term "bounded professionalism" to refer to teachers' a-theoretical and school-bounded perceptions of educational issues. Sachs (2003) has argued for an active, flexible and transformative professionalism that links teachers' professional lives with civic meanings within broader social goals.

Evidence showed that teachers could respond to policy changes and work environments differently in order to regain their authority and autonomy (Don et al., 2000). Teachers are not passive "dupes" and "helpless agents in the reproduction of the relations of production" (Ball and Goodson, 1985:7). Instead, they are perceived by scholars as "active agents" who can resist and exert influences on the control strategies of the neo-liberal state, thereby actively constructing meaning around their work (Apple and Christian-Smith, 1991: 14). Day and Sachs (2004) identified the differences between two major discourses of teacher professionalism, namely managerial professionalism and democratic professionalism. Instead of treating teachers as belonging to only one category, these authors recognise the contingencies and overlap between the two conceptualisations. Other empirical studies have also identified the mix of managerial professionalism and democratic professionalism in teachers' work (e.g. Hargreaves and Goodson, 1996; Helsby, 2000; Webb et al., 2004).

Hoyle and Wallace (2010) focus on the impact of an accountability agenda on teachers' work and lives and use the concept of *situational irony* to convey the unstable and unpredictable outcomes of the reciprocal relationships between centralised policies, policy implementation and teachers' strategies to cope with the policy demands. The authors pointed out three major modes of teachers' responses to the incorporation of professionalism within managerial trends in British schools: acceptance, resistance and mediation. The *persistence of professionalism*, as the authors further argued, calls for the support of school leadership and management development. In this sense, teacher professionalism is interpreted as a context-bounded phenomenon reflecting the changing nature and value of professional teachers in its social and historical contexts (ibid.). Milner (2013) based his discussion on a descriptive study of three high-profile reform policies in the USA—teacher evaluation policies, fast-track teacher preparation interventions and scripted curricula—to identify conflicting influences on teacher professionalisation in each reform. In the UK, Goodwyn (2010) argued that teachers still struggle with defining themselves as professionals. Fuller et al. (2013) used survey data from 849 teachers and in-depth interviews with 31 advanced skill teachers to explore how this designation influenced teachers' perceptions of their professional identity and status. The researchers found that teaching grades that recognise and reward teaching excellence exerted a positive impact upon teachers' sense of identities due to the increased sense of recognition, and the rewarding job satisfaction. They further called for objectifying the value of all teachers by finding ways of recognising and rewarding good practice more generally to improve teachers' sense of identity and status (ibid.). So far, there has been little research into the role of teachers' professional bodies, such as teachers' unions and professional associations, in teachers' sense of their professional identities, which could be an area worth exploring for a better understanding of the interactions between teachers' professionalism, agency and sense of vocation.

3.4.3 Communities and Collaborations

Other literature on communities and collaborations had led to a deeper understanding of the ways different communities negotiate the meanings of policy demands with their own needs and practices (e.g. McLaughlin and Talbert, 2006). Researchers have focused on the interplay between teachers' collegial relationships and their professional development, and found that positive social interactions bring positive changes in teachers' learning and educational changes (e.g. Graham, 2006; Lieberman, 2008; Vescio et al., 2008). Various terms have been employed, including "learning community" (Oxley, 2001), "community learning networks" (Chen, 2003) and "communities of continuous inquiry and improvement" (Hord, 1997). The concept of CoP seems to have particularly significant relevance for research on teacher identity. In developing the theory of CoP, Wenger highlights the profound connections between identity and practice. According to Wenger (1998), developing a practice requires the formation of communities whose members have common interests and engage with one another to improve the status quo. Thus, members of the community need to be acknowledged by each other as participants. A CoP is defined as a sociocultural context of situated learning in which groups of individuals interact with each other and engage in common interests (Lave and Wenger, 1991). The development of a CoP, however, is not an automatic or a smooth process. Instead, members' interpersonal relationships and social identities vary according to different stages of their engagement. As Varghese et al. comment, under the theoretical framework of CoP, the focuses of researchers are on the "structure of group practice in which identities are constructed" (2005:30). Professional identity is developed in relation to the practice of the individual's working context. Individual teachers' participation and learning are a necessary part of social processes:

> [...] learn through practice (learning as doing), through meaning (learning

as intentional), through community (learning as participating and being with others), and through identity (learning as changing who we are) [...] rooted in the human need to feel a sense of belonging and of making contributions to [the] community where experience and knowledge function as part of community property. (Lieberman, 2008:227)

Drawing upon the conception of a CoP, researchers have investigated the influences of the interactions in the immediate workplace on structuring teachers' identities (e.g. Brown, 1997; Tsui, 2007). Although some studies have advocated the benefits of CoP for teachers' learning and development (e.g. Zboralski and Germunden, 2005; Harris, 2003), I will focus on the challenges identified in existing studies. Tsui (2007), for instance, explored teacher identity formation through a narrative inquiry into professional identity with an EFL teacher in China. In this study, two sources of identity formation were reported: "The individual recognises that he or she possesses competence that his or her community values, and the individual is given legitimacy to the access of practice" (2007:675). In other words, participation plays a central role in the process of teacher identity formation; equally important is the legitimacy of access, which is often shaped by power relations in communities and broader social contexts (Tsui, 2007:676). In an ethnographic study that explores the identity formation of language teachers, Varghese (2000) looked at language teachers in professional development programmes and highlighted the importance of "the interaction between learners and the layers of [the] sociopolitical-economic structure that is surrounding the community and the activity" (2000:30). The interaction, according to the author, is crucial to teachers' "legitimate participation" in the second language teaching profession. Anderson's qualitative research into part-time lecturers also focused on how "institutional policy and procedures can significantly affect the development of a shared repertoire within CoPs" (2008:96). In their study of teachers in an Australian university, McDonald and Star (2006) found five major challenges in the development of the CoP:

1. the need for financial support;
2. time pressure and institutional demands on academics;
3. the lack of well-placed leadership;
4. problems in quantifying the outcomes of CoP; and
5. issues in ongoing support and programme sustainability. (2006:72)

Educational research must therefore focus on not only the possibilities, but also the restrictions on teachers' work across different contexts in order to understand how teachers' professional and learning communities might be cultivated, and how teachers' communities might influence the development of TPIs.

3.4.4 Sense of Vocation and Personal Values

Another focus of the TPI literature is the development of teachers' sense of vocation and its intersections with teachers' personal experiences and values. Britzman (1993:24) summarises that "role and function are not synonymous with identity; whereas role can be assigned, the taking up of an identity is a constant social negotiation". In this sense, teachers' roles and functions in their work, however, may not be the defining elements of teachers' personal values and identities. We need to investigate teachers' own values to education and their understanding of children's learning embodied in their specific cultural and historical contexts in order to understand teachers' perceptions of themselves and their work. Teachers' perceptions of who they are might be more closely linked with their relationships and daily interactions with their students, colleagues and parents. Therefore, the macro-level theories on teachers' work and professionalism need to be supplemented by the micro-level insights into teachers' interactions and social relationships in school contexts.

Researchers need to be cautious of the tendency to perceive teachers as rationalistic, scientific and cognitive beings when we rely only on theories of teacher knowledge. An account of teacher identity may appear disconnected from teachers' personal experiences of themselves and their changes in their work environments. The notion of teachers' personal, practical knowledge is defined as a set of cognitive beliefs and attitudes developed from wide-ranging personal experiences and backgrounds, which is considered as the centre of TPIs (Golombek, 1998). In a preliminary study of the career stories of 12 teachers in six Belgian primary schools, Kelchtermans and Vandenberghe defined five related parts of TPIs:

1. self-image: how teachers describe themselves throughout their career stories;

2. self-esteem: the evolution of the self as a teacher, how good or otherwise, as defined by self or others;

3. job motivation: what makes teachers choose, remain committed to or leave the job;

4. task perception: how teachers define their jobs; and

5. future perspective: teachers' expectations for the future development of their jobs. (1994: 55-56)

Other empirical studies identified key influences on teachers' identities. In a longitudinal study of 14 teachers' professional experiences in the first two years of their careers, teachers' biographies, pre-service training, and the school culture and leadership were found to constitute key influences on the stability and instability of TPIs (Flores and Day, 2006).

A number of studies attempt to integrate teachers' emotions in understanding teachers' lives and identities (e.g. Hargreaves, 1998, 2000; Zembylas, 2003; Day et al., 2007). In her study of primary school teachers in England in the 1980s, Nias explored the "me" of the teachers' selves, as situated in their working lives, as well as the "I" that was considered the affective component of the self. She distinguished the personal and professional elements of teachers' identities and found that the social identity as "a teacher" is incorporated into an individual's self-image over time. Nias (1989) warns that an examination of teachers' experiences would be incomplete if it did not incorporate a discussion about emotions. This seems to be particularly the case when a teacher's identity is challenged by changes in schools, educational policies and sociocultural contexts (Woods and Carlyle, 2002; Flores and Day, 2006; Darby, 2008; Yin and Lee, 2011a). As Hargreaves emphasises:

> Educational change initiatives do not just affect teachers' knowledge, skill and problem-solving capacity. They affect a whole web of significant and meaningful relationships that make up the work of schools and that are at the very heart of the teaching process [...] Teachers make heavy emotional investments in these relationships. Their sense of success and satisfaction depends on them. (1998:838)

In other words, teachers' emotions, which are embedded in meaningful social relationships, compose an integral part of their lives. Teacher vulnerability, for instance, is found to be a recurring theme in educational changes (Kelchtermans, 1996). In describing the impact of teachers' values and choices, Kelchtermans (1996) noted that teachers' feelings are heavily determined by their social, historical and biographical context and by their own perceptions. Cultural influences on the perception and expression of emotions have also been raised. Yin and Lee (2011b) have described the emotional rules governing Chinese teachers' emotions in their professional practices. According to the researchers, teachers perceive their emotions as at the core of their work, and a significant component of "heart-consuming" (caoxin in Chinese) labour is identified in teacher interviews. Two major interpretations can be identified in explaining teachers' "heart-consuming" labour. Yin and Lee (2011b: 63) argue that the emotional pressure a teacher feels could be grounded in the Chinese tradition of a familial relationship between teacher and students, which is consistent with the Chinese saying that "he who teaches me for one day is my father for life"[①]. Others have used the term a "paradox of power" to describe the situation whereby teachers with high social status in China are placed under a great burden to follow society's moral norms, which makes them more vulnerable to being shamed if they

---

① 一日为师,终身为父。

fail (Gao, 1998; Yin and Lee, 2011b).

Although one cannot be certain whether teachers' emotional discourses actually affect how teachers really feel about themselves, teachers' talk about their emotions could reveal important aspects of their lives influencing how they perceive themselves as teachers. School cultures and teacher education, for instance, might inform what ought to be felt in pre-defined classroom teaching and workplace relationships; understandings of ways to "properly" express themselves could be another influence on teachers' emotional experiences. Zembylas (2005) proposed a different theoretical perspective for defining teachers' emotional work. On the basis of a poststructuralist perspective of identity and place of emotion, Zembylas asserted that a teacher's emotion, as a part of the teacher's discursive practices, is more than a psychological phenomenon located in individuals. Instead, emotion is a social construction based on teachers' social and political experiences. In Cornelius' words, "the experience and expression of emotions is dependent on learned convictions or rules and that, to the extent that cultures differ in the way they talk about and conceptualise emotions, how they are experienced and expressed will differ in different cultures as well" (1996: 188). In Zembylas' discussion, the emotional discourse constitutes a crucial part of teacher identity and is found to be closely linked with teachers' self-knowledge in the process. The "emotional geography" approach taken by Hargreaves (2000, 2005) defines emotional labour as:

> The spatial and experiential patterns of closeness and/or distance in human interactions and relationship that help create, configure and colour the feelings and emotion we experience about ourselves, our world and each other. (2005: 968)

These "emotional geographies" include sociocultural, moral, political, physical and professional dimensions, and are ways teachers describe their relationships to others. As Hargreaves points out, the nature of "emotional geography" will vary in accordance to culture and context, the rules of which are neither natural nor universal. So far, I have reviewed the empirical literature on TPIs and summarised four major domains that could demonstrate a holistic view of factors that influence the development of TPIs: (1) teacher training and education; (2) teacher professionalism and policy demands; (3) teacher community and collaborations; and (4) teachers' sense of vocation and personal values (Figure 3-3). I developed the literature review mainly from school TPIs in other different institutional, social, political and cultural contexts. Though these are all helpful in informing this study, there have been limited studies on teacher identity in the Chinese context.

Figure 3-3　Factors influencing factors on TPIs

3.5　Developing a Conceptual Framework

This DPhil research project focuses on groups of teachers and sets out to ask about the roles that school contexts may play in the realm of their identities and the particular changes and challenges in different identity development. In her study of Chinese teachers' cross-cultural learning experiences in the UK, Gu (2004:122) defined a teacher as primarily "a social being and teaching as a social activity, which bears distinctive meanings and values in specific sociocultural settings". A teacher's identity, which generally refers to ways that teachers see themselves and their work, is a term widely used to explore the interactions between individual teachers and the given social and cultural conditions. This tension is commonly referred to as a tension between agency and structure in social theories. In a systematic investigation of the literature about TPI from the years 1998 to 2000, Beijaard, Meijer and Verloop (2004:108) identified four fundamental features as essential to the definition of TPI:

Dynamic: Identity is an ongoing process of the interpretation and re-interpretation of experience.

Contextualisation: Identity involves both the person and the context. Within the context, teachers learn professional characteristics while attaching their personal values to these characteristics.

Multiplicity: Sub-identities exist within teacher identities, which may be in conflict or harmony with one another according to the context.

Agency: Identity construction comprises teachers' active participation and control over teaching and their pursuit of professional development and learning.

According to the authors, there is a general acknowledgement of the multi-faceted and dynamic nature of identity, which is influenced by both internal (e.g. emotion and stories) and external (e.g. contexts and relationships) factors. In social theories, the use of "agency" often embodies the idea of individuals' or groups' beliefs and desires that drive individual or collective decision-making capacities and goal-oriented behaviours in changing certain aspects of their surroundings; the term "structure", when it is used in relation to agency, often signifies forms of material and possibly ideological forces that explain the behaviours of an individual or group. The above discussion sees teacher identity as neither located entirely within the individuals nor entirely a product of their social settings. Rather, an emerging perspective on teacher identity supports the idea of the coexistence of teachers' agency and structure. Figure 3-4 demonstrates the concept map that I have developed to guide this DPhil study. It is informed by the literature review and my earlier MSc pilot study of 10 private tutoring institute teachers in Shandong (Liu, 2012), which was informed by an empirical study that bridged agency and structure in a four-year longitudinal study with 300 primary and secondary teachers in England (Day et al., 2007). In this study, the researchers identify three interacting and competing dimensions of TPI: professional, situated and personal identities:

> The professional aspect of teachers' sense of self is described as "open to the influence of local and national policy as well as social trends".
> The situated or socially located aspect is defined as the aspect of teachers' sense of self within a particular school, department or classroom.
> The personal identity is the dimension that relates to a teacher's personal life outside school. Various influencing factors are suggested, including gender, family and friends.

They concluded that teachers' identities are constructed from their personal lives outside schools, but also from organisational, professional and cultural influences on their perceptions of being a teacher. Recognising a wide range of personal, social and professional influences, the researchers argue that TPI is "neither intrinsically stable nor intrinsically fragmented"; rather, it is "more or less stable" depending on teachers' ability to manage the interaction and dominance of those dimension(s) in various social settings (Day and Kington, 2008:9). Teachers are found to take a combination of strategies in managing their identities: accommodation, tolerance, resistance, acceptance, engagements, adaptation and subjugation, etc. (ibid.). Although the research context of this study is different, my analysis resonates with the researchers' efforts to develop a holistic perspective that sees TPI development as a dynamic interrelationship of different aspects of teachers' knowledge and experiences in the policy-making process of education reform in China. As shown in Figure 3-4, multiple layers of interactive influencing factors may contribute to the development of TPIs:

1. Factors in the category of *personal experiences* include the teacher's gender, his or her relationship with families and friends, the perceived

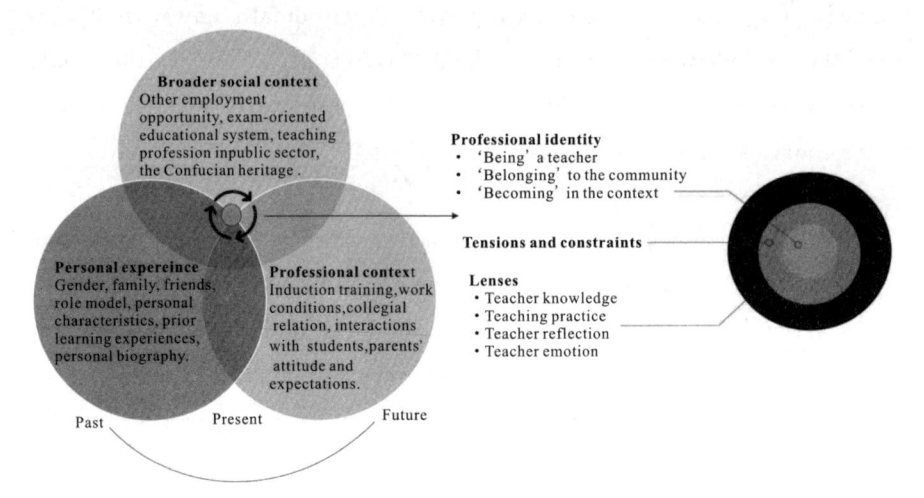

Figure 3-4 The conceptual framework (Liu, 2012)

characteristics of the teacher's personality and his or her role models, prior learning experiences and personal biography. These influences could be from outside of the workplace of the specific school, yet they may create a significant impact on the teacher's values, commitment and emotions.

2. Factors in the categories of *professional context* focus on the school or other organisations that provide support or regulate a teacher's work. A wide range of influences are identified in the process of professional identity formation, including induction training for the teacher, the work conditions, the teacher's relationships with colleagues, interactions with students, and the role of pupils' parents and their attitudes and expectations for schools and teachers.

3. Given that teaching is also a social activity, the development of TPIs could be influenced by the broader social context. Limited employment opportunities with bianzhi and the exam-oriented educational system in China could significantly influence how teachers perceive themselves in teaching. The framework also draws attention to the cultural contexts of the Confucian heritage in education in China. In the previous MSc study, I found that most of the private tutoring school teachers

considered their job as only temporary; they all hoped to teach in state schools and attain the bianzhi status, while they may have different perceptions of the teaching profession in the public/state sector. Therefore, I included "the teaching profession in the public sector" as a potential influencing factor in this DPhil study as well.

In this framework, I included the indicator of time which was directed to the past and to the future. This is to show that TPIs, in the multiple contexts, could change and transform when they were narrated across chronological orders. In the centre of the three contexts is an arrow that lead to the manifestation of TPIs, that is, what TPI actually means or is constituted of. As shown in the bottom of the graph, the framework defined professional identity using three main aspects: (1) "being" a teacher, which includes the teacher's definition of a good teacher, teaching practices and experiences, as well as the teachers' professional qualifications; (2) "belonging" to the community, that is, a teacher's sense of connection with the students, colleagues, the school management and significant others; and (3) "becoming" in the context indicates teachers' aspirations, and their sense of satisfaction and professional status. The literature examined helped to define four main conceptual lenses that may mediate the manifestation of TPIs: teachers' knowledge and beliefs, teachers' practices, teachers' personal and professional reflections, and teachers' emotions. This framework also highlighted the characteristics of tension and constraints in the exploration process, as it is a necessary yet undeveloped area in the field of TPIs.

3.6 Summary

In this chapter, I reviewed the literature on both theories and empirical studies of TPIs. The review covered four main topics:

1. The broad implication of identity in different disciplinary areas

and different theoretical perspectives on identity in educational research.
2. The co-existence of personal and social identities.
3. The effect of TPIs on teachers' performances and practices.
4. Influences on TPIs in different social and cultural contexts.

The concept of TPIs has been broadened out in a growing number of empirical studies. There is a broad recognition of the multidimensional, dynamic and complex nature of TPI and its development. One of the key findings in reviewing the literature is that TPIs cannot be understood using a single approach. Instead of being a homogeneous concept, identities vary between individuals, groups and communities, and over time. While the formation of TPIs is certainly important for teacher effectiveness and professional development, there are often multiple layers of, and rapidly changing, contexts that shape the process of becoming a successful teacher and the composition of what it means to be one. There is also usually great differentiation of TPIs even within a particular group of teachers. Both positive and negative connotations are found to be related to the idea of forming an integrated professional identity in ever-changing educational contexts in China and around the world.

The literature included a wide range of factors and contexts that various authors viewed as being particularly important in developing TPIs. Few are backed up by a comparative analysis of different groups of teachers and focus almost exclusively on the effectiveness of a particular teacher education programme. In teachers' everyday lives, it is almost impossible to balance the various factors claimed as important for the development of TPIs. But teacher commitment, professional reflection and professional community are the most supported items in the literature. Gradually, teacher vulnerability, identity crises and tensions have appeared in recent empirical studies, yet there is a lack of well-developed theory and accepted indicators for further identification and measurement. There do not appear to be many generalisable findings in the literature about tensions and teachers' coping strategies.

A few research requirements and gaps would be of particular importance in the field of TPI. Firstly, research is needed into the types and perhaps the prevalence of tensions in the process of developing TPIs, and the main factors influencing how changes in TPIs can be assessed. How does TPI development in different cultural and social contexts equate professional identities in other school contexts and in the service and industrial sectors? How can cross-sectoral learning be improved (e.g. health and education, technology and education, public and private sectors, higher education and primary education, etc.)? What are the means by which barriers to the formation of TPIs at the institutional level could be removed? Studies are also needed on the contributions of individual and professional strategies in supporting the development of TPIs and negotiating barriers and boundaries. The impact of technology on TPIs also requires better understanding and further exploration.

In addition to identifying the gaps in existing studies, the literature review has also allowed me to develop a concept map to organise key topics related to TPIs and has assisted the framing of the RQs (Section 4.2). In terms of RQ 1, the literature review has aided me by identifying the three theoretical approaches to identity—symbolic interactionism, the sociocultural perspective and poststructuralism—and the different focuses in exploring TPIs in the Chinese context. It has also aided me to adjust the conceptual framework to connect the major topics and concepts for a more coherent picture of how the ideas might be related to TPIs within the research. These topics and concepts include teachers' knowledge, teachers' emotion, professional reflections and teachers' engagements with tensions. As for RQ 2, the literature examined has helped me to be aware of multiple layers of contextual influences on TPIs in different school contexts in China. In the literature, it became evident that variable personal, social and professional factors could exert a significant impact on the development of TPIs. Scholars have adopted both constructivist and pragmatic approaches to map the complex influences on teachers' experience of the formation of their TPIs. In practice, the concept of TPIs is also used as a pedagogical tool for education innovation and evaluations of teachers' learning, professional development and policies.

Furthermore, the literature review has also helped me to identify the lack of comparative studies on TPIs in state schools and private schools.

Although the literature review is specifically focused on TPIs, in the broad scope of professional learning and development, it should not be forgotten that educational research can gain a great deal from other fields of academic research and general models of professional development. Nevertheless, the literature examined has helped me to frame this DPhil research by identifying the different focuses of the different theoretical perspectives on identity and by indicating key influences, issues and gaps related to the TPI concept.

Chapter 4
Research Design and Methodology

This chapter presents the methodological approach I adopt to investigate TPIs in four different state and private schools in China. The first section outlines the RQs derived from discussions in the literature review. This leads to the subsequent discussion of the use of the narrative approach to investigate and compare TPIs in private and state primary schools in China. The second section explains the sampling scheme adopted in this research, including purposive sampling and snowball sampling. It also gives an overview of the school contexts. The third section deals with the process of data collection and covers such issues as the development of the interview guide and the negotiation of entry to the research field. In the following section, I will present procedures for data analysis, which focus on individual teachers at this stage. Issues related to assessing the quality of the qualitative research are discussed in the fifth section, with the strategies adopted to build upon the rigour of this research study. The final section draws this chapter to a conclusion through discussing issues of reflexivity, research ethics and some limitations of the research study.

4.1 Origin of the Study

This research stems from my personal experiences teaching English to primary school students in a local private school. In this role, I witnessed the efforts made by teachers to support students' learning. Teachers are considered key to the success of schools and education in general in modern China. As I communicated with the students and their parents, I became aware of their different attitudes towards teachers in state and private schools. On the one hand, there are teachers who are highly respected for their professional skills and ethical conduct; those well-recognised teachers are always in very high demand. On the other hand, I also heard students and parents complain about the low quality of teachers, which is closely related to the phenomena of corporal punishment and fee-charging tutoring in schools. I became increasingly interested in understanding the changing attitudes to teachers and how they themselves understand their lives and negotiate their own positions in the wider educational environment.

My own story as a teacher in a private tutoring institute led me to ask myself: "What is important for teachers? What do teachers want people to know about their profession and lives? What strategies do teachers take to resist discouragement and what helps them to define themselves as teachers? How do teachers know where they really belong?" The research methodology emerged as my interest in the teachers' stories grew. I wanted to embrace different modes of understanding while exploring ways in which teachers' experiences and beliefs are linked and integrated with the personal, social, cultural and political contexts. To achieve this objective, I needed a research approach that enabled me to focus on the lives of individuals and groups and co-construct meanings while participating in the study.

This research adopts a narrative inquiry approach because the nature of narrative inquiry applies most aptly to the objectives of this research. I would argue that one way to improve existing theories about the professional identities developed in the context of neo-liberal educational reform is to incorporate the patterns and changes in non-Western societies, which is also a challenge faced by scholars in the field of education. To transcend the limited knowledge about teacher identities and professionalism, I believe that I need to turn to teachers' narratives to consider how their professional identities and cultures are actually established through processes of contested negotiation, rather than through abstract theoretical models. Before explaining the application of narrative inquiry in framing this research, the following section begins with a review of research aims, objectives and questions.

4.2 RQs and Research Strategy

4.2.1 The RQs

As mentioned above, this study investigates and compares the development of TPIs in private and state schools in Nanqi in China. My aim is to find out how PSTs' experiences and identities differ from those of SSTs. As stated in Section 1.2, the main research aims of this DPhil study are: (1) to explore the processes and influencing factors of professional identity constructions in different primary school contexts; (2) to investigate teachers' strategies to reconcile tensions and uncertainties in these processes; and (3) compare the characteristics of TPIs across individual and school cases in both state and private schools.

The following research objective (ORs) seek to facilitate the achievement of these aims.

RO 1: To identify the perceived factors impacting the changes and development of individual teachers' sense of identity at work.

RO 2: To assess teachers' perceptions and experiences of their engagements with others in their particular school contexts and how this might influence teachers' professional self-efficacy and sense of belongingness at work.

RO 3: To identify the tensions that teachers experience in constructing their professional identities and their perceived conditions and strategies to address those tensions.

RO 4: To further record and theorise teachers' narratives of the processes of reacting to these perceived tensions and uncertainties, which may or may not further influence teachers' sense of their professional identities.

RO 5: To identify the differences and similarities of school contexts that are relevant to TPIs.

RO 6: To identify characteristics of individual TPI constructions and compare these characteristics inside and across four school cases.

Embedded in the general inquiry are the following specific RQs:

RQ 1: What characterises teachers' sense of their professional identities in the four different primary schools (two state schools and two private schools) in Nanqi in China?
- Sub-question 1: How do teachers within each school construct their professional identities?
- Sub-question 2: How do teachers experience tensions in each school?
- Sub-question 3: What are the other characteristics of TPIs?

RQ 2: What personal and social factors do teachers consider important in shaping their professional identities?

RQ 3: What are the differences and similarities in the TPIs in the two state schools and two private schools in Nanqi?

To achieve the primary purpose of the enquiry, I chose to explore the comparative characteristics of TPIs by using an interpretive approach and adopting interviews as the method. I investigated the meaning-making practices of individual teachers in different school contexts through their narratives about their work and roles. Thus, the first RQ identifies the characteristics of teachers' personal experiences and reveals the ways in which teachers construct their sense of professional identity in their narratives. The second RQ investigates the perceived personal and social factors that may influence teachers' sense of self and of their own professionalism; it also attempts to explore how individual teachers respond to multiple structural restrictions and opportunities in their professional lives. This question also brings an exploration of other factors that may shape teachers' experiences beyond the school context. The third question further examines the similarities and differences of TPIs in the four different private schools and state schools.

4.2.2 Narrative Inquiry

Because the focus of this study is teachers' personal and social experiences and the quality of their working lives, I consider narrative inquiry to be the most appropriate approach to address my RQs. The narrative approach helps me to bring together the multiple layers of the personal and socio-cultural aspects of teachers' lives, and how these lead to changes in TPIs. The shapes of teachers' stories also support my attempt to understand the ways in which teachers interpret key events in their personal and professional lives and how their values, beliefs and experiences guide those interpretations in this study. The local knowledge gained, which is characterised by multiple voices and perspectives, helps me to better identify social discourses that may impact teachers' knowledge development in their own specific contexts.

Narrative inquiry is increasingly used in educational research to explore the phenomena of human experiences (Connelly and Clandinin, 1990). Connelly and Clandinin (2006: 477) support the narrative view that takes human experiences as "storied lives":

> People shape their daily lives by stories of who they and others are and as they interpret their past in terms of these stories. Story, in the current idiom, is a portal through which a person enters the world by which their experiences of the world is interpreted and made personally meaningful. Viewed this way, narrative is the phenomenon studied in inquiry.

Bruner (1987) also distinguishes two ways of knowing: (1) the paradigmatic mode of thought; and (2) narrative knowing. The paradigmatic mode of thought is described as the process of reasoned analysis, logical proof and empirical observation used to explain "cause and effect" and to create unambiguous, objective "truth" that can be proven or disproved. In contrast, the other side of the mind, namely the "narrative mode", is the human act of imagination, which constructs knowledge and creates meanings through stories of lived experiences, helping people to make sense of the ambiguity and complexity of human lives. In this sense, knowledge is not a fixed entity; instead, it is socially constructed and changes according to contexts and social relations. By translating knowing into story-telling, individuals can make meanings and link their experiences of the world together. Of course, there is no single perspective about the centrality of narratives in human experiences. Polkinghorne (1988) claims that narrative is the impetus for those seeking to create coherence in interpreting human existence. He suggests that experience forms and represents itself in one's awareness of narrative in its original literary form. In this view, actions will be inconsistent, and time will be experienced as incoherent without the use of the narrative formation as a sense-making device. Packer (1991) considers narrative not as a primary mode, but as a need of human beings to engage with and construct meanings in particular situations:

> Understanding is, first and foremost, a way of grasping the entities around us in the active and engaged manner. Through this grasping, we comprehend ourselves at the same time. Mostly, these entities, and the network of interrelationships among them, are transparent and invisible to us, but when practice breaks down, the entities [that] are their interrelationships stand out and [get] troublesome. At this point, in our practical deliberations on breakdown, we undertake interpretation articulating aspects of our project, its objects, and its setting, in order to resume smooth practice [...] Interpretation is the articulation—the laying out and explication—of possibilities that have been projected and have become available in practical understanding. (1991: 71)

White (1980) supports the idea of story-telling as a primary tool for meaning-making by stating that our initial experience is not as fluid as narrative. Instead, narrative serves as a representation of the meaning we give to that experience. Lived experiences cannot be presented as "objective" facts. It is subjective, and it is situated in time, language and culture, and limited by the memories that are used to interpret the experiences. Connelly and Clandinin (1987) define "narrative unity" as a person in place and time, claiming that the desire for coherence and unity emerges in narratives of experiences.

Bruner (1991: 21) further argues for sociological concern with group lives in narrative inquiry by claiming that the "cultural tool kits" and "exchanges in a linguistic community" support narratives, as a "conventional form of knowing". In other words, stories have a typical structure. An important development of the idea here is that narratives are not merely personal constructions of meaning; they are developed in particular social contexts. By drawing on narrative inquiry, this study also conceptualises research as an active and constructive process, one through which I can pursue a deeper understanding of teacher identity development by integrating my own role and viewpoints with those of the participants. This point is further supported by the interpretative tradition of hermeneutics and selection, and by the framing of research methods, as I now explain.

4.2.3 The Tradition of Hermeneutics

From within the discipline of anthropology, Michael Agar (2008) describes the process of interpretative qualitative research as a dialectic cycle in which the researcher goes back and forth between data collection and analysis in attempting to negotiate the shared interests, knowledge and intentions of the researcher with his or her participants. The methodological approach of this study is influenced by the interpretative tradition of hermeneutics, which originates from the Greek word *hermeneuo*, meaning "to interpret". Hermeneutics is conventionally understood as a methodology for reading and interpreting texts (Davey, 2013). It was developed for use in biblical interpretation and philological investigation of the classics and has been extended to the reading of non-biblical texts. The contemporary understanding of hermeneutics is strongly influenced by Hans-Georg Gadamer, who argues that the process of textual interpretation is constituted by continuous interactions or conversations between authors' and readers' "horizon [s] of understanding", that is, "the range of vision that includes everything that can be seen from a particular vantage point" (Gadamer, 1979:143). This means that interpretations are influenced by the preliminary experience of personal life, lifestyle and culture of the participants (both the actors and the researchers) (Hekman, 1984; Patterson and Williams, 2002). Unlike more relativistic interpretative paradigms that seek to set aside researchers' prior knowledge, hermeneutic epistemology explicitly recognises the positive function of researchers' primary understanding, or "prejudice[s]", on their conclusions (Hekman, 1984). In this sense, a teacher's professional identity can be understood as constructed in a dialectical process in the encounters between the participant teachers and the researcher throughout the process of research.

Instead of assuming objective structural similarities based on predetermined theories, a hermeneutic epistemology suggests beginning with the analysis of individual cases (i.e. idiographic-level analysis) and then combining conclusions with other individuals (i.e. nomothetic-level analysis) at a later stage (Terwee, 1990). The focus on individual cases in hermeneutic analysis reflects the belief that each situation should be recognised as unique. This is not to deny the existence of shared meanings. The flexible and open-ended nature of narrative inquiry enables me to trace the twists and turns in the conversations, in which certain topics are chosen or avoided by the teachers. In this process, I can explore how the research process and my own identity help (or hinder) teachers in making meaning of their work in relation to their professional identities. For example, teachers in this research may not want to explicitly discuss the curriculum or educational reform. They might instead recount their stories of learning, teaching, working and family lives. Themes such as the perceived characteristics of a successful teacher might not be highlighted but might emerge as a topic within detailed accounts of different teachers' narratives.

4.3 The Pilot Study

Before the main qualitative investigation, a pilot study was carried out in April 2011 as an MSc thesis project. This aimed to offer a first glimpse into TPIs in the context of private educational institutes in China. This pilot study grounded the topic of TPIs in the context of PTIs. Combining the research aims, research questions and the pragmatic concerns of time and resources for conducting the research, I adopted an interpretivist perspective using semi-structured qualitative interviews with a purposive sample of ten teachers of English from three PTIs in Shandong province in China. The consent form and interview guide were developed and used to collect narrative data about teachers' experiences in PTIs and their reflections on their professional practices, decisions and identities. This process helped me to refine the interview guide and its Chinese version to avoid vagueness and misunderstandings. I was also able to get feedbacks on my interview techniques and gain an initial understanding of the significant experiences of teachers in this study. Below is a brief summary of the key points and processes in developing the interview guide and the key findings from the pilot study.

4.3.1 Purpose of the In-depth Interview

1. To gain detailed and in-depth information about individual teachers' subjective perceptions of their work.

2. To build personal rapports with participants and encourage them to provide more information on issues that might be sensitive.

3. To co-construct the narrative that allows participants to reflect on their assumptions, emotional engagement and experiences in the research.

4.3.2 Drafting the In-depth Interview Guide

1. To confirm that the potential respondents are aware of the purposes and scope of the research and the amount of time the interview would take, I drafted and used a consent form and probed for teachers' concerns before the interview questions.

2. The interviews were audio-recorded with the participant's permission. All interviews were conducted and later transcribed (in Chinese) for analysis. Two transcripts were translated into English for the purposes of transparency.

3. The interview guide was developed to address the research questions and informed by the reading of literature on TPIs.

4. According to the initial conceptual framework, aspects of the interview guide included:

(1) Personal background: the teacher's age, education and position.

(2) Knowledge: what a teacher knows and thinks about specific aspects of teaching and his or her work in general.

(3) Behaviours: what a teacher does at work and in the classroom, as well as how he or she plans to achieve his or her career goals.

(4) Feelings: how a teacher feels about specific issues in his or her work.

4.3.3 Wording of Questions

1. To keep the questions neutral and open-ended, I avoided questions with yes or no answers or those that might generate strong emotional reactions.

Example: Instead of asking "Are you satisfied with your performance in teaching?" (你对自己的教学表现感到满意吗?), I asked, "For you, what are the most satisfactory things about teaching?" (对你来讲,教学当中最让你满意的事情有哪些?).

2. To keep the wording clear and simple, I avoided jargon and technical terms.

Example: Instead of asking "What is your career plan?" (你有哪些职业规划?), I asked: "Where do you see yourself in five years' time?" (你怎么看自己 5 年以后的样子?).

3. To keep the interview more natural, I also shared personal knowledge and experiences in the questions.

Example: Instead of asking "How do you compare yourself with state school teachers?" (你怎么拿自己和公办学校教师比较?), I asked: "Some people say that teachers in PTIs are different from those in state schools, what's your opinion?" (有人说培训学校教师和公办学校教师不同,你对这一点怎么看?).

4.3.4 Order of Questions

1. To engage participants in the interview, I started the interview with less controversial questions, for example those about educational background, age or career choices.
2. The interview questions were ordered chronologically to support teachers' reflections on their current perceptions and circumstances.

I asked the participants to give feedbacks or talk about any issues they thought important and which had not been addressed in the interview.

4.3.5 Key Findings

The findings indicated the differences as well as the commonalities in the negotiation of the professional identities of PTI teachers. Both contextual and personal factors were identified as contributing to the participants' understanding of themselves as PTI teachers; at the same time, conflicts and tensions were apparent in the negotiation of their identities in their workplaces. The result led to a refinement of the initial framework.

4.4 The Sampling Scheme

A sampling scheme is defined as the specific method used to select the data, including where the study is to be conducted, who and what events it includes and how the participants are to be identified (Onwuegbuzie and Leech, 2007). For the optimal selection of the research participants in the main study, I used two sampling strategies in accordance with the research design: purposive sampling and snowball sampling. In this section, I will first introduce the research site, providing the specific contexts for the sampling before describing the sampling strategies I used in this research study.

4.4.1 The Research Site

Gatekeepers control access to schools and teachers; therefore, they played a significant role in this research (Miller and Bell, 2002). In my attempt to gain access to schools, my experience of working in Nanqi gave me an advantage in building trust with the school principals and teachers. As Lee suggests, "social access crucially depends on establishing interpersonal trust" (1993:123). I will now move on to explain how I chose and accessed the research field for this research study.

This study was conducted in Nanqi (a pseudonym), which is in the north-eastern part of Shandong province. In China, the word county (xian) is used to refer to a settlement at the third level of the structural hierarchy of administrative division. Shandong province has 136 counties in total. The county is on the lowest level of the administrative hierarchy of urban areas in China. Since the 1980s, the demographics of Nanqi have seen a trend towards rural-urban integration due to the dramatic urbanisation process. The vast majority of Nanqi's population, however, are rural residents. Many families from rural areas have moved to urban areas to work, and in the hope of getting their children enrolled in good urban schools. This has resulted in increased pressure on both the parents and schools to compete for better educational resources. As the birthplace of an ancient Chinese philosopher and educator, Nanqi's development has always been shaped by its cultural significance. Since the 1980s, Nanqi has been considered a successful example of China's socio-economic development in harmony with cultural richness. Education is considered one of the major drivers for building a harmonious and prosperous community. This process is fueled by a strong demand for education and the development of cultural industries in Nanqi (i.e. commercial production or arts, crafts and other artistic output).

The six-year primary schooling period is one of the four major parts of China's education system, achieving a 99.93% enrolment rate in 2016 (Ministry of Education, 2017). According to Nanqi's *12th Five-Year Plan for Education Development* (Bureau of Education, 2013), in 2013 there were over 120 schools and about 60,000 students in this county. The numbers of primary, junior secondary and senior secondary schools were approximately 90, 20 and 2, respectively.[①] There were also 5 junior vocational training schools and over 140 kindergartens. In terms of the teaching profession, Nanqi had about 5,500 full-time state teachers. Primary school teachers account for about half of the total and make up the biggest proportion of the state-employed teaching population. Nanqi also has a large proportion of older teachers: about half are over 40 and over one-fifth are in their 50s.

The gap between the greater demand for high-quality education and the restrictions in terms of finances and spaces facing state schools represents a huge challenge for local governments and schools. In the state schools that I visited, the numbers of students in each class exceeded 80, a tremendous challenge for teachers and schools in managing their classrooms and guaran-

---

① I used the approximate number to maintain the confidentiality of the county and the school information.

teeing the quality of teaching. In 2015, the provincial government released the *Notice on Solving the Problem Related to Overcrowded Classrooms in Urban Areas*, requiring local government to "solve the problem of overcrowded classrooms" by the end of 2017, directly suggesting the principle of "city-district planning, county-leading, one policy for one county, mainly through school expansion and amplifying the urban educational resources". In the policy document, the number of newly established schools is specified. This is to encourage innovation by the school management and the "civil force" (shehui liliang) to establish new primary and secondary schools in different types of state-private partnership (private school, state-sponsored private school, hybrid school, etc.). In 2016, Nanqi had one private charity school, with two more private schools under construction. While I was doing my fieldwork, I was also aware of the influences of another international private school on educational experiences and choices in Nanqi. Some parents in Nanqi are considering sending their children to that school despite its location (about one and half hours by car from Nanqi) and the high tuition fees (in comparison with the free state schools).

For the state schools, the increase in demand for high-quality education in the era of urbanisation is a major issue. Although the government has increased its investment by improving the infrastructure to cope with the increase in students, the number of qualified state teachers remains a main obstacle to solving the problem of overcrowded classes and meeting the need for high-quality education in general. In China, however, state primary schools have no authority to determine the number of students and staff they recruit. Instead, the local government allocates the quotas, which largely determines how the school is funded, and how the teacher shortage is dealt with. On the other hand, the shifts towards decentralisation in China are "giving more autonomy and responsibility to local authorities for primary and secondary schools and strengthening the power of principals to make decisions regarding their schools" (Lewin et al., 1994: 202).

I chose Nanqi as the research site for three major reasons. First, the societal context of Nanqi is characterised by a mixture of influences of the government, the market, the traditional culture and broader international trends in education. Although they do not show all the characteristics of the education system in China, schools in Nanqi have played key roles in the recent national education reform and typically reflect the educational contexts of a small, third-tier city in northern China. Secondly, considerations of personal and practical issues have been included in making the research decision. My experience has also provided familiarity with local educational contexts. This was a very important factor in facilitating my approach to potential participants, particularly when the rapport between the researcher and the participants became a primary factor in validating and applying the research findings. Thirdly, geographical proximity was a factor. Through personal connections, I was able to get in touch with schools in Nanqi. Also, given the city's particular socio-economic situation and cultural historical legacy, my research findings may indicate how the local context might influence teachers' social relationships with parents and students, as well as their changing roles and identities in state and private schools. This research could provide new insights into the question of alternative ways of thinking about the role of the market, resource distribution and local contexts in education in contemporary China.

4.4.2 The Sampling Strategy

Tashakkori and Teddlie (1998) classify sampling techniques into two broad types: probability sampling and purposive sampling. Probability sampling is described as a method of randomly selecting a relatively large number of units from a group or subgroup population. In this sense, the inclusion of every unit in the samples is determinable. As a result, the research finding can be generalised and applied to a larger defined population or setting (ibid.). Purposive sampling, on the other hand, is based on the assumption that the researcher needs to identify and select the sample that can provide valuable information or develop or test certain theoretical ideas (Maxwell and Loomis, 2003). This sampling strategy is often used in exploratory and descriptive qualitative research.

As I mentioned at the beginning of the section, this study employs a purposive sampling strategy to determine the target population and to select participants who can provide rich information with respect to the goal of the study (Kemper, Stringfield and Teddlie, 2003; Patton, 1990). This is in line with Maxwell and Loomis' (2003) claim that the selection of a sampling scheme is closely related to research questions, research methods and available resources. This study has an explicit focus on TPIs in both state schools and private schools, and proper participants need to be selected to answer the research questions.

There are no clear rules on the size of samples in qualitative research; size is informed by "fitness for purpose" (Cohen, Manion and Morrison, 2011: 161). Considering the depth of the investigation, and the time limits on the data collection and analysis, I decided to interview four teachers from each of the four schools in Nanqi. My intention in this study is not to generalise from the findings of a limited group of teachers, but to offer an in-depth picture of a group of teachers' perceptions and experiences in specific contexts. This will allow me to identify the relevant factors that contribute to differences and similarities among the participants and to compare them. Given the exploratory nature of this study, I include teachers from a wide variety of age groups, occupational life phases and types of school. Another factor in the sampling decision is the practical limit on the scope of this doctoral study. In this project, I interviewed four teachers from each of the schools, with varying characteristics in terms of gender, professional life phase, work organisation and location. The criteria were:

  1. Participants must be interested in the topic and willing to participate;
  2. Participant teachers will be drawn from either a private or a state school in the purposive sample of four schools (two private and two state schools);
  3. Both state teachers and private teachers must be included; and
  4. Participants must be at different professional life phases (e.

g. less experienced and more experienced).

Snowball sampling was used to gain access to participants. According to a definition provided by Vogt (1999), snowball sampling is a useful tool for researchers to find research subjects, who will then introduce another subject and so on. Snowball sampling seeks to take advantage of the social networks of identified respondents to approach potential contacts (Thomson, 1997). In Nanqi, teachers are considered key representatives of school qualities and some may define themselves as part of the urban elite in Nanqi, which adds to the difficulties in gaining access to the participants. By using snowball sampling, I sought to build trust with them. The involvement of the school principal in this study might lead to a more complete perspective on the school context. This is also informed by some research that identified the influence of school leadership on TPIs (e.g. Day et al., 2007). Because the school principal is responsible for school management, he or she can offer complementary perspectives on school changes, the quality of education and teachers' development. Therefore, the sample includes both teachers and the school principals in the four schools. Having introduced Nanqi as the research site and the sampling strategy, I now delineate the four types of school I chose for my fieldwork.

4.4.3 Brief Introduction to the School Sites

4.4.3.1 The Willow School (the sub-district state school)

The first school is a sub-district primary school, which is located in the rural-urban continuum of Nanqi. In 2000, the Willow School was merged with another local school due to the policy of optimising the school layouts in Nanqi. As a sub-district state school, the Willow School is also administered by a district secondary school. The school is under the command of the Education Bureau at the county level, which means the county government is responsible for funding and managing the school. This school runs the six-year-long national standard curriculum. In 2016, it had 36 classes with 2,400 students and 160 teachers and staff in total. This means that each class had over 80 students and the number of teaching staff fell seriously short of what was needed.

4.4.3.2 The Aspen School (state school directly under the city/county government)

Aspen is the second sample school, which is a school under direct city/county government control (shizhi). This means the school is subordinated directly to the Education Bureau at the county level. Established in 1933, Aspen has been a demonstration (shifan) school. This school is located in the centre of the old county and is very close to the tourist area. Aspen covers the largest school district area population and is the biggest primary school in terms of student population. It currently has more than 60 classes and over 4,000 students. It has also been evaluated as one of the best schools in Nanqi.

4.4.3.3 The Redwood Charity School (private charity school for "sub-orphans")

Redwood is a charity school that accommodates the educational needs of children with special needs and those in poverty. Unlike charity schools that are funded by non-governmental and charity organisations, Redwood is fully funded by a local estate development company and runs as an "enterprise-run school". As the third charity school established by the same company, Redwood is located in the development area of Nanqi and has about 800 students, 23 classes and 40 teachers, who work on a contract basis. It uses the "6+3+2" model: students receive 11 years' education, which includes six years' primary education, three years' lower secondary education and two years' vocational training.

4.4.3.4 The Ash International School (private international school)

Ash is an international school located in the high-tech development zone of Nanqi. This zone was established in 1992 as a provincial development area. The school was first established to provide primary and secondary education for the children of employees of foreign companies in this area. To develop its capacity for setting up and managing an international curriculum, as well as to help the process of internationalisation, the school established collaboration with a local state school (Acacia) from another province. The managing team has been taking charge of the school curriculum, teacher recruitment, management of foreign teachers, teaching, etc. The collaboration took the form of a cross-regional school partnership overseen by the local management committee. The Ash International School is considered a sign of internationalisation in Nanqi and a new experiment in cross-regional school partnership.

Table 4-1 The basic characteristics of the four case schools

	State schools		Private schools	
	Willow	Aspen	Redwood	Ash
School type	Sub-district primary school	City primary school	K-12 charity school	K-12 international school
Number of students	About 2,400	About 4,000	About 800	About 3,000
Number of teachers	About 160	About 300	About 40	About 200
Funding source	County government	County government	A local real estate company	The development district of Nanqi
Management	Bureau of Education	Bureau of Education	Professionals employed by the funding company	An independent educational cooperation
Curriculum	National curriculum	National curriculum	National curriculum	National curriculum and international curriculum

Table 4-2 Teacher participants in this research

School	Pseudonym	Gender	Teaching experience	Subject	Educational background
Willow (State school)	(A1) Xiwen	Female	1 year	Chinese	MA
	(A2) Haoting	Male	10 years	Maths	College diploma
	(A3) Yifan	Female	30 years	Maths	College diploma
	(A4) Ruolan	Female	3 years	Chinese	BA

Continued

School	Pseudonym	Gender	Teaching experience	Subject	Educational background
Aspen (State school)	(B1) Qizhen	Female	20 years	Chinese	College diploma
	(B2) Xinxin	Female	3 years	Maths	BA
	(B3) Zhe	Male	3 years	Chinese	BA
	(B4) Jianguo	Male	5 years	Maths	BA
Redwood (Private school)	(C1) Linjia	Female	1 year	Maths	College diploma
	(C2) Ting	Female	1 year	Fine arts	BA
	(C3) Meng	Male	2 years	Maths	BA
	(C4) Wei	Male	1 year	PE	BA
Ash (Private school)	(D1) Zhulin	Female	8 years	English	BA
	(D2) Cong	Female	20 years	Maths	College diploma
	(D3) Baihe	Female	10 years	Maths	BA
	(D4) Yu	Female	4 years	Chinese	BA

4.5 The Use of Interviews

How to turn the theoretical concepts of narrative inquiry into a practical interview process was my primary concern. Various researchers have written about interviews and interview conversations, including Briggs (2003), Gubrium and Holstein (2003), Kvale (1996) and Mishler (1986). An in-depth interview can be a powerful research method that generates narrative accounts of individuals' lives and everyday experiences (Elliott, 2005; Kvale, 2009). As Kvale (1996: 5-6) states, the purpose of an interview is to "obtain descriptions of the life world of the interviewee with respect to interpreting the meaning of described phenomena". Tuckman (1972: 197) provides a more specific description of the merits of a qualitative interview: "By providing access to what is 'inside a person's head', [it] makes it possible to measure what a person knows (knowledge or information), what a person likes or dislikes (values and preferences), and what a person thinks (attitudes and beliefs)." In order to understand the school context and the influences on a teacher's perceptions and work experiences, I adopted the interview as the primary method to collect rich qualitative data about teachers' lives. This allowed me to explore teachers' knowledge of the school contexts, and their educational values and teaching beliefs. I also invited participants to reflect upon issues of teacher quality and education and elicited the stories they told in making sense of other aspects of their working lives.

Bryman (2008) also argued that semi-structured interviews could help by assuring cross-case comparability, which suits the purpose of this research project in comparing TPIs in state and private schools. To summarise, I used an interview guide in this study for three reasons:

1. To keep the conversation fluid and foster a good sense of timing;

2. To include specific issues indicated in the literature view, such as teachers' educational backgrounds, workplace relationships and their outlooks; and

3. To help to offer a comparative dimension in analysing patterns of experiences in different personal and work contexts.

To bring teachers' rich self-narratives, voices and experiences into the research process, I gathered their narratives from different private and state schools. As reviewed previously, existing literature indicates that aspects of teachers' identities could be influenced by their earlier education and personal backgrounds, as well as by access to participation in school communities. Hence, I included four key topics in the teacher interview guidance:

1. Teachers' educational background and earlier experiences;

2. Teachers' career decisions and motivations to work in private and/or state schools;

3. Teachers' perceptions/experiences of their work; and

4. Teachers' expectations of school education and their career aspirations.

In this research study, I also included interviews with school principals to gain familiarity of the school contexts and negotiate access to interview teachers. I consider school principals as important informants and gatekeepers. Interviews with them helped me understand the different situations of school management and the expected roles of school leaders. The school principal interview protocol includes three main topics:

1. Introduction to the school;
2. School policies on teacher recruitment and education; and
3. Leadership and organisational vision.

It is important to note that I use the interviews with principals only as supplementary contextual data to discuss the findings in the analysis. Meanwhile, I am aware that teachers' narratives are more than the objective description of discrete experiences. Rather, narratives as a "text" also take into account how and why stories are presented in certain ways.

4.6 Data Analysis

In analysing the interview data, I am aware that my authority as a researcher needs to be supported by a rigorous scientific research method in creating the portraits and generating and interpreting findings. I drew on Miles and Huberman's (1994) suggested framework for the process of coding and data display; this focused on three components throughout the analysis:

1. Data reduction: the component that includes the coding of data (transcript) without losing the context. In the authors' words, it is "a form of analysis that sharpens, sorts, focuses, discards, and organises data that conclusion can be drawn" (Miles and Huberman, 1994: 10).
2. Data display: the process of displaying data with diagrams, charts or models, which runs alongside the data reduction components.
3. Conclusion: drawing conclusions throughout the data analysis process. Early conclusions may be vague but are verified during the analysis.

In addition to Miles and Huberman's (1994) framing of the analysis process, I used three structured tools to ensure the validation of the process:

(1) a hybrid approach to thematic analysis with inductive and deductive coding to demonstrate the reliability of the analysis (see Figure 3); (2) close attention to the transcribing and translation process to enhance the validity of cross-language qualitative research; and (3) reflexivity to examine my own assumptions and preconceptions that I may have brought to the research.

4.6.1 Transcribing and Translating

After the fieldwork, I first transcribed the recorded interviews on spreadsheets for further analysis. This process served as the initial stage of the data analysis process. By listening to and typing out my conversations with teachers, I was further able to embed the analysis of teachers' narratives into the framework of the study. Glaser (1992: 27-30) used the term "theoretical sensitivity" in order to "define the process of generating concepts from data and systematically developing the concepts in relation to the data during different stages of the research study". In this research, the process of transcription required me to draw on more implicit information, such as body language and the tone of voice, for the data analysis and this can be considered a facilitating stage contributing to my reflection of the content and context of the interviews. I also developed some of the initial codes as I transcribed the interview data.

After I had transcribed all the interviews in Chinese, my primary concern in data analysis became the language which I should use to analyse the data. From an interpretative perspective, as Berger and Luckmann suggested, language "is capable of becoming the object repository of the vast accumulation of meaning and experience, which it can then preserve in time and transmit to following generations" (1966: 52). Accordingly, language is key to tracing the participants' generalised patterns of meaning and experiences (Inhetveen, 2012: 29). In qualitative studies, the close distance between experienced meanings and interpreted meanings is crucial to research validity (Polkinghorne, 2007). My background as a native Chinese speaker gives me the advantage in the analysis of the data in its original verbal form (Chinese). The first language differences occur when interpretations are discussed with my supervisors in the form of writing pen portraits for each teacher and in creating codes. Multiple meanings were revealed and discussed in this process. For the discussion, I first translated two interview transcripts in full and then listed the codes and their explanations in English. In this process, it is crucial to be sensitive to both the verbal form and meanings to address issues of the representation of the main concepts in English.

Use of "back-translation"

Back-translation is to translate the target language (i.e. English) back to the source language (i.e. Chinese) to allow the equivalence between the source language and the target language to be evaluated (Brislin, 1970). Figure 4-1 shows the process of back-translation in this research study.

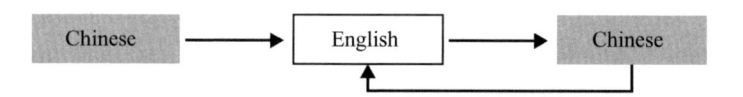

Chinese → English → Chinese

Figure 4-1　The back-translation process

In this process, I draw on observations of two main characteristics that differentiate Chinese from English:

1. Chinese is characterised by parataxis and English is characterised by hypotaxis (Nida, 1982:16), which means that Chinese tends to have loose and unclear relations between sentences, while English speakers give more attention to cohesion.

2. In Chinese, different ideas seems to be equally important, and so the relationships between ideas are often not very clear, while in English, people tend to place the most important information in the statement first.

To further demonstrate, the process of back-translation can help achieve dynamic equivalence. Maintaining the quality of data analysis is a crucial aspect to educational research. As a part of the data analysis process, rigorous translation is important to enhance the quality of the text narrating the meanings as perceived by the participants.

4.6.2 Writing Up and Using Teacher Pen Portraits

It is crucial to understand individual cases as a whole for further references to the interpretation of the data. In this research, I use pen portraits to frame teachers' accounts of their working lives. One aim of teacher pen portraits is to make the participant "come alive" for the reader. The pen portraits are largely descriptive and provide enough information against which subsequent interpretations could be assessed. In this way, the reader can gain a grasp of the participant who figures in the findings chapter, allowing what is said about him or her to be meaningful. To grasp the "whole" in the pen portraits does not mean that the teachers need to be perceived as consistent, coherent or rational beings; rather, the characteristics of teachers' identities might become visible by concentrating on the "fractures" in teachers' narratives. The focus on the fragments could serve as stimuli for deeper reflections on the reason for their existence.

Portraiture can be a highly useful tool for examining the culture of educational systems by illustrating the ways in which different individuals appear to understand events and environments. The technique of portraiture to discuss individual teachers has also been used in other studies of their professional lives (e.g. Day et al., 2005; Cassie et al., 2013). Without the use of portraiture to give richness and complexity to teachers' perceptions of themselves as teachers, we would lose the dynamic and storied nature of teachers' identities. The variation of teachers' perceptions can provide a composite representation of various beliefs regarding an individual and a group of teachers' views of their role in their specific school setting through the integration into the "'canvas of the institutions' portrait" (Hackmann, 2002: 57). In this research study, more specifically, I developed 16 pen portraits using the conceptual framework to illustrate the characteristics of teachers' identities and how they experience the factors at work that influence their identity constructions.

4.7 Strategies of Comparative Analysis

One goal of this study is to establish elements of analysis for teachers' construction of their professional identity in private schools and state schools in China that accord weight to themes and dynamics distinctive to the school cases. The second goal is to account for similarities and differences between sectors of schooling—the state and the private—recognising that these two sectors are not necessarily separate from each other, so as to better understand the differences in their particular social and organisational contexts.

As I have discussed in the introductory chapter, professional identity constructions in private schools are under-investigated, but they are not necessarily worse or better than comparisons made from other perspectives. But how can our understanding PSTs' lives not be reduced to be either "in the shadow" or "the parallel" of the SSTs? Here is my strategy. First, I compare the main themes of SSTs' professional identity construction to the changes and characteristics in PSTs' professional identities. I then explore the rationales, contexts and significance of the differences. After analysing the characteristics according to the framework, I evaluate possibilities for SSTs according to the private school standards in order to introduce comparisons not usually made by contemporary analysts. This strategy allows me to qualify and revise existing insights rather than just discard them as inappropriate for the context of my study. These comparisons then can be used to extend and revise the common existing frameworks in the field of TPIs (see Figure 4-2).

Chapter 4 Research Design and Methodology

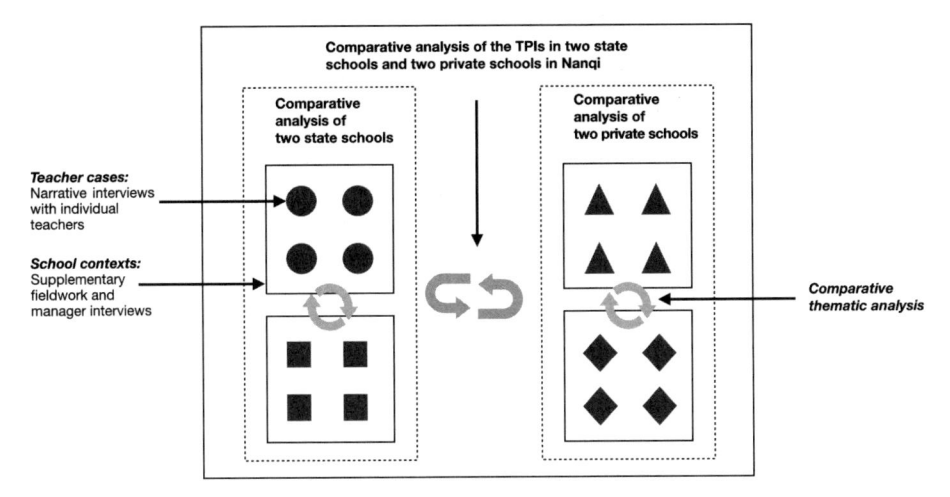

Figure 4-2 Cross-case comparison of the role of contexts in the construction of TPIs

4.8 Ensuring the Rigour and Quality of Qualitative Research

Working within the narrative field, I do not assert research rigour in the positivist claim upon the analytic approach, which relies on the criteria of validity, reliability and generalisability, but rather refer to the field of qualitative research, which addresses the analytic value in the "apparency, verisimilitude and transferability" of social experience provided by public and personal narratives (Connelly and Clandinin, 1990: 7). The differences between quantitative and qualitative studies are increasingly recognised. Scholars have constructed alternative terms to evaluate the quality of research projects, such as *trustworthiness* (Winter, 2000), *credibility* (Lincoln and Guba, 1985), *consistency* (Kerlinger, 1973) and *legitimacy* (Onwuegbuzie and Johnson, 2006). Other scholars have provided more systematic criteria. For instance, Yardley (2000) put forward the following criteria for assessing a successful qualitative study:

1. Sensitivity to context

Theoretical; relevant literature; empirical data; socio-cultural setting; participants' perspectives; ethical issues.

2. Commitment and rigour

In-depth engagement with topic, methodological competence/skill; thorough data collection; depth/breadth of analysis.

3. Transparency and coherence

Clarity and power of description/argument; transparent methods and data presentations; fit between theory and method; reflexivity.

4. Impact and importance

Theoretical (enriching understanding); socio-cultural; practical (for community, policy makers, health workers).

Despite the concerns surrounding the use of terminology in quantitative research, as compared with qualitative research, Maxwell (2010: 279) redefined the term "validity" in terms of qualitative research, identifying it as a component, instead of an outcome, of a successful research project. As he argued:

1. Validity is a goal rather than a product; it is never something that can be proven or taken for granted.

2. Validity is relative: it is to be assessed in relation to the purposes and circumstances of the research, rather than being a context-dependent property of methods or conclusions.

3. Threats to validity are reduced by evidence, not methods; methods are only a way of obtaining evidence that can help the researcher rule out these threats.

According to this view, validity is no longer a series of scientific rules or methods for eliciting the "objective truth", but a critical component of the qualitative research design that builds up the credibility of different sorts of accounts of a certain phenomenon (description, interpretations, explanation and conclusions, etc.).

The following table (Table 4-3) presents a simple representation of the strategies that I adopted to rule out specific threats to meet the criteria for interpretations and explanations in this study. Recognising that validation frameworks cannot be taken as mandatory guidelines to ensure research rigour, I borrowed from Guest, MacQueen and Namey (2012: 99-101), with relevant criteria (Bassey, 1999; Charmaz, 2006) to enhance the development of this research design. The developmental stages of the study are divided into three major parts, all of which are connected: research design; data collection; and data analysis. Researchers can go back and forth between different stages in developing the study.

Table 4-3 Methods used in addressing issues of validity

Criteria and developmental stages	Methods used
Research Design — Has the researcher achieved familiarities with the topic and the research settings (Charmaz, 2006:182)? — Has the researcher engaged with research participants (Bassey, 1999:75)? — Is the research giving sufficient account and sensitivity to the context (Charmaz, 2006:182)?	1. Drawing on literatures of the research topic and backgrounds to form the development of research design and use of research methods. 2. Using informal observations and conversations inside and outside schools to gain familiarity with the research setting and research participants. 3. Employing multiple methods, including document analysis, observations and interviews to provide oppotunities to compare findings in analysis for convergence or divergence. 4. Piloting research instruments to ensure questions and concepts make sense to participants. 5. Developing a comparative sampling frame to compare and contrast those teachers inside and outside of the interest group (i.e. teachers in private schools) to add on insiights of difference in experiences that arise from different social settings and attitudes and the connections between broader practices of education policy.

Continued

Criteria and developmental stages	Methods used
Data collection — Are the data sufficient to merit claims about the reserach aims in this study (i.e. the range and depth of interview and observations) (Charmaz, 2006: 182)?	1. For the exploratory pupose of this research, the maximum variation sampling strategy is employed. The researcher will deliverately seek out teachers with varing age, experiences and backgrouns (Willington, 2015: 199—120). 2. In an exploratory study, researchers need to keep the flexibility in using the research instruments and be able to make adjustments according to changing contexts. 3. Adjustment could also be informed by emerging themes when the researcher goes back and forth to fieldwork memos, literatures and previous studies to improve the quality and consistency of data collection. 4. Eliciting feedback from participants after summarising the interview and previding clarification when needed.
Data analysis — Has your research provided enough evidence for your claim to allow the reader to form an independent assessment and agree with your claims? — Are there strong logical links between the gathered data and your argument and analysis (Charmaz, 2006: 182)?	1. Using transciption to provide the verbaltim account of the data collection event. 2. Analysing data in Chinese langauge and providing translation for reviews of coding and summaries. 3. Keeping documentations of analysis steps and codebook revisions to make the analysis process more transparent for others to assess. 4. Conducting constant comparison to validate convergence of data from different data souce; Providing potential reasons for divergence of data. 5. Using verbatim quotes in the presentation and directly connecting the researcher's interpretation with the empirical data.

4.9 Research Ethics and Limitations

Qualitative research is based on human interactions and involves the development of human relationships. Such relationships are particularly important when they involve narrative interviews and personal stories. This leads to the acknowledgement of ethical issues in research and strategies to address transparency, as well as to protect the anonymity and confidentiality of participants. This section considers some of the relevant issues and how I employed strategies to recruit participants and enable teacher engagement in the qualitative research exploring different characteristics of TPI construction.

4.9.1 Engagement and Ethical Concerns

Kimmel (1988: 36-40) argues that three levels of the research process can be affected by ethical problems: (1) individual participants; (2) the broader society; and (3) the community of social research. My constant and explicit self-analysis throughout the data collection and analysis remains a crucial tool in addressing the ethical issues and integrity of the study within the wider social and research community. Patton (2002: 495) argues for three categories of questions that must be asked: (1) self-reflexivity (e.g. What do I know? How do I know what I know?); (2) reflexivity about the participant (e.g. How do the participants know what they know?); and (3) reflexivity about the audiences (e.g. How do those who receive my findings make sense of what I give them?). These three categories are employed in this study to minimise the bias that could result from the influence of my personal assumptions and prior experiences.

This study also follows the guidelines laid out by the British Educational Research Association (2011) for obtaining ethical approval from the Central University Research Ethics Committee before conducting a pilot study and fieldwork. School principals' letters and informed consent forms were provided when I established contact with the schools for interviews and collected further data from teachers. I also carefully addressed the principles of voluntary participation and confidentiality throughout the research process. Participants were informed that their rights to refuse to answer certain questions and limit the time of their participation would be respected. I provided and explained the consent form in Chinese and asked for participants' permission (in the form of a signature) before the interview. I also asked questions about the consent form to help participants understand the practical and ethical considerations surrounding the research project. Before recording the interview, I also asked for participants' permission to do this.

4.9.2 Power and Reflexivity

In this research study, I attempted to reduce the power differences between the participants and me and encourage disclosure and authenticity. During the data collection process, I aimed to create an open, safe and relaxing environment in which my participants were willing to share personal stories. However, the reliance on human relationships in data collection introduces issues of power that are also influenced by broader social structures. According to Grenz (2005), power is fluid in that nobody actually possesses it; we could define power in terms of its movement between the researcher and the participants. Such movement is influenced by the different positions that different actors take in a given context.

Although I am aware that my identity as a student researcher will appear non-threatening and non-authoritarian with different participants, one particular aspect of being an overseas student placed me in a vulnerable position, so that I often felt unsure of the cultural and organisational norms in specific schools. Unlike researchers who had worked with or within certain types of organisations, I had not had formal collaborations with the participant teachers. Social capital and networks are crucial for building rapport and gaining access to the participants. It was also my identity as an overseas research student that shaped most of my encounters with the participants. For the aims of exploration and learning, I encouraged help from the local community and school principals to connect me with individual teachers and used snowball sampling to invite more teachers to participate afterwards.

4.9.3 Limitations

This research carries with it several limitations. This study is limited to the development of TPIs in the two private schools and two state schools in Shandong province. Both the state and private education sectors in China are very large, so limiting my analysis to a small number of schools in Shandong province restricts my ability to generalise beyond teachers from these schools. In addition, this study is also limited by time and scale as a doctoral study, the financial resources available and restrictions on access to schools and teachers.

4.10 Summary

The motivation for this project originates from my experiences working in a private tutoring school and my interest in the potential differences between PSTs' and SSTs' experiences in their work. A pilot study was carried out during my MSc programme, during which I conducted semi-structured interviews with ten teachers from three private tutoring schools. This doctoral thesis aims to extend the study to teachers in different private and state schools and to focus on the implications of policy changes in China.

The literature on TPIs is reviewed in Chapter 3. Given that this research study is exploratory in nature, the themes and categories defined in this chapter are useful for informing the research design and providing the basis for comparison and consensus in data analysis. To understand teachers' work contexts and experiences, I employ interviews and non-participant observations in this study. This study also involves an awareness of my position as a private teacher and research student.

Chapter 5
Characteristics of TPIs in Willow School and Aspen School (State Schools)

5.1 Introduction

This chapter explores the main characteristics of TPIs based on an analysis of data collected from teachers in one of four different primary schools (two state schools and two private schools) in Nanqi. It focuses on analysing interview data obtained from four teachers working in each of these schools to explore the main characteristics of TPIs in different school contexts. The teacher cases are presented and discussed as embedded in the context of the school. The purpose of the analysis is to deconstruct and reconstruct teachers' narratives and explore the characteristics of TPIs in the Willow School context. It also aimed at exploring the relationship between TPIs and teachers' experiences, and the negotiation of tensions in the context of work. To address the first research question on the basis of findings in the context of Willow School, I present findings based on the analysis of data collected from each school. Figure 5-1 demonstrates the structures within each of the four schools in this chapter. Each school section includes two parts:

1. *School contexts*. I will describe the characteristics and contexts of the school based first on the qualitative fieldnotes of observations made during my school visits, school documents (school websites and reports) and principal interviews. Themes drawn from interview data are

Chapter 5　Characteristics of TPIs in Willow School and Aspen School (State Schools)

used to examine the perceived characteristics of the school contexts and possible impacts on teachers' construction of their professional identities.

2. Teacher cases. I will present four teacher cases after introducing the school context. The purpose of this section is to organise and describe the data set in rich detail and to examine the ways in which events, school contexts, teachers' experiences and other aspects of their work life affect the range of discourses about their professional identities. Mainly on the basis of Day et al.'s (2005) conceptual framework of TPIs (see the literature review chapter), I included three main components in presenting the findings. The three aspects of teachers' professional identity examined based on this conceptual framework are: (1) teachers' *social selves*—what it means to be a professional teacher; (2) teachers' *personal selves*—what defines teachers' learning and professional development; and (3) teachers' *professional selves*—what characterises teaching as a profession. The organising structures are indicative of a range of professional, personal and social contexts that teachers engage in to construct their professional identities.

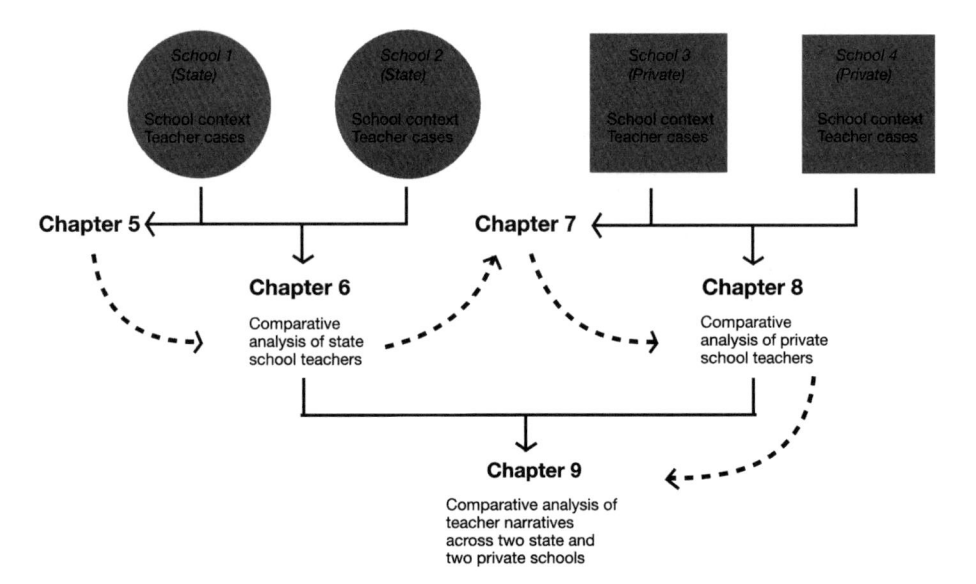

Figure 5-1　**Structures of the finding chapters (Chapter 5-Chapter 9)**

To sum up, in this chapter, I address the research questions via three layers of presentations: the school; the teacher cases; and the cross-case analysis of teachers within each school. These findings will be used as the basis for further cross-case analysis and discussion of the overall patterns that emerge in teachers' narratives in each school context.

5.2　Introducing Willow School (State School)

Willow School is a primary school with 2,400 students and about 100 teachers and staff in total (2015 figures). This sub-district primary school is located in the developing residential area of eastern Nanqi and it is close to the centre of the county. The residential area is composed of a few major housing estates, shops, shopping malls, banks and a sports park. According to the local policy of the *Area-Divided Enrolment and Exemption Admission*[①], Willow School is assigned an area that serves many rural-to-urban migrants. The street in which Willow School is located is alive with a large number of grocery and stationery shops, learning centres, restaurants, salons, bookshops and fast food chains. Many cars, electric vehicles and bikes run through the willow trees by the street, especially during rush hour.

The open gate leads to a named road and on to the main buildings. The campus is beautifully decorated with lawns, a small pavilion and a long corridor with blossoming Chinese wisteria by the left side of the building. The corridor leads to a further open space between two teaching buildings. Trees surrounded by stone chairs create more space for students to sit or play. The main teaching building is a five-floor modern building, which is also equipped with a reading room, a computer room, an auditorium, a laboratory and an audio-visual classroom. Each class is equipped with two blackboards (one in the front

---

① This policy was first released in 2014 by the MoE to ensure the admission of students in primary and lower secondary schools without entrance examinations. According to the policy, each county government will set out the priority admission area for each school according to the school scale, the student population and distribution of schools.

and one in the back), a computer, a projector and an air conditioner. By the side of each classroom are displays of students' works, including colourful paintings, clean and appealing brush drawings, literary works and calligraphy.

When I visited the school, the large number of students in each class was noticeable. Each classroom had about 80 student desks in alignment, using the traditional side-by-side rows-and-columns setup. This left only one to two aisles for students and the teacher to walk and move about in. In the centre of the front of the classrooms were large computer desks, behind which were the teaching platforms. Although equipment and facilities had been significantly improved, there seemed to be an urgent need for more classrooms and qualified teachers given the student numbers and cramped space. As the school principal, Mr. Chen, said, one of the major issues facing Willow School is over-crowding classrooms.

The campus was also extremely crowded, where students were walking and running energetically through corridors, stairways and the sports field. The large sports field was located in the eastern side of the campus. It was equipped with a red plastic running area and a large field of plastic lawn. In the middle morning, all the students were required to gather in the sports field to take part in exercises. All the students would stand in lines that could extend outside the sports field and on to the pathways, which again shows the lack of space in the school.

5.2.1 School-Based Changes to Address Students Learning Needs

I was allowed to shadow Mr. Chen for an afternoon. Most of his working hours in the school seemed to be spent on hosting management-level meetings and supervising teachers' instructions and learning outcomes. He told me he was also involved in teacher meetings and parents' meetings. According to Mr. Chen, this summarises the nature and form of classroom reform to achieve better learning outcomes and improve students' learning capacities. Chen explained that he encouraged teachers to pay close attention to classroom behaviour management: "We borrowed this policy from other schools.

Teachers need to first pay attention to keeping students' focus in listening and learning in classes. Before implementing this policy, our classes were muddled up. The school was at the bottom of the district school ranking." As Mr. Chen described it, classroom discipline remains the priority of classroom teaching and a pre-condition for student engagement in learning.

Almost each class took 40 minutes and students could have 10 minutes' break between. There were also two longer breaks that were used for specific exercise: the morning session for diabolo and afternoon break for eye-relaxing exercises. Diabolo is a traditional Chinese yo-yo sport, in which Willow School had won a series of national and international awards. "Next month, the Bureau of Education and Sports will hold an announcement conference to promote this sport," said Mr. Chen. He was eager to improve the school and construct a distinguished identity for Willow, which seemed to be an important part of his responsibility as the leader of the school. He later talked about the "experimental class" in which students were given the cucurbit flute (a traditional Chinese music instrument) class. After the class team successfully won the Shandong TV prize, Chen aimed to offer the lessons for more students. In his own words: "This will become another distinguishing feature of our school. [...] This is all very good preparation for our kids."

5.2.2 Implementing the School Reform and Enhancing Teacher Quality

Like many primary and middle schools in Shandong province, Willow School began to adapt the well-known model of Dulangkou Middle School and implement the school-based teaching reform as the main approach for school improvement[①]. To match the pedagogical and managerial demand, teacher

---

① According to the limited literature on this model in China, the headmaster of Dulangkou Middle School first named this model the "10 + 35 classroom" in 1997, which meant "10 minutes" for teachers to give lectures and "35 minutes" for students to lead the discussion. According to the test results, students from Dulangkou School had made significant progress. It is believed that Dulangkou's success was related to this strategy, which led to huge improvements in students' test scores.

Chapter 5 Characteristics of TPIs in Willow School and Aspen School (State Schools)

training has become a key focus in Willow. One problem in the teaching staff in Willow was the aging teacher group. According to Mr. Chen, 30 out of 90 teachers in Willow are over 50 years old. The difference in age groups could add a challenge for school leaders to address the needs of a heterogeneous group of teachers in achieving the goals for school improvement. Nevertheless, a series of school-level and county-level training sessions have been held to enhance teachers' professional skills: this has involved lesson observations and the weekly open demonstration classes, teacher reading groups, teachers' collaborative learning group, school visits and exchanges, expert teachers' lectures and teaching competitions. At the school level, Willow School's teacher-training scheme included three main parts to improve young teachers' practices and meet external accountability. These three parts are:

1. Sending "backbone teachers"[①] to rural schools: Experienced teachers in urban schools were assigned the role and responsibility to teach in rural schools for a few months to share professional expertise. This is also considered as a learning opportunity for the urban teachers to adapt their teaching to different groups of students.

2. Daily appraisal: Each teacher was assigned to demonstrate their classroom teaching in the auditorium for other teaching staff. The principal would attend the demonstration classes and could give the teacher feedbacks based on his or her teaching on the stage. The open appraisal took place in the afternoon of every working day.

3. Teaching competition: Teaching competition was considered as an important activity for evaluating the teachers' competencies. Teachers were encouraged to select a topic, design, and demonstrate the teaching of the selected topic to the students, evaluated by a group of experienced teachers and educational advisors from the local school community or the Education Bureau.

---

① 骨干教师

Mr. Chen said that significant attention is given to developing the young teachers in the school. According to Chen, staff and teachers in leadership roles, for instance, are required to observe teachers' classes and give direct and constructive comments to young teachers. The daily appraisal was a very intensive and potentially stressful event for teachers in Willow. Although direct instructions and supports were given to young teachers in terms of their teaching practices, the school seemed to pay less attention to teachers' emotions and self-assessment. In the following sections, teachers were asked to reflect upon their experiences and the effectiveness of these professional learning tasks.

5.2.3 The Demand for Better Education

There is a growing number of parents, especially from suburban areas, who have noticed the opportunities to send their children to better schools by moving to the expanding commercial real estate in this area of Nanqi. Purchasing apartments near Willow School is considered as the simplest way to locate their children to an urban school. Even so, however, parents need to negotiate with the school and their efforts may still be in vain.

Many of the parents associated with Willow School are from poorer socio-economic and educational backgrounds. The parents attempted to seek additional support for their children in various school subjects and extra-curriculum learning as well as after-school care. Alongside Willow School, there were over 30 chain tutoring centres, fine arts centres, and after-school care centres or "little dining table" (xiaofanzhuo), many of which are run by non-professionals without legal registration. While I visited some of the centres, parents often complained that children are doing too much, but they still do not want their children to "lose at the starting line". The high demand and pressure to improve children's learning outcomes were apparent in these expanding commercialised learning centres.

Chapter 5 Characteristics of TPIs in Willow School and Aspen School (State Schools)

5.2.4 The Crisis in School-Parent Relationships

Although Mr. Chen had positive relationships and shared information and gained emotional support from local leaders and other school principals, he summarised his experiences as the school principal: "Recently, parents have expected much more than before. Everyone wants to enjoy a good education. But the quality of state schools cannot meet that expectation. My job has become very exhausting." Mr. Chen also spoke of the urgent need for legal protection for schools and teachers when the school authority is threatened by the demands of the "new generation of parents".

"The school cannot develop without a consensus with parents," Mr. Chen said during the interview. He added that the relationship between the school and parents was "very strained" and that the excessive number of students had added extra administrative burdens. Later in the teacher interviews, the four participant teachers also supported Mr. Chen's claim and talked about the complexity added to their work in managing their relationships with parents. The most commonly mentioned issues included the permissive parenting style (four teachers), a lack of understanding and collaboration in managing students' homework (three participants), corporal punishment in school (two teachers) and the inadequate school safeguarding (one teacher). There seemed to be a consensus among educators that the tradition of "honour teachers and esteem teaching" was being destroyed because of the lack of financial support and professionally qualified teachers to meet parents' growing demand for better-quality education. Table 5-1 summarises the school context based on the interview with the principaland observations in the field.

Table 5-1 Characteristics of Willow School

Location	Busy residential area near city centre
Neighbourhood	Expanding real estates and increasing residents
School finance	Determined by school of higher administrative level and supplemented by profits from the kindergarden
School staffing	Determined by local government Shortage of teachers
School facilities and equipment	Good facility but short of classrooms and school spaces
Number of students	About 2,400 students
Number of teachers	About 100 state teachers
School-parent relationship	Barriers and conflicts
Role of national curriculum	Remain dominant, but supplemented by two extracurricular activities as school charateristics
Staff support and supervision	Strong and high intensity in training for better teaching skills, with a focus on young teachers
Focus of class reform	Promoting group learning, and encouraging students' engagement and focus on the learning outcome
Teacher job progression	Stable but lacking in progression
Leadership	Institutional and administrative leadership style

5.3 Example Teacher Case: Ruolan

Basic biographical information
Age: Late 20s
Gender: Female
Education: Bachelor of Primary Education (Normal College)
Current position: Chinese teacher
Years of teaching: 6 years

Ruolan is a Chinese teacher in her late 20s. She graduated from a local teacher education college and started to teach at Willow School six years ago. I met Ruolan in her open class and Mr. Chen introduced us to each other. She needed to return to her classroom, so I text messaged her to confirm another date for the interview. Ruolan has a Bachelor's degree in primary education. After graduating from college, Ruolan did not want to become a teacher. She liked music and dancing and hoped she could find a relevant job.

5.3.1 Choosing and Being Chosen as a State Primary School Teacher

Before becoming a state school teacher, Ruolan had to follow her parents' suggestions to work in Willow School as a substitute teacher. This is mainly because being a state teacher offers the stability and status as a state employee, therefore is considered as most ideal for female college graduates in small towns like Nanqi. However, the status and payment for a substitute teacher was very different from those for government-employed teachers even inside the same school. Ruolan believed that she was disadvantaged and marginalised as a substitute teacher in Willow, so she quitted her job to explore better opportunities. During this time, she shared her thoughts with her friends. She was finally convinced that teaching is the best available opportunity for her. As she described:

> I talked with many other people about work, the future and what's next. And I felt, at that time, just as what my friends agree on, the "iron rice bowl" is the best job, especially for a girl.

Ruolan prepared for two years to pass the teacher exam in 2013. After that, she became a full-time, state-employed teacher at Willow School. Although gender stereotyping from family and friends seemed to have been a major driver of her decision, the success gave her a sense of achievement and offered her the status of a legitimate and deserved member of the teaching profession. As Ruolan reflected:

> After that (I became a state teacher) I was considered someone who is guaranteed food and clothes for life. Also, I remember how parents and students looked down their noses at me because of my status as a substitute

teacher. [...] This hurt my feeling, so I must leave and pass the exam. I must show them that I can pass the test and become a state teacher one day.

Despite the sense of achievement as a state teacher, Ruolan also reveals the struggle with the stereotypes and unfair public opinions about having the "iron rice bowl". She said that state teachers are often seen as those who only kill time, which is hugely mistaken. As a teacher, Ruolan described her work as one with a tight schedule, heavy workloads and a tremendous amount of emotional labour with children and students's parents. As she described:

> Let me put it this way, teaching is not an easy job. Teachers are facing the future and the owners of our future, so we all hope for the best and to be helpful for students' development. Honestly, teaching is very tiring. Some people think we could have more personal time after work, while that's not true. Especially when it is close to the exam period, we need to bring back the test papers and grade them at home. Think about it, 80 papers, 3-4 minutes for each one, it would take over 3 hours to finish marking them. It is very demanding. Students in higher grades also have writing tasks; the teacher then needs to read, evaluate, praise, correct the errors, plus leaving space for students to reflect on their own. It really is tiring. I had to work at home while I taught grade 5.

5.3.2 The Emotion Work in Teaching and Caregiving

Among her busy schedules of activities, Ruolan considered safeguarding as the most important part of her work in Willow School. She explained that all the details could have educational impacts. Ruolan said she observes very carefully when students walk out of the school gate. According to her, she could know if students had a good day by simply observing them. In addition to this, Ruolan said, supporting the development of students' characters is another professional responsibility for primary school teachers. For Ruolan, students' character development and positive life-attitudes can also benefit students' future lives. Ruolan often defines herself as someone who takes care of other people.

In terms of classroom teaching, Ruolan claimed her professional goal was to bring a joyful climate to the classroom and encourage students to engage with her questions. She believed that a teacher's emotions play a vital role in changing the class atmosphere, and hence in addressing students' engagements:

> I think teachers' emotions exert an influence on students. For example, if I'm happy today, the class will be relaxing. That would be how the students feel. They would be very active and look happy in responding to my questions in class. But if I'm in a bad mood because of their poor performances, I'm sure students will be very quiet in class. Their attention would begin to wander.

Ruolan considers a "lively but harmonious" class atmosphere as essential for successful teaching, while she finds keeping good order with 80 students in one class very challenging. Although Ruolan had close relationships with her students, it had been very difficult for her to include everyone in her teaching. As a result, Ruolan seemed to be burdened by the students' expectations for emotional support and guidance in learning. The demand for communication and caretaking in primary teaching is a demanding aspect of teachers' everyday lives. When it comes to very difficult situations, Ruolan often finds herself incapable of controlling her emotions. As she spoke out: "I'm not the God, and I can't control my emotions all the time."

The frustrations were also from the mixed demands and lack of collaborations from the parents. While feeling frustrated, Ruoban seemed to internalise the parental demand for students' good academic outcome. She used the Chinese phrase "hen tie bu chenggang" (What a let-down) to describe her inner struggle when her students could not make satisfactory academic progress. She argued that the responsibility for students' learning and development needs to be shared by families, and Ruolan seemed to have a sense of helplessness in carrying out her professional responsibility when students are not supported by their parents:

> The parents really pay zero attention to their kids. How can we help? If the kids already know that no one cares about them, no matter how hard the teachers work, the kids will not be well off.

5.3.4 Lack of Time and Effective Support

In terms of her relationship with the curriculum, Ruolan considered her responsibility as to deliver the "messages" from the textbook in the pre-defined process. Although she tried to incorporate her own ideas, she found hard to realise these ideas due to the limited time she had to cover the contents of the textbook. Regarding teachers' in-service learning, Ruolan enjoyed informal learning opportunities in the school, such as discussing key knowledge points with her colleagues in the office. In contrast, formal learning in the school context was mainly public lectures, which she found difficult to guide her practices. Ruolan's following comments on these programmes are rather negative:

> In fact, theory is theory; what we need is practice. No matter how good or persuasive the theory is, it needs to be grounded in real practice.

Her negative attitude to theories might be aligned with her identities as a *practitioner* and *caregiver* in Willow School, as this can be identified in the following claim:

> Because I'm a practitioner and I'm with children most of the time, it is pointless to have so many theories without applying these to real lives.

5.3.5 Summary

To summarise, Ruolan's identity as a teacher appears to be characterised by

Chapter 5 Characteristics of TPIs in Willow School and Aspen School (State Schools)

the tensions between different professional goals. Although Ruolan could draw on some strategies and resources to help keep herself emotionally resilient, her overall experience of teaching seems to be characterised by emotional exhaustion, particularly in negotiating the realities of multiple and seemingly contradictory expectations for good teaching in the context of educational reform. What she chooses to do is to manage her identity as a "happy teacher" by using the "mirror rule" as a self-love exercise: "When you wake up every day, and before you go to work, you can smile to yourself in the mirror and tell yourself 'today will be a happy day'."

5.4 Introducing Aspen School

Aspen is a primary school under direct county government control (a "shizhi" school), which means the school is subordinated directly to the Education Bureau. Established in 1933, Aspen has been a demonstration school ("shifan" school). This school is located in the centre of the old county and is very close to the tourism area. During the pick-up hours, the road to the school would become extremely congested. Due to the fact that it is located in the very centre of the tourist town, the school was surrounded by small shops and shopping malls. It was very difficult to find any free parking and waiting space nearby. According to the *Area-Divided Enrolment and Exemption Admission*, Aspen also covered the largest school district area's population in the county and the biggest primary school student population (about 4,000 in total). It had more than 60 classes and had also been evaluated as one of the high-achieving schools in Nanqi.

The red Chinese-style school gate was about 15 meters wide with the school guard office by the side. Walking into the school, visitors could see a quiet courtyard area on the left-hand side. I was told that the courtyard was built for staff meetings and offices for top and middle-level managers in the school. Bamboos were planted in the yard. I thought anyone who walked into this area would feel relaxed seeing the sunshine dropping on the green leaves and hearing children's voices from afar. In the centre of the school was a large open area surrounded by three teaching buildings. Teachers' offices were located in these different buildings. Children and teachers walked through this open area for different classes or meetings. During the 20 minutes' break time in the morning, this area would be used for the national broadcast gymnastics.

Space inside the teaching buildings was small, especially when each of the classrooms was filled with up to 80 students. Students had their own desks that was facing the stage. The classrooms were equipped with a computer, a projector, a blackboard and an air conditioner. Teachers were encouraged to use Information and Communications Technology to facilitate students' learning. In the offices, teachers' desks were laid in pairs. The school arranged same-subject teachers to share an office. While doing my interview, I heard teachers discussing their classroom experiences and problems with students' learning. Table 5-2 demonstrates the characteristics of Aspen School.

Table 5-2 Characteristics of Aspen School

Location	Busy commercial and tourist area in the city centre
Neighbourhood	Refurbished commercial area
School finance	Determined by the government
School staffing	Determined by local government Shortage of teachers
School facilities and equipment	Good facility but short of classrooms and school spaces
Number of students	About 4,000 students
Number of teachers	About 200 state teachers
School—parent relationship	Barriers and conflicts
Role of national curriculum	Remain dominant, but supplemented by two extracurricular activities and the Chinese classics reading
Staff support and supervision	Strong and high intensity in training for better teaching skills, with a focus on young teachers
Focus of class reform	Promoting group learning, and encouraging students' engagement and focus on the learning outcome
Teacher job progression	Stable but lacking in progression
Leadership	Administrative leadership style

Chapter 5 Characteristics of TPIs in Willow School and Aspen School (State Schools)

5.5 Example Teacher Case: Xinxin

Basic biographical information
Age: 30s
Gender: Female
Education: Bachelor of Primary Education
Current position: Maths teacher
Years of teaching: 3 years

Xinxin loved arts when in school and always wanted to become an art student. To secure a good job after graduation, Xinxin followed her parents' advice to attend a teacher college and majored in primary education. In the teacher college, Xinxin did not have many opportunities to teach. Rather, the courses were heavily based on learning information and theories. After graduating from the teacher training college in 2006, Xinxin decided to prepare for the local teacher recruitment examination. At the same time, she worked as a contract teacher in the kindergarten attached to Aspen School. Four years later, Xinxin successfully passed the exam and became a state teacher in Aspen School.

5.5.1 Tensions

Xinxin was arranged to teach a general subject called "Morality and Society". Six months before Xinxin's maternity leave, the school asked if she could substitute as a maths teacher. Without enough time and training, Xinxin was unprepared to take the responsibilities. As she recalled, it was a relief when she left that position for her maternity leave six months later. After she was back to the school, Xinxin started to teach maths to two grade-four classes. Each class has about 70 students. She told me she was still stressed because of disagreements with students' parents, the crowded classes, and the constant pressure to improve students' exam outcomes.

> I want to help, but in the circumstance of such a large class, it is challenging to take care of everyone. Now, I can take care of two-thirds of the students, and the left is probably marginalized or sandwiched. I probably pay less attention to those who are just ordinary, and I won't pay any attention to those who are doing well. To the poor students, even if you try to help, your efforts would probably be in vain.

The contrast between her expectations for students and the real working conditions seemed to leave Xinxin with contradictory goals and conflicted feelings in teaching. On the one hand, Xinxin had to distinguish her students according to their academic performances; on the other hand, she felt ashamed to consider herself failing to lead an inclusive class. The new 1980s parents, according to Xinxin, are more critical with teachers; they often question the teachers' qualifications and tend to hold higher power over teachers. As a novice teacher, Xinxin often finds herself unable to claim her authority. The personal relationships as "friends" with parents seemed to pose threats to Xinxin as a teacher, as she thinks her professional status could be easily questioned and judged. Meanwhile, Xinxin seemed to struggle with understanding and handling of others' opinions and feedback, even though she was well aware of her tendency to deny her real motives, ambitions, and achievements. To make her point, Xinxin quoted another teacher's compliment, which failed to turn her focus away from the reinforcement of others' criticism:

> I don't know (what others think of me). One day, a teacher said I am very clever and that I am a fast learner. I cannot agree with her. Some teachers might think I'm flexible. Maybe I am more sensitive to others' comments, and that makes me appear to be flexible. But I have low self-identity, because I know I'm not that good. It might be harmful as well. I have not heard about those (she laughed), there must be some, some negative evaluations.

In this context, Xinxin's reflection did not seem to help her to become an autonomous teacher. Noticing her right to become rebelling, she felt a stronger

Chapter 5　Characteristics of TPIs in Willow School and Aspen School (State Schools)

inner conflict as she also wanted identification with others in the school.

> Recently it would be that I don't follow others's advice and insist on my thinking. I might be a bit stubborn. Maybe I'm sensitive, so I know that from others's facial expressions (she laughed). Especially in a class, they will tell me this is good, but I would think I'm OK this way. I don't follow them. I feel sorry though. They give me advice, but I don't accept it. Here I think I still identify strongly with others. It's conflictual.

This tendency is not only limited to her classroom teaching but influences various aspects of her professional life in the school. In her own words, she lives "under others's evaluations" and unable to develop her critical thinking skills. According to Xinxin, this might be a result of her cultural background and growing experiences in a collectivist environment. In the process of negotiating her growing professional autonomy and group identifications in her daily practices, Xinxin needs to make sense of her fear to confront others' criticism and to reconsider her tendency in maintaining an ideal professional image.

Although Xinxin said she feel happy about the rapport between her and her students, the tension she experiences is so overwhelming that while talking she burst into tears. I was first shocked by her reactions and did not know what to do in such a situation. I handed a paper handkerchief when Xinxin shed tears and stopped the tape recorder for a short while. Thinking of myself as a friend, I was just quiet and getting prepared to be emotionally available to her. I kept silent and later on asked if she would like to terminate the interview. She said that she was okay to carry on the interview. I then moved on to less sensitive issues and asked her how she would describe the different stages of her teaching experiences. Later on, Xinxin told me that it was a relief for her to tell the stories and share with me these feeling. In this sense, I could perhaps claim that the context of a research interview also created a meaningful interaction through which Xinxin was able to express and make sense of how teachers feel and who they are, even though the sense of shock and empathy remained when I reviewed the transcript and the field notes.

5.5.2 Growth and Development

Xinxin's professional identity construction is crucially influenced by the way she understands and pursues her personal and professional development, as she tended to continually reflect upon her practices and developed the narrative of personal growth. Balancing a wide range of demands in teaching seemed to be the focus of the process of personal growth. According to Xinxin, these demands included higher self-esteem, professional skills in instructional design, supporting family education, reading books and taking care of her own well-being as a teacher. Xinxin also utilised her reflections as well as retelling stories to define primary school teachers' professional competency as to focus on pedagogical knowledge and instrumental skills to support young learners. After a few years of self-reflection, Xinxin said that she considered herself unfavourable of complex bureaucracies and language uses at workplace. She appreciated the "simple" work of state teachers through which she can learn and focus on her classroom teaching. A developmental perception of CPD seemed to help Xinxin frame her experiences and expectations.

As she could deepen her understanding of teaching and school lives, Xinxin could easily understand situations and gradually make decisions on her reactions and responses and become more strategic in solving specific problems. She identifies a stage of suppression of innate attempts to take action and only focus on the essential steps to take in the process of problem-solving. However, Xinxin still needed to bear the anxiety and worry, especially when she feels the challenge exceeds her skills. Unsolved problems, the overcritical self-assessment, negative feedback and the sense of inferiority could cause her great distress and uneasiness. Xinxin hoped to move towards what she framed as the "stage of flow". According to her, the professional skills to master instructional design[①] serve as a vital bridge between the two

---

① 教学设计

stages. Xinxin's description of the stages seems very general, and she stressed the idea of capacity to know what and how to do with "all kinds of things", by which she might indicate the necessity for her to extend her focus from classroom teaching to more general affairs. She used the proverb "still waters run deep" to describe the image of a teacher who is in a calm manner that conceals a wise and passionate nature.

Xinxin considers her participation in the school's "Quality Teacher Competition" as a critical event in her professional life. She described the competition as more formal, so she needed to make more efforts. Xinxin also consider teacher competition as a way to assess her progress. She set herself higher objectives to progress to provincial-, national- and international- level stages. Narrating her experiences and sense of transformation seemed to bring out her hope in becoming a high-achieving teacher and an "authentic person" through recognizing, challenging and improving herself in teaching and professional skills. Xinxin defined herself as a "lifelong learner" and considered teaching as a job in which she could develop her professional skills to achieve a sense of flowing in various situations. It is important to note here that professional skills and professional images still compose the crucial parts of TPI in Xinxin's case. Consistent practices, observations, deep understanding and active engagement to improve constitute the core elements that contribute to her sense of progress and achievement in teaching.

5.5.3 Frustration with Family Education

Although Xinxin tried to build rapports with her students and the parents to support students' learning, the situation was often more complex and devastating than she expects. Xinxin has given advice for parents through a range of school activities, such as parental meetings and public lectures on parenting, yet she doubts if her words or deeds could make any significant effect, given the limited time for each parent, the problems of parents' absence in their children's education as well as the limitations put by their social backgrounds. She thought most of the meetings lack interactions. She said: "Only teachers talked, and the parents just listened." The lack of communication between parents and students could become a hurdle for students' character development. According to her, some parents tend to be static concerning parenting styles that are either "too rough" or "too weak", others are reluctant to get involved in children's education.

> Of course, it is my honour to have the trust, but I also feel helpless. There are too many students. If everyone relies on me, whom shall I take care of first? Everyone? Of course, a teacher needs to be fair and to pay attention to every individual kid. But when I'm told these, I feel I have such a grand responsibility and burden.

Her expectations for the flexibility in parenting strategies became almost impracticable. Xinxin emphasized the challenging issues in family education and hoped that the integration of family education ard school education could make a difference. Xinxin attempted to show her firm belief in the role of teachers' professional skills and willingness to acquire a professional qualification as a psychological consultant to enhance the teacher-parent partnership so as to help students make more significant progress, as she claims:

> Suddenly I feel I want to be a consultant and give them some advice (she laughed). But I don't have much experience, nor do I have any qualifications. I think family education is not a simple problem. If family education and school education can be integrated, then students can make more significant progress. Yes.

5.5.4 Summary

Xinxin also included four other aspects of her perceived professional lives as a novice teacher: 1) her relationship and interactions with others; 2) her perceived progress in competency building that could also be recognized and rewarded; 3) her willingness and endeavour to learn and engage with academic studies to address issues in students' learning and family education; and 4) the journeys teachers took in pursuit of moral quality, long-term impacts on student and authenticity. Teachers' identity formation is an on-going, fluid process, while conflicts and dilemmas between teachers' personal and professional identities seemed to be a significant part of Xinxin's recent experiences. The sub-identity as a lifelong learner seemed to help balance the tension. As she argued, she needed to maintain a positive attitude towards others' critiques and accept one's imperfections, so as to become a "living spring of knowledge" for students rather than just a "cup of water". By employing the metaphor of transforming from a "cup of water" to a "living spring of knowledge" that can continuously provide creative insights and learning experiences for students, Xinxin seemed to indicate the necessity for her to keep learning as a teacher.

Chapter 6
Comparing State School TPIs

In this section, I will compare and contrast themes emerging from the SSTs' narratives. Before that, I will first review and compare the school contexts for the construction of TPIs. Willow and Aspen Schools were the state schools in the sample that were similar to many state primary schools in Shandong province in terms of class size, implementation of the national curriculum and school administration. The school leaders and teachers of both schools thought that many of the problems the schools face stemmed from the shortage of teachers and space, as well as parents' high expectations for their children's educational outcomes and often negative attitudes towards teachers. At neither school did the school leaders think that parents were sufficiently actively involved in children's school and family lives. For instance, the parents would visit the schools with their problems, rather than to provide help and support students' learning activities. Willow's school leader described this as a "crisis in school-parents' relationship", while Aspen's said that parents were often too emotional and unreasonable when it came to conflicts among students. In both of the schools, the school leaders and teachers emphasised the importance of effective teaching in supporting students' academic progress and stressed students' social and moral development as an essential part of their learning.

However, in other aspects, the administrative nature and hence school strategies deployed were somewhat different. One of the main differences between these two state primary schools was their relationship with the local government. Willow was a suburban school financially and administratively managed by a rural secondary school. Aspen, in contrast, was directly regulated by the local government. According to the school choice policy, Willow and Aspen were assigned different geographical areas from which to recruit groups of students, leaving Willow (in the suburban area) with challenges to face when there was a significant increase in the number of migrants from the rural to the urban area against the background of urbanisation. At Willow, one of the strategies the school leaders had taken was to extend the buildings and organise extracurricular activities (i.e. diabolo and an experiment with cucurbit flute), which in turn helped the school attract interest from the local government and broader communities.

Regarding participants' perceptions of themselves as professional teachers, all sample teachers addressed their commitment to students' academic and character development as the focuses of teachers' work. To achieve their professional goals, teachers felt that they needed to be flexible to adapt to students' needs. At the same time, carrying out their dual responsibilities to maintain classroom discipline and keep students engaged in classroom activities was very challenging. Concerning teachers' professional development, all the eight teachers reflected upon changes they want to make to improve students' learning experiences in their classroom. They also addressed the significance of community and school-based learning in their learning experiences at work. All these teachers commented on the negative social image of teachers in the media reports and the disruptive attitudes of parents for their children's education. Even though all these teachers have the status of state employees, they considered their job to have a low social status and often feel vulnerable and stressed because of the need to meet the social expectations for children's schooling in China. The comparative analysis of teachers' narratives also showed the differences in teachers' strategies in responding to tensions they experienced at work. The eight SSTs engaged with two kinds of narratives in negotiating their identity tensions: (1) a narrative of a lack of career choice; (2) the need to address challenges in students' learning. Each of these is discussed in turn below.

6.1 Narrative of a Lack of Career Choice

Although all teachers considered they became SSTs for extrinsic reasons, such as family expectations, gender stereotypes and other circumstances over which they had little control, the data analysis revealed that teachers expressed a sense of conflict regarding their career choice. This sense of conflict in career choices is particularly intense for young teachers (Xiwen, Ruolan, Haoting, Xinxin), those in their 20s and 30s. This group of teachers also seemed to have lower-level job satisfaction due to their crowded work environment, heavy workload and lack of social and community support in the early stages of their teaching. The list below demonstrates the range of different challenges and barriers that these state teachers faced during the interviews.

Extrinsic reasons: lack of options; family influences; teacher recruitment policies; gender stereotypes.

Unsatisfactory treatment: low pay; low social status.

Heavy workload: overwork in terms of correcting homework; large class size; administrative responsibilities; coping with class and school inspections.

Although all the participant teachers thought they faced these challenges, the comparative analysis also suggested that teachers considered job stability as the benefits of teaching in state schools; meanwhile, they could engage with the conflicts in career choice differently. More active teachers tried to tackle the tension by engaging with others, fixing relationships and changing their attitudes. They tended to believe in their capacity to improve the situation. Other teachers had the intention to withdraw from the conflictual situations.

6.1.1 The Case of Willow School

In Willow School, most of the teachers thought that becoming a state teacher meant they could gain a sense of job stability and higher social status with the bianzhi status. Meanwhile, the teacher recruitment structures seem to have exerted a significant influence on teachers' employability and hence the way these young teachers perceive themselves in this research context. According to Xiwen, she had difficulties adapting to her role and building her confidence as a primary school teacher at the beginning of her career. Xiwen said she could not accept herself becoming a primary school teacher. Her self-esteem and confidence were low as she felt inferior among her college classmates regarding job and social status. Haoting is a maths teacher in Willow. He obtained the higher level of teacher qualification to teach in junior high schools when he graduated, but none of the junior high schools was recruiting new teachers in that year. Becoming a primary school teacher was "horrible" for him in the beginning, which Haoting mainly attributed to the training he received in the teacher college. This finding has alarmed educational researchers in that these young teachers did not seem to have the choices and decisions that teachers in contemporary Western culture must make in choosing their jobs. In such cases, younger teachers might need to take a different approach to develop a strong sense of their professional identities as teachers.

A wide range of factors exerted influences on the way teachers negotiate these conflicts in making sense of their career choices. These teachers took two different approaches to address the challenges they faced: the involved approach and the uninvolved approach. That is teachers who tended to take the involved approach were able to adopt multiple internal strategies in addressing the tension and challenges they faced at the beginning of a career that did not meet their initial expectations. For example, both Xiwen and Ruolan noticed a lack of understanding, mutual support and trust among stakeholders in Willow School. They both found parents were demanding and unreasonable. The negative experiences significantly threatened Xiwen and Ruolan's sense of self-efficacy. Both of the teachers claimed that they were able to adopt a range of strategies and became more resilient in adversity. These strategies included:

1. Striving to demonstrate competence by taking teacher exams and becoming a SST.

2. Actively engaging with colleagues, parents and students to promote learning and better understanding.

3. Changing their attitudes and reflecting on the educational value of teaching in the primary school.

4. Self-motivation to learn to improve the status quo.

The teachers' narratives demonstrated their capacity to exercise their professional agency to learn and adapt to unexpected circumstances and the willingness to be flexible and learn from others, which in turn encouraged them to reflect on the value, purpose and nature of teaching in Willow School. Meanwhile, the other two teachers, Haoting and Yifan, tended to take a more accepting attitude towards the structural restrictions, such as family roles and teacher policies, and were less involved in coming up with personal strategies to resolve the tensions. Haoting, for instance, developed a sense of alienation in his narrative of the conflicts between his ambition and the lack of opportunities for a better and more stable income. Although Yifan did not state any kind of personal feelings about her career choice, her narrative also focused on the social and political context in which she was "selected" rather than "she chose" to be a primary school teacher.

6.1.2 The Case of Aspen School

Similar to the teachers in Willow School, job stability was the most commonly mentioned reason for the participant teachers in Aspen to choose the job. All the participant teachers referred to the lack of alternative job opportunities after they graduated from teacher training institutes and the benefits of job stability in teaching.

Because this job is very stable; it is not like any other jobs, where you might be fired at any time. Besides, my experiences showed me that this job fits me pretty well. I don't have the talent for business, nor do I like politics. I want to be with friendly people. (Xinxin)

It's complicated to find a proper job here. It's even harder for teacher trainees because we are not considered skilled workers. Becoming a teacher or a state employee is the best choice for us. (Zhe)

Both of the female teachers, Qizhen and Xinxin, considered teaching to be a job that fitted their introverted personalities. They recognised teachers as public service professionals who enjoy social respect and positive collegial relationships. Moreover, Qizhen and Zhe also have a sense of personal connection to their families as state teachers; they had other family members who had worked as school teachers and government officers. In this sense, having family members who had similar careers might be helpful for teachers to maintain a sense of self-efficacy in their career paths.

When it came to the everyday experiences of working, however, some teachers' narratives reflected a lack of self-efficacy with regards to their career choices. Xinxin, for instance, said that she considered herself as lacking a strong character and the courage to act on her own as she concluded that staying within a "simple environment" where she does not need to deal with "business or politics" would fit her personality. Xinxin also tended to link her lack of a sense of agency at work to her personality test result, which stated that she needed more extended time to process negative feelings. Such a conflicted sense became especially strong when she began to act on her own initiative. Xinxin seemed to feel extremely guilty about not following others' advice and guidance. She thought part of the reason was the link with her role as the oldest daughter in her family, someone who needed to show her capability and tolerance of others as an excellent role model.

I need to say I'm the oldest and I'm eager to do well in everything. In others' eyes, I'm a good girl. I think it must be related to my performance at work. I follow the rules docilely and do whatever asked by the leader. I won't be secretly doing other kinds of things. I will do whatever I'm told. I'm a typical follower and I don't have my own ideas.

On the one hand, Xinxin seemed to be desperate to become more autonomous in making her professional decisions and remain positive in collegial and parental communications in the school as a young teacher. On the other hand, she felt overloaded with the stress and sense of insecurity in starting to pursue her personal goals. In this sense, although Xinxin seemed to be involved in negotiating the tension between her pursuit and the fear of her own choice in a hierarchical social structure, she could not come up with a solution for such tensions, which might lead to further issues such as downplaying her professional achievements as mere luck, and profound frustration when students' academic outcomes do not meet her expectations.

Jianguo also claimed that the social environment and school leaders needed to be responsible for teachers' sense of professional identities. Unfortunately, Jianguo declined to answer my questions with regards to his own experiences and ideas about how teachers might respond to adversity through their actions. In summary, these teachers' responses reflected slightly different patterns in the way teachers make sense of their career choices. Three kinds of approaches could be identified in the samples: 1) satisfied and personally connected (Zhe and Qizhen); 2) negatively involved (Xinxin); and 3) uninvolved (Jianguo).

6.2 Addressing Challenges to Support Students' Learning

The data analysis also brought to light the teachers' perceptions of their beliefs and their practices in supporting students' learning and development. The comparative analysis revealed some of the common themes of teachers' reflections on students' learning needs:

1. Students need an open and supportive family environment for their

moral development.

2. Students need to follow classroom discipline.

3. Students need to be supported by a favourable classroom climate.

4. Students need diversified pedagogical practices that can help and adapt to their unique and different learning demands.

5. Students need to improve their academic performances.

6. Students need supportive parents to oversee and provide constructive guidance.

The major concerns among the SSTs are: 1) the students' poor academic performance; 2) the lack of pedagogical ideas to diversify students' learning experiences; and 3) meeting students' different development needs. The oversized classrooms had also left teachers in a particularly disadvantaged position to bring changes to students' learning. Moreover, teachers felt particularly conflicted when the accountability system is heavily reliant on assessing students' test scores.

6.2.1 The Case of Willow School

In Willow School, Haoting and Ruolan had experienced intense challenges in negotiating the tension between their beliefs and the realities of classroom teaching. Haoting and Ruolan tended to advocate their professional role as caregivers and the significance of cultivating students' moral and character development due to their personal preferences and previous experiences. By contrast, Haoting and Ruolan tended to take a more reluctant and helpless position when it came to the workload of implementing the curriculum reform.

There is just too much work, both the quantity and the content. The national curriculum added too much pressure on teachers, students and parents. The students must do well in the exams, and there is no other choice. This is the situation in China; scores evaluate students. We can't do anything about it.

Xiwen's tensions, however, originated from more practical aspects of teaching, including her concerns about classroom discipline and the use of one pedagogical model advocated during the teaching reform. Nevertheless, Xiwen was able to reconcile these tensions by drawing on a wide range of alternative resources and methods, such as assigning roles and responsibilities for students, focusing on the textbook while encouraging students to read broadly and maintaining her own understanding of the strict accountability scheme. As she said in the interview: "I think every teacher is different and does their best. It's not about which methods they use, but how they bring changes to children's lives."

For Yifan, the most critical part is to focus on students' learning and to adopt a student-centred approach in implementing the curriculum reform. A range of factors seemed to contribute to this phenomenon, including her status as an established teacher, one who had returned from retirement, her understanding of her role as an experienced teacher in Willow and her interest in teaching. Although she considered the crowded classes as a challenge for Willow, she focused more on the positive outcomes of the curriculum reform and its impact on students' learning. As she summarised:

> I think it is good. We used to put teaching before learning. During the curriculum reform, students are at the centre and teachers merely give guidance. In this way, students can understand better and remember more accurately. There's a saying that experiences are the most unforgettable. If students could participate in group activities and count the numbers themselves, they will remember more easily, because their learning has started with practice.

Yifan supported that the use of learning groups is beneficial for students' learning in mathematics. She did not consider issues such as subject knowledge and the pedagogical models as problematic. In contrast to everyone else, Yifan seemed to have the least tension between her beliefs and practices during the curriculum reform.

In summary, differences in teachers' perceptions of the influencing factors and coping strategies led to marked professional identities in teachers' narratives of students' learning and development. Xiwen's narrative, for instance, seemed to reflect the teacher's sense of agency that is contingent on contexts. She was able to critically reflect and adjust herself to fit into the relationship to which she belongs and strive to meet her duties and educational visions for her students. Yifan could also focus on selecting useful methods based on previous experiences in implementing the school vision. For the other two teachers, they might focus on adjusting internal attributes (i.e. emotions, ability and personality) to address the sense of self-esteem (Ruolan) or bearing with the dilemmas and considering the problems as impossible to solve (Haoting).

6.2.2 The Case of Aspen School

Teachers in Aspen School also emphasized the importance of students' moral and character development in primary schools and worried about the lack of parental support for students' growth. All the four participant teachers mentioned the erosion of teachers' professional authority among young and educated parents of students in this school. These teachers claimed they could not make much difference to students' learning and development without parents' collaboration. These four teachers were still able to draw on resources and address some of the significant challenges in achieving their professional goals.

To support students' moral and character development, teachers perceived themselves as role models who needed to be people of integrity in their daily behaviour and in the management of their classrooms. Three of the teachers focused on the importance of treating students in an equal and respectful manner and giving equal opportunities for all the students; one mentioned teachers' dress codes and daily behaviour. Also, all the four teachers pointed out the importance of and their willingness to invest in developing their professional skills at work. By "developing professional skills", teachers seemed to focus on the methods and skills involved in effective classroom teaching, through which teachers take the role of the "guide" of students' learning and development.

Despite the common focuses on their work ethic and professional skills, teachers' subject knowledge and years of experiences seemed to have significant influences on their sense of competency to support students' learning. For instance, Qizhen had taught Chinese for over 20 years. She considered herself an experienced teacher, who was willing to keep learning, adapting to the changes and helping young teachers. She focused on reflecting and developing an understanding of Chinese education as language training to better support students' learning in the classroom. In this process, she needed to transform her role from an instructor who used to "tell everything I know about the texts" to one who "helps students read and write and gives them enough time to learn on their own". She supported her claim by emphasizing the emotional aspect of language learning and the importance of scaffolding in teaching primary school students in her discussion with her colleagues. She later summarised that Chinese education should pay attention to students' emotional experiences, and that teachers could help by integrating different methods and tools in classroom teaching.

For the younger teachers, however, learning to teach could be a frustrating process and the teacher needed to cope with multiple demands from the students and the evaluative feedback from experienced teachers. As a maths teacher, Xinxin often felt frustrated by the students' lack of interest and passion for learning maths. As she claimed,

> Unlike Chinese, maths is very rational. I need to make maths learning fun and attractive for my students. […] Students would complain when given extra maths classes. I hope to make my classes more interesting. However, it's so difficult. […] I don't feel good about myself or any of my classes. "Oh my God, it is finally the end", that's like how I felt after class. It's torture for me and my students.

In her narrative, Xinxin seemed to be more concerned about her work performances, rather than reflecting on students' learning needs and being critical of structural limitations. In this sense, it is more difficult for Xinxin to lay claim to her professional authority in the face of others' criticism and to come up with solutions for the challenges she hoped to address.

To briefly summarise this section, the participant teachers from Willow School came up with a wide range of strategies in negotiating the tensions to meet their professional purposes in supporting students' learning, including:

1. teachers' self-assessment;
2. knowing the teaching goals;
3. connecting subject knowledge with students' overall learning needs;
4. understanding the curriculum and students' learning;
5. thinking of alternative solutions and resources for current challenges;
6. employing self-care techniques;
7. motivation to learn from others;
8. appreciation of collegial rapport;
9. years of experiences in teaching; and
10. a sense of vocation.

6.3 Summary

In summary, the participant teachers' narratives reflected highly conflicting professional self-images in Willow School. There was a consensus on the benefits of current curriculum reform, which aimed to transform the traditional classroom teaching to one that is more engaging for students. At the same time, the teachers were aware of the adverse social and educational trends that challenge teachers' authority in classrooms as well as their relationships with parents. These teachers also talked about the impacts of the media in terms of creating a negative professional image of teachers among the general public.

There were more universal than different themes across the two school cases. Generally speaking, teachers were exposed to highly intensive professional training and worked in a comparatively stable system yet one with static promotion. Both of the school leaders mentioned that they found it challenging to help promote teachers in the system and most of the focus on teachers' professional development was given to training young teachers in classroom teaching. Such a strategy was also informed by the theoretical framework employed for teachers' professional development stages. Older teachers demonstrated a strong sense of vocation and took a leading role in helping young teachers, yet young teachers were more frustrated and conflicted than the older teachers.

All the eight SSTs demonstrated their commitment to students' learning. In the interviews, all the teachers had addressed the problems of family education and its influences on their sense of professional authority. Positive teacher-student interaction is a significant contributing factor to those teachers' sense of achievement and their satisfaction at work. Teachers were engaged with policy and social issues in education in negotiating the challenges they faced in their everyday lives. The sense of a threat to their professional authority was a distinguishing theme in these SSTs' identity narratives, one that might exert both positive and negative influences on teachers' development of identities. Some teachers were able to express their political opinions. Others showed a sign of vulnerability. Teachers' narratives also reflected the influence of political and cultural factors on TPIs (see Chapter 9).

Chapter 7
The Ash International School and the Redwood Charity School (Private Schools)

7.1 Introducing the Ash International School (AIS)

The Ash International School (AIS) is a state-funded and privately managed K-12 school. It is located in the high-technology industrial development zone in Nanqi and occupies an area of 140,000 square metres. It was about 30 minutes' drive from Nanqi county and another 20 minutes' drive to the city centre. Located at the intersection of counties and at an upper administrative level, AIS is surrounded by wide, newly built roads and scattered residential areas, high buildings and large mansions. It was not easy to find the kind of small shops or banks I was used to seeing near other schools. Setting up a high-quality K-12 international school became a part of Nanqi's global vision. It is believed that a good school is essential to attract foreign and domestic talents and promote this area for economic development. The collaboration took the form of a cross-regional school partnership overseen by the local management committee. Huawen Education was responsible for implementing the international curriculum and issues such as student enrolment, teacher recruitment and the management of foreign teachers, etc.

7.1.1 Diversifying the Curriculum

The media portrays AIS as a strong sign of internationalisation in Nanqi and a new experiment in cross-regional school partnership. In the interview, Jiang (member of the vice principal team) said that the AIS' goal for its primary school was to cultivate students' independent personalities and behavioural habits. The official website introduced the primary school of AIS as follows:

> Under the guidance of Huawen Education's 6C concept, the primary school is committed to cultivating the international citizenship of physical and mental health, rich in Chinese civilisation background, full of all-round ability and with elegant temperaments. Here is the fertile soil every student can benefit from; what's more, here is the sailing start for every student to pursue the dream.

The 6C philosophies are "Confident, Caring, Committed, Creative, Cooperative and Communicative", which is put forward by the principal. To achieve the goal, the school paid a great amount of attention to the diversification of the curriculum and the enrichment of students' experiences. Within each level of education, AIS provides different kinds of courses varying in terms of tuition fees. Regarding primary education, there are three types of classes: the experimental class; the international class; and the international girl's class. The following table (Table 7-1) demonstrates the characteristics of the curriculum, the organising of the class masters and the learning goals.

Table 7-1　Characteristics of different classes in AIS (primary education)

	Experimental class	International class	International girl's class
Curriculun	• National curriculum • School-based English • Optional courses • Social practice • Chinese classics chanting	• National curriculum • International curriculum • School-based English • Special lessons (piano and calligraphy)	• National curriculum • International curriculum • School-based English • Special lessons (piano, *zheng*, dancing, physique, vocal music, calligraphy, pottery, chess, etiquette, cooking, etc.)

Continued

	Experimental class	International class	International girl's class
Organising of class masters	One class master	Two seating in class masters (one Chinese teacher and one foreign teacher)	Two class masters (one Chinese teacher and one foreign teacher)
Learning goals	Focusing on developing one's speciality and cultural identity Cultivation of modern citizenships	Integrating Chinese and Western education to cultivate globally competitive talents with outstanding English and comprehensive capacities	Focusing on the quality of "versatile and elegant characteristics of future outstanding women models"

In addition to the curriculum, AIS holds three to four extracurricular events every month during term time. The reality, however, was more complicated and unpredictable. The director of teaching of AIS told me that AIS faced tremendous challenges in adapting to the local educational context of Nanqi. As he commented:

> Since international education does not have a long history in this city, there was a lack of correspondence between the educational vision and parents' expectations.

He said that the parents, who are also the "customers" that pay for their children's school education, tend to expect more and tend to be too reliant on the school to prepare their children to attain good academic outcomes. According to Jiang and the participant teachers, some students' parents still maintain a result-oriented mindset that focuses only on academic progress and often overlooks the value of students' experiences of cultural difference and diversity. Despite the challenges, Jiang argued that the second-child policy would bring more opportunities for private schools. The key for private schools to bring changes, as he argued, is parents' humble expectations and clearer planning for their children's education.

7.1.2 Structural Restrictions on the Development of Private Education

Jiang also stated that the lack of economic development hinders the funding resources for the development of private schools. Jiang took the example of foreign teachers and argued that one of the greatest expenses for an international school is the employment of foreign teachers. In his view, it is increasingly difficult to employ and pay for qualified foreign teachers to implement the international curriculum and to provide an international environment for learning to maintain the school's attractiveness for students and parents.

At the same time, he pointed to the danger of a system that increasingly takes education as market behaviour. For him, the market environment is not sufficiently developed yet to guarantee the quality of private education. Jiang took the recent close-off policies for coal-mining industries in Shandong as an example. According to the news, the policy resulted in thousands of laid-off workers, who could quickly receive licences to set up kindergartens and private tutoring centres. The expansion of short-term, profit-driven businesses and the low quality of these private educational institutes, according to Jiang, would exert a significant negative impact on education quality. In other words, educational choices could be risky when neither the competitive supply sides (schools and institutes) nor the utilitarian demand sides (parents and students) are equipped with sufficient knowledge of what constitutes a good education to make a good choice for the children.

7.1.3 Teachers' Roles and Professional Development

Regarding teachers, Jiang stated that teachers need to "make the finishing point by painting the dragon's eyes"[①] in classroom teaching. This is a famous Chinese idiom and its story is often used to phrase an artist's exquisite skills to bring his painting alive. What he wanted to indicate here seemed

---

① 画龙点睛

to be the teachers' role to bring enlightenment to students rather than spoon-feeding them. The use of group work and discussion are encouraged to engage students in their learning. To train new teachers, AIS employs the system of apprenticeship, in which an experienced teacher guides the new teacher in familiarising teaching and the schoolwork in general. The school also organises activities such as a teaching competition and classroom demonstration to encourage and reward effective teachers. According to Jiang, a three-year plan for professional development is an essential requirement for teachers. The project includes: 1) the first year of course delivering; 2) the second year on course design; and 3) the third year on teaching style[①]. The development needs a professional community where teachers can support each other.

In the early years of development, AIS recruited and allocated teachers through the local government to give teachers bianzhi status. Jiang said that this model has been successful in attracting some of the best qualified and most experienced teachers. Since 2015, the government decided to cut the number of bianzhi quotas; therefore, AIS needs to hire more contract teachers. Jiang said this could be a positive change, for those teachers with bianzhi often "lack a sense of crisis". On the basis of his own experience, Jiang claimed that teaching in private schools is often "only suitable for certain personalities". How to strengthen teachers' identification with the school organisation is a priority for Ash to attract and support new teachers. Jiang said that school improvement is the key to developing such a sense of identification and ownership: teachers are expected to benefit from the development of the school in terms of their social status and income. Table 7-2 demonstrates the key charactersitics of the Ash International School.

---

① 教学风格

Table 7-2   The key charactersitics of the Ash International School

Location	A high-technology industrial development zone between the county and city
Neighbourhood	Wide, newly built road and scattered residential areas, high office buildings and large blocks for industrial purposes
School finance	Dtermined by the government and supplemented by profits from tuition fees
School staffing	Initially recruited through local goverment as state teachers and moving to school contract-based employent with better payment
School facilities and equipment	Large campus with good facilities
Number of students	About 3,000 students (K-12) and about 100 classes
Number of teachers	About 300 Chinese teachers and 40 foreign teachers
School-parent relationship	Mixture of collaboration and high demand
Role of national curriculum	Remain dominant, and supplemented by international curriculum and a wide range of school-based curriculum and extracurricular activites; Varies according to different types of class
Staff support and supervision	Systematic training for teacher induction; Strong focus on professional collaboration
Focus of class reform	Promoting life skills such as communication and leadership skills; Encouraging students to express and particiapte in a wide range of school activities; Setting high starndard for academic progress
Teacher job progression	Stable and with opportunities for professional pogression with bianzhi
Leadership	Instructional and administrative leadership style

7.2　Example Teacher Case: Baihe

Basic biographical information
Age: Mid-30s
Gender: Female
Education: Bachelor of Arts in Chinese Literature (Normal College)
Current position: Maths teacher
Years of teaching: 10 years

Baihe decided to become a teacher when she was 17 years old; her father, who had been a teacher for over 30 years, influenced such decision. Before joining AIS, Baihe had worked in another private school in Yishui for 6 years. Back then, Baihe thought the school management was corrupt, and there was a lack of professional training for teachers. As a private school teacher, she did not find a sense of security and belonging. After the school board decided to close the school due to financial problems, Baihe chose to move back to Nanqi, which was also her hometown. Although she experienced uncertainties in her earlier years of teaching, Baihe thought teaching had become an excellent job for her, as she said: "Unlike banking or the telecommunications industry, I can spend my days with children. Teaching brings me happiness. It is the happiest occupation in the world."

7.2.1 Realising Personalised Learning

There were 31 students in Baihe's class and she needed to take a significant amount of time to manage student lives in school. "In private schools, you have to pay attention to individual students, while in state schools, because of the large number of students, teachers tend to focus more on the commonalities," she said. In addition to teaching students according to their different levels, Baihe believes that teachers not only need to be professional in terms of classroom teaching, but they also need to be a "scholar of flourishing thoughts", so as to influence students in various aspects of life. Baihe perceived her educational background in the normal college to have been beneficial to her work in AIS. In particular, she appreciated the teaching of critical skills such as performance skills, public speaking and the spirit of teamwork. As Baihe stated:

> When I was in college, I was the class leader in arts. I learned a lot including singing, dancing, volleyball, public speech and piano [...] I can hardly remember any of these, but these improved my overall attainment. Without these, I could barely give any advice for my students (for school performances) now.

Baihe suggested that offline-learning opportunities, such as school visits and class observations, are the most helpful methods for teacher learning. Having visited one school in Singapore and the Dulangkou School in Shandong, Baihe identified the general characteristics of each school. She argued that students in the Singaporean school were more relaxed than students in AIS. In contrast, Baihe was less convinced by the Dulangkou model, which for her seemed to be more of "just a form than the deeper educational philosophy that 'touched my heart'". "What do you mean by that?" I asked. Baihe drew on her detailed observation of an art teacher to demonstrate her point: "I wanted to cut a few pieces all together, so I stapled them, which left small holes in them," Baihe explained. The art teacher's attention to detail and concern for accuracy was very touching for her.

She told me about Linlin, a student who just transferred to AIS. Linlin used to be disruptive and rude to his classmates and teachers. With her support, Linlin could accept criticism and express himself with confidence. Baihe thinks this is an example of her success as a class master in paying close attention to individual students in her class. Seeing students' progress in their development is what makes Baihe most satisfied, as she stated: "It's hard to quantify this feeling. It is invisible. But in my heart, I feel a strong sense of achievement."

The idea of achieving excellence and perfection seemed to be an impor-

Chapter 7 The Ash International School and the Redwood Charity School (Private Schools)

tant aspect of the school culture that drives Baihe in her work. As a member of the middle management team, she also thought of the school principal as a role model for her in the leadership role. She stated that on top of Chinese teaching she was someone who could exert a positive influence on children. For the idea of teachers-as-role-models, she felt teachers need to behave in a good way regarding their lifestyle and their etiquettes so that a student similarly conducts his or her life, and to pay attention to every aspect of conduct to improve general competency. The phrase "competency"[①] was first introduced to Chinese educational policy discourse in the 2014 MoE *Suggestions to Deepen Curriculum and Pedagogical Reform and Verify the Fundamental Goal of Strengthening Morality Education*. It was also used to replace the concept of "quality" to incorporate values, attitudes and capacities, and to employ multiple skills and knowledge to meet specific needs in one's academic and personal lives. What Baihe indicated here, however, seemed to focus more on the alignment of teachers' behaviour in both personal and professional aspects, a coherent identity that integrated the teacher's personal "lifestyle" with social etiquette and relationships. In this sense, Baihe's sense of social status is closely related to her identification with a particular style of life as a teacher. To connect with what she had described before, Baihe did not focus on the subject and pedagogical knowledge of Chinese; instead, the "lifestyle" might include her dressing, classroom practice, activities to do with her personal relationships, decorating style and child-care practices, etc. This tendency might be closely related to Chinese culture, which focuses on the behaving part of "cultivating one's moral character"[②] for a man (or woman) of noble character[③]; that moral cultivation relies heavily on putting principles into practice.

7.2.2 Roles and Respects

In the international class, Baihe had taken the role of teaching assistant

---

① 素养
② 修身
③ 君子

to help students interpret and collaborate with students' parents. Baihe said she appreciated foreign teachers' flexible approach to teaching: "They have lots of new ideas and know lots of handcraft skills." However, Baihe needed to take care of discipline. Also, Baihe spends more than half of her working hours in school activities. In this process, Baihe felt she needed to negotiate her identity as an educator and a teacher:

> If I have a choice, I hope I could focus on teaching. But as an educator, we need to exert subtle influences and "cultivate the students" through [a] series of activities. Teaching is for students' learning, which is also crucial in schools. Someone must do the job.

Although Baihe felt teachers are respected in her school, her experience informed her that, in the digital age, people could form opinions on any profession through online platforms and social media. The negative social images could also affect teachers and how people treat them. Like other teachers, Baihe claimed that the traditional authorities given to teachers are under threat by public opinion. She expressed her concerns about changes in parents' attitudes: "Parents will respect you if you are a good teacher; in the opposite, they won't pay you any respect if you can't get your work done." Baihe expressed that she felt teachers' social status has been enhanced because of the school's improvement. Despite occupational conflicts between parents and schools, Baihe thought parents of students from AIS paid more respect to teachers than parents in other schools due to the school reputation.

7.2.3 A Sense of Happiness

Teacher-student relationships are crucial to Baihe's sense of joy and job satisfaction in Ash. Baihe talked about a teaching diary she posted on the class blog about a playful conversation she had with her students. Through the communication, she felt intimately connected with her students. She said in addition to her daughter's love, she could also receive her students' love

Chapter 7 The Ash International School and the Redwood Charity School (Private Schools)

for her. Tellingly, she noted proudly, "Sometimes, they would call me mother." She also enjoyed her relationship with colleagues. According to Baihe, not only would other teachers provide emotional support when she was ill, but they also help each other in organising school activities. "We are very different from the state schools. Teachers are very honest with each other, and we are often very direct." She later explained that this is because PSTs need more collaboration in carrying out their work and rarely have time for politics in schools.

Due to the rapid pace of work in Ash, Baihe found it challenging to balance her work and life. In her spare time, she likes to go for walks, surf the Internet, watch TV and take a spa. "When I'm at home, I'm as lazy as a pig; when I work, I will burn out like a dog. This is the very private part of teachers' life. When I'm home, I don't want to move at all." Like many other teachers, Baihe does not have much time to spend with her family and her daughter. Baihe told me that she and her husband have been planning to have a second child. When I tentatively asked if that would create even more of a burden on her, she answered two children would make them happier, especially since China has an ageing society. In the end, she does not want to lose her family because of her career:

> I think I must have both a family and a job. I'm happy if I can just get my work done. I don't want to spend too much of my energy on it because social positions do not determine our happiness.

In this portrait, I talked with Baihe through aspects of her personal and professional lives and attempted to gain a glimpse of her professional identities. Baihe had unique experiences as a teacher trainee in college, through her many years of teaching experiences in private schools, as well as her current leadership roles in AIS. Baihe's interview indicated that she is a mother in pursuit of her happiness in both her personal and professional lives. The major challenge she faces is to balance her work and family life.

7.3　Introducing the Redwood Charity School (RCS)

RCS is located in the high-speed rail development zone (HRDZ) in the Southeastern area of Nanqi and is about 8.5 miles away from the city centre. This area used to be a small village before the HRDZ was built. Redwood is entirely financed by a real estate development company and operates as an "enterprise-run school" (Qiye Banxiao). According to the official introduction, RCS adopted the "6+3+2" model that both of the previous two schools had employed. Students receive 11 years of education including six years' primary education, three years' lower secondary education and two years' vocational training. In 2015, RCS had about 800 students, 23 classes and 40 teachers who worked on a contract basis.

After receiving the permission to visit the school through personal connection, I took a taxi alone and began my fieldwork in Redwood. It was around 2 p.m. when I arrived and the road to the school was empty. The front of the school gate was wide and deserted, facing which was a large construction area. All the school buildings followed the style of ancient Chinese architectures with grey-colored brick walls and the xieshan roof[①]. The classes had already started when I arrived. By the right side of the school, I saw a few small restaurants and shops on the road that leads to the village. These small shops made the school look even more ornamental.

The school occupies about fifty thousand square meters. By the side of the path to the main administration building were some small trees. A few displays stand with picture posters were hanging inside. By the right and left sides of the path stood the large-scale indoor sports centre and the dining hall.

---

① Xieshan roof is a type of roof in Chinese architecture with four slopes and two triangular vertical planes added on the lateral slopes. In terms of social position, this kind of roof is only next to the hipped roof (wudian roof) that's only used by the royal family and Confucius.

Chapter 7 The Ash International School and the Redwood Charity School (Private Schools)

Despite the size of the campus, I rarely saw any cars or bikes inside. In front of the entry path was a large open area surrounded by three major spaces with mid-rise buildings: the administration building (the front), the dormitory space (the left) and the teaching buildings (the right). According to the principal, RCS has over 100 classrooms that can accommodate 3,000 to 3,500 students. The school corridors were furnished with white ceramic tiles, making the buildings look simple and clean. Compared to the two state schools I had visited, RCS was certainly more spacious. Three teaching buildings were still under construction. Sitting in the stone chairs, I faced a large outdoor sport area with an outdoor swimming pool, a sports ground with a red plastic runway, two basketball courts and a few tennis courts. After classes, this space became the major area for students to play. Looking through the trees behind the area, some small residential buildings of the village were still visible. Table 7-3 demonstrates characteristics of Redwood Charity School.

Table 7-3 Characteristics of Redwood Charity School

Location	The high-speed rail development zone
Neighbourhood	Away from the city center nd the "new city" built in a village
School finance	Funded by a real estate company and managed by its own educational office
School staffing	Determined by the company, mainly young teachers with high turnover rate
School facilities and equipment	Good facilitiates with a new campus in construction
Number of students	About 800 students
Number of teachers	About 40 constract teachers
School-parent relationship	Low level of school-parent engagement
Role of national curriculum	Remain dominant, while supplemented by extracurrciular activities
Staff support and supervision	Strong and high intensity in training
Focus of class reform	Promoting group learning, encouraging students' engagements and foucing on the learning outcomes
Teacher job progression	Mainly relies on school rating system and lacks job security
Leadership	Instructional and administrative leadership style

7.4 Example Teacher Case: Ting

Basic biographical information
Age: Late-20s
Gender: Female
Education: Bachelor of Arts in Calligraphy (Normal College)
Current position: Maths teacher
Years of teaching: 1 year

Ting is a first-year Fine Arts and Chinese teacher in RCS. Ting was born in Sishui county in Shandong and migrated to a far-western province with her parents. She grew up in Gansu until the age of primary school. She received her first year of primary education in Gansu province before returning to Shandong due to family reasons. Coming from a background of a migrant child, she defined herself as less academically capable than other students in her class. She told me her classmates often laughed at her for her rather rustic dressing. Even her teacher did not show sympathy and support to her. "My teacher didn't even want to look at me," Ting looked very disappointed. Her traumatizing experiences in primary school led her to become socially anxious. We met in front of the teaching building on my second day of fieldwork in RCS. When I met her, she looked like a confident and caring person.

7.4.1 Exerting Positive Influences on Students

As a past victim of school bullying as a student herself, Ting said she wants to make a difference to the life chances of vulnerable students such as those catered for by RCS in her career as a teacher. She thinks that keeping a positive attitude to deal with students' disruptive and bullying behaviours in school is an important way of shaping students' character development:

"We need ten years for good teaching and a hundred years for good nurturing"①, right? Education is a long-term process. What we do at one time might influence students for a while, but to shape a character needs constant influence. Of course, everyone has different characteristics, but if I keep my positive attitude, I can support their personal growth in the long term.

The notion of personal influence emerged as an essential component of teachers' professional identity in RCS. Like other participant teachers, Ting hopes to exert a constant and positive influence on students' character development and future employability. This seems to be a fundamental principle that guides one to become a good teacher in RCS:

> Students in this school are very different from others. I want them to have a healthy mindset rather than thinking of themselves as victims of the society. From this perspective, I can be a good teacher if every student in my class become strong and calm enough to deal with difficulties and instabilities in their life. I will define that as my success. Rather than improving their academic performances, I think they need to be tough first. Otherwise, it will be tough for them to survive in the society.

In her view, to successfully exert personal influences requires the capacities to build a good rapport with students, which seems to be challenging for other participant teachers from RCS.

7.4.2 Influence of Others

Ting told me that before she met her best friends at high school and college, she had been a very introverted person. The change in her life took place after she transferred to a school in her hometown, where she found security and happiness. In her own words: "Because there was no insolence, no isolation, so I could be really happy." She enjoyed her college life with

---

① 十年树木,百年树人。

some of her best and most extrovert friends. After graduating from college in N. county, Ting found a teaching position in a private tutoring institute (PTI). In the PTI, Ting worked overtime and was ill-paid. She also thought that her relationship with her students and their families were often jeopardised by the commercial nature of her work. Most importantly, Ting realized that she simply could not afford her living expenses in Nanqi by working as a private tutor.

In 2015, Ting decided to accept her friend's advice to work in RCS. The free teacher accommodation in RCS alleviated Ting's financial pressure for living. She now has a busy life in RCS. As a class master of one class in grade four, Ting is very conscious of the fact that many of her students' particular family backgrounds would hold them from flourishing academically. In teaching, Ting used to focus on the organisation of the contents; while after the curriculum reform, she noticed that she needed to "cultivate students' active learning, self-management and deep understanding". "I must be very passionate when I teach. That's what defines successful classroom teaching," Ting said. The application of new teaching techniques including asking students to practice and demonstrate their work in classes was very helpful for Ting to achieve her goal. She also thinks it is important for students to collaborate in their groups, which in turn could help to develop their own learning community. Like Linjia, Ting was also concerned about the issue of discipline. According to her, the combination of the "vividness" and "discipline" in class became the everyday challenge.

7.4.3 "Nurturing" Is Crucial

In addition to her role to organise and facilitate the effective classroom teaching and learning, Ting defines her priority as making sure that all her students could become healthy and confident. Hence Ting has to spend lots of her energy in pastoral care and life coaching. During the interview, she mentioned the feeling of closeness she shared with her students. Ting told me that one day, when she went to the school dining hall to have lunch, a student sitting near the south gate burst into tears. Ting walked to her to

Chapter 7　The Ash International School and the Redwood Charity School (Private Schools)

calm her down. "Tell me what happened, maybe I could help?" Ting asked. The student raised her head and looked at Ting's face and said: "I want to see my grandparents; I'm scared I won't see them again." Ting wondered what had happened, so she kept asking for more information. It turned out that the student learned from her uncle that her grandma was in the hospital. The student became extremely anxious and worried about losing her grandma. Since then, Ting would often find and talk to this student. "This kind of things happens here every day," Ting told me. Once before, Ting had a self-harming student in another class. When he receives criticisms from teachers, he would often hit himself. "Why would you do this? Why can't you be kind to yourself?" Ting asked him and talked with him for a long time. Afterwards she would allow the student to find a quiet place to let off his feelings. This seemed to work for Ting and this student. "Whenever he feels down, he will find a place to be alone." According to Ting, the student's condition seemed to be improved. There are many other students who are under severe pressure to become academically capable and competitive. She said many of them have very low self-esteem. Ting would show her sympathy to these students when they feel low. She often tells her students that it is important to study, but more importantly, they need to be happy. "In this school, it's not just about teaching; it's about sharing most of your love with your students," Ting said.

　　Ting thinks that she plays three key roles in RCS: the teacher, the family member and the life coach. She mentioned the Chinese proverb "jiaoshu yuren[①]", which defines teachers' roles as to "teach the texts and nurture the person". What Ting understands is that "teach the texts" is important, but "nurture the person" is crucial. She believes that the formation of her students' personalities is rooted in their daily encounters and experiences. "I hope I could somehow influence them by showing them how I deal with problems and difficulties in life," Ting said. She hopes her students will find happiness in learning and have a strong mindset and develop their critical

---

① 教书育人

thinking skills to face future challenges. "I need them to become tough; that defines my success." Although her parents still encourage her to become a state teacher, she thinks, "Every job is the same, no matter where it is."

7.5 Summary

Findings in this section show distinct characteristics of the interaction between teachers' identity and professional learning. It is important to note here that this research does not focus on teachers' learning on a particular event context; instead, by paying attention to individual teachers' personal experiences in general, I hoped to gain a holistic view of how teachers make sense of their learning experiences at multiple levels, be that physical, emotional, cognitive or spiritual.

All the participant teachers in the AIS were female teachers and they had bianzhi status, yet they had diverse professional and personal experiences of teaching. During the data collection process, teachers were actively engaged with the questions. Two teachers (Cong and Yu) had worked in rural schools for 15 years and 3 years, respectively, before quitting their job and transferring to AIS; Zhulin and Baihe only had short-term experiences in state schools. The four teachers shared most similarities in their personal experiences of being a professional teacher. They were: (1) committed to students' learning and holistic development; (2) developing a sense of satisfaction and happiness in teaching; (3) facing challenges in taking additional responsibilities in the school context and engaging students in extracurricular activities; and (4) acknowledging the importance and influences of students' parents for their work. In terms of their professional development, all four teachers' narratives demonstrated a sense of actualisation of personal potential, or a sense of personal development, and the core of professional knowledge and skills to achieve their ambitions. Teachers did not seem to share the same perception of how the teaching profession is perceived in policies and society in general. Teachers' perceptions

Chapter 7　The Ash International School and the Redwood Charity School (Private Schools)

seemed to vary according to the extent to which their career choices and personal lives had been influenced by changes to and restrictions on teacher policies. Throughout the analysis, I also noticed a stronger influence of school leadership and school vision on TPIs, as compared to teachers in the first school case (Willow School). A more comprehensive comparative analysis will be presented in Chapter 8 in the book.

Chapter 8
Comparing Private School TPIs

Studies have illustrated that the process and organisation of schools tend to reflect the socio-economic backgrounds of the communities and families they serve. That is to say, the agency of teachers and school leaders is not the only contributing factors influencing the activities and social relations in the schools. For the most part, teachers and school leaders experience the local context and school organisations that might restrict or enable their work and the ways in which they can exercise their agency. A better understanding of the local contextual complexity could therefore help us to understand the process of TPI formation. This section aims to compare and contrast themes emerging from the PSTs' narratives with a particular focus on the influence of school contexts. As presented in detail in the previous chapters, the two private schools extend and complement each other inside the current categories of private education in China, as they represent respectively a socially advantaged school (the international school) and a socially disadvantaged school (the charity school).

Ash was an international fee-charging school that was managed by a private educational corporation. It was located in the high-technology industrial development zone between the county and the city. Founded and permitted by the government, the Ash school was allowed to hire foreign teachers and promote an international curriculum. It was a selective school and considered attractive for well-off parents. The school leader described how the wealthy professional parents at Ash constituted a different demographic from that found at many primary schools. Having the parents' support was helpful financially and socially for Ash. At the same time, the parents were ambitious for their children and could sometimes be very demanding towards the school for their children's academic progress.

In contrast, the Redwood is a disadvantaged private school that was founded and fully funded by a private real estate company to accommodate the sub-orphan students' learning needs. The school's teachers were recruited by the school directly and were working on the contract basis.

8.1 Narratives of Students' Learning and Development

All the eight PSTs demonstrated their commitment to supporting students' academic and moral development. All teachers addressed the significance of students' learning needs in defining their professional values, which seemed to reflect a fundamental element of their professionalism. Nevertheless, different teachers seemed to take a range of positions in their narratives of students' needs, which seemed to be related to their professional attitudes, job involvement and professional images. Below is the list of students' needs which these teachers mention in their narratives:

1. Students need care and love.
2. Students need to learn flexibly and actively.
3. Students need to become responsible for their behaviour.
4. Students need to develop their planning, social and vocational skills for future education and employment.
5. Students need to have positive social relations and guidance on moral and emotional development.
6. The sub-orphan students need a role model who leads and guides them to make changes to their learning and lives.
7. Students need to live in an open and safe environment, one where they can be respected and feel that they are being treated fairly and hopeful.
8. The sub-orphan students need better opportunities for their career de-

velopment and long-term well-being.

9. Students need guidance, support and positive influences from their families.

Positive teacher-student interactions seemed to be one of the significant contributing factors to the eight PSTs' sense of achievement and satisfaction at work. These teachers' perceptions and engagement strategies, however, seemed to differ according to school contexts in meeting students' learning and development needs, and are closely connected to teachers' professional roles and identities. This section organises the findings according to the various themes and summarises the commonalities and differences in the TPIs between the two groups of PSTs under each theme. I will summarise the implications for the current understanding of these private school TPIs at the end of this section.

8.1.1 The Case of RCS

The four teachers from RCS considered schooling as the key to helping students cultivate a strong mind and a healthy lifestyle for happier and more satisfying lives in the future. To achieve the development vision for the sub-orphan students, all the participant teachers from RCS emphasized their roles in cultivating students' moral development for their future success. Ting and Wei claimed that teachers needed to take the role of family members, role models as well as life coaches to inspire students. As Ting stated: "I need to do my work wholeheartedly. When my students see what I do, they will follow." Wei and Linjia also share their observation of students' great potential for good friendships and understanding with each other, which gives them a great deal of confidence in their students' potential for success in guiding students to enhance their motivation and pursue academic progress.

Nevertheless, all the participant teachers from RCS faced challenges in their everyday interactions with students and classroom management. Due to the sub-orphan students' poor mental health given their low-income family backgrounds and lack of social support, these teachers have to cope with a wide range of disruptive behaviours, emotional demands and identity crises in their teaching. The RCS teachers' work seemed to be heavily involved in correcting students' disruptive behaviours, helping with students' low self-esteem and building teacher-student relationships with mutual trust. Communicating with students became extremely challenging in RCS, so teachers often needed to be more engaged with students at a very personal level. The absence of parents and a low level of engagement of other family members in the schoolchildren's education also meant that teachers felt that they needed to take over roles as close family members.

In this context, all the RCS teachers' narratives demonstrated a strong sense of empathy through the secure connection between their personal experiences in schools and colleges and their visions for students' moral development in RCS. Wei, for instance, told the story of his college coach, who inspired him to develop his ambition and personal integrity in the face of life challenges; Ting considered her devastating experiences of school bullying as a student herself as a driving force for her to make a difference for her students; and Linjia acknowledged both her failure in academic performances and success in engaging with others in college as examples (both negative and positive) to motivate her students in both their academic studies and socialisation. In this sense, teachers consider themselves as empathic agents sharing similar experiences, therefore having a sense of mission to shape disadvantaged students' moral compass. Ting's statement is a vivid example of this:

> This [bullying] had happened to me before, so I must stop this from happening again to my students [...] They must be strong-minded; they must know they are no worse than others.

Like other teachers from RCS, Ting intended to demonstrate her understanding in guiding her students to move on from their personal sorrow and self-pity without parental support and given social stereotype as the sub-orphans. Such an endeavour is closely connected with teachers' sense of professional identities as educators, often with a strong sense of the acceptance of uncertainty as a feature of teachers' work. Wei's comparison between an educator and a mechaniec is an example of such acceptance of the risks and imperfections that being a professional teacher involves:

> Human beings are subject to changing moods and have mixed feelings. A machine might never develop a sense of identity. However, we, as educators, could affect students with our thoughts and spirit.

8.1.2 The Case of AIS

All participant teachers from AIS took teaching as their first job and had generally longer teaching experiences than those from RCS. Teachers' previous experiences differ regarding the kind of schools they had worked at before AIS. Baihe and Zhulin had worked in private schools; Yu and Cong had transferred from state schools.

Despite the differences in these teachers' career paths, teachers seemed to have developed similar focuses for their narratives of students' learning. They highlighted the importance of students' interest, curiosity and learning habits, as well as building individual character and moral qualities. Teachers often considered the attention and guidance given to individual students as a merit of private schools, hence as distinctive characteristics of their professional identities, as Baihe described:

> The difference between a state school and a private school is that here we focus on details and students' individual character development, their feelings and living habits, etc. We care for students' development, while state schools (do not) because they have too many students. They focus on the shared characteristics rather than individual situations. At least concerning the subject of Chinese, I think private schools show higher quality in stratified teaching and considerations for students' personal development.

The international school teachers' narratives seemed to be less engaged with their personal learning experiences when it came to students' learning and development. Instead, these teachers addressed the influence of the school's global visions, school leadership and parents' lifestyles in shaping their personal lives and sense of professionalism. In this sense, being a teacher is no longer limited to seeing oneself as a professional practitioner in the context of formal schoolwork but as being represented as members of a community where they are engaged to be positively influenced by other stakeholders (i.e. school leaders, parents and students). The role change was particularly significant for Yu and Cong, who used to teach in rural state schools. They considered that teaching in AIS has helped them "upgrade" their professional knowledge as well as the quality of their own lives. Such an adaptive attitude is also reflected in teachers' agreement about the superiority of the international curriculum and the roles of foreign teachers in bringing about better academic outcomes and improving students' cognitive and communication skills (see next section). This can be identified in Cong's claim:

> I will certainly recommend the international class for parents. Although foreign teachers do not give students as much content knowledge as in the preparatory courses, students can become more confident and creative.

As members of the sub-group of native Chinese teachers in the international school context, participants in this research also tended to perceive themselves as being stricter with classroom discipline. As the teachers (Zhulin, Baihe, and Cong) described, Chinese teachers tend to be more direct in pointing out students' mistakes and giving criticism when necessary.

> Because of the cultural and language barriers, it takes longer for foreign teachers to become familiar with Chinese students. So, in this aspect, Chinese teachers are better.

Nevertheless, these teachers also tended to take the adaptive approach to understand their roles in the school and showed less tension with regards to the school's strategies for students' learning and development.

> Now we belong to the culture of an educational cooperation, I had expanded my vision and changed my attitudes. As a result of this, I developed a better understanding of parenting and children. (Cong, maths teacher, 20 years of teaching experience)

8.2 Narratives of the Curriculum

8.2.1 The Case of RCS

The implementation of the school curriculum exerted a crucial influence on teachers' experiences in the two private schools. The charity school was going through a period of significant organisational transformation, from adopting the school-based curriculum for orphan students to implementing the Dulangkou model with a strong focus on the national curriculum. Teachers were invited to attend talks, pay school visits and carry out classroom observation to learn techniques to improve classroom effectiveness and students' academic outcomes. During the interviews, teachers identified a series of benefits and challenges of the curriculum reform as presented in Table 8-1.

Table 8-1 Teachers' perceptions of the benefits and challenges of the curriculum implementation

Benefits	Challenges
• Group collaboration activities that help students to learn from peers. • Tools that support teachers' assessment of students' academic progress. • Engagement of students to develop communication and presentation skills.	• The inadequacy of the objectives and activities to meet students' cognitive development needs. • The managerial approach of curriculum implementation and heavy workload. • The lack of evaluation in measuring the effectiveness of the curriculum change. • Lack of teachers' professional autonomy.

On the one hand, teachers held mixed perceptions of the curriculum change. The implementation process was also tightly connected with the teacher appraisal system, under which teachers awere assessed based on their capacity and performance in implementing the curriculum reform. According to the interviewees, the school will select outstanding teachers and award a position in the new school with bianzhi status. Teachers seemed to take different views of the external motivation in their narratives. For instance, Linjia's narrative demonstrated a strong sense of commitment to the career path in the school, yet others seemed to distance themselves from the school policy and to prioritise teaching in the mainstream state schools in their career perspectives.

> I want to try my best to go to the new school. (Linjia, maths teacher, 1 years of teaching experience)

Despite the external motivation, teachers often feel pressured and showed a certain level of resistance to implement the curriculum reform.

> The reform requires a student to be an independent learner who is capable of doing his or her research or preview before classes, yet most students are not capable of doing so. I also don't think students need to do written demonstration every day or at every level. (Meng, Chinese teacher, 3 years of teaching experience)

All four teachers pointed out the adverse impact of their heavier workload and showed a lower level of satisfaction concerning the significant drop in free time during the curriculum reform. Such a change, according to the teachers, could also cause unnecessary stress for students. Meanwhile, teachers (Linjia, Meng, and Wei) expressed their sense of inadequacy and confusion concerning peer pressure, professional training backgrounds, subject knowledge and communication skills.

Teachers in this school push themselves hard at work [...] If everyone is doing their best, I would feel bad not to do so. (Meng, Chinese teacher, 3 years of teaching experience)

It is a long time since I graduated from college. I'm not very confident in my subject knowledge for teaching the higher grade, though I was pretty good at maths in college. Plus, the textbooks are different from the one I used in schools. (Linjia, maths teacher, 2 years of teaching experience)

I always have some distance from my students because I'm very strict. I want to correct students' behavioural problems before they become more serious issues. My students are scared of me in the beginning. I also speak very loud and tend to speak in a direct way. (Linjia, maths teacher, 2 years of teaching experience)

8.2 2 The Case of AIS

When it comes to teachers' perceptions of the school curriculum, Ash school teachers' narratives show a lower level of variation. Teachers seemed to develop strong preferences for the international curriculum based on their evaluations of students' cognitive development. In this sense, teachers showed a higher level of agreement with the school curriculum and a sense of superiority when comparing themselves with teachers in other schools. Students' social and emotional development composes a crucial part of teachers' evaluation of the school curriculum. Besides, to exert positive influences on students' personality and school lives in a holistic and experience-based way, teachers felt that they needed to perform a wide range of professional roles and undertake a broader set of responsibilities.

If I can choose, I'd like to focus on teaching. However, for children, experiences in extracurricular activities are essential. Someone has to do it. (Baihe, Chinese teacher, 7 years of teaching experience)

These teachers are not only classroom practitioners, but organisers of educational activities that engage students in multiple ways. Ash school teachers claimed that extra-curriculum activities added to their workloads and learning gaps as they adapted to the school culture and work environment. Such a change is particularly significant for Yu and Cong, the two teachers with previous teaching experience in rural state schools.

> In the previous school, teaching maths was the only thing I focused on. My job was to teach in the classes. My relationship with students was straightforward, and I did not need to do much extra. Here, however, I need to take care of a range of tasks. Without anyone to teach me, I must adapt to the environment. Suddenly, I have more colleagues, and communication with students' parents also became a demanding task [...]. In addition to the regular teaching, I need to collaborate with others in school activities: making lecture slides, organising events, rehearsing with others. I used to be just a maths teacher who teaches equations and solves maths problems, [...] now I need to seize both teaching tasks and school work. (Yu, maths teacher, 2 years of teaching experience)

Yu's statement reflected her experiences in a school that diversifies teachers' tasks and professional skills. As a young teacher, Yu needed to be willing to learn from others and slowly build her confidence at work. Her family support, as well as positive feedback from students' parents, helped Yu develop a strong sense of identity as a learner at school. Baihe, who is an experienced teacher, also commented on her preference for observing other teachers and pursuing continuous practice at work as a method of professional learning.

> Other teachers' developed approach to carrying out specific tasks pull at my heartstrings [...]. I learned these small details from working with them. Being a teacher is a gradual process of growing by doing.

Cong also claimed that her school identity developed through five years of experiences in Ash. In her own words:

> I grew a firm sense of identification with the pace of work and school culture. I think I'm slowly immersed in this culture. It [the school culture] is compelling.
>
> The parents influenced me by showing me their expectations for and investment in their children's education. Those outstanding parents mainly had an impact on me.

To summarise the characteristics of TPIs concerning the school curriculum changes, teachers in the RCS seemed to experience a higher level of tension in the context of the curriculum change. When teachers perceive the curriculum reform decision as being made in a coercive way, teachers felt that they had to follow the guidelines of teaching. The strong focus on instrumental techniques might, however, undermine teachers' sense of well-being and integrity. Teachers in RCS relied heavily on their personal experiences and inherent resilience to make sense of the curriculum change and the value of their work in the school. In contrast, AIS teachers tended to take pride in their work environment in the international school. To better understand the underlying factors, we need to ask whether AIS teachers have more organisational and domestic resources in constructing their professional identities, including a developed professional community, school culture, effective leadership, feedback from parents and positive teacher-student relationships.

8.3 Narrative of Job Involvement and Professional Image

PSTs' narratives of their job involvement and professional images comprise another important aspect of teachers' identity narrative. A wide range of social, cultural and personal factors contributed to teachers' professional attitudes with regards to students' need in primary schools. Some teachers drew on their own educational experiences (e.g. Ting, Linjia), interactions with students (e.g. Meng) or previous work experiences (e.g. Cong) in forming their attitudes towards students' needs. They also drew on cultural resources to support their claims. Teachers also recalled professional attitude changes, as influenced by their work experiences in general (i.e. Cong), critical events in professional lives (Meng, Yu), school community (Yu, Cong) and role models (Wei). Through the comparative analysis, I identified four apparent types of job involvement:

    1. Professional learning as a pathway to integrity (internal), career services to others (external) and services (relational). (Cong, Wei, Yu, Linjia, Ting)

    2. Seeking and engaging with opportunities for constant improvement and progress in teaching. (Meng, Yu)

    3. Low expectations and a strong sense of responsibility to meet expectations for the school and students. (Ting, Meng, Yu)

    4. High professional standards and critical self-evaluation. (Baihe)

Despite the similarities and overlaps in teachers' perceptions about their students' needs and their job involvement among the selected two groups of teachers, a key observation from the comparative analysis is the school differences in teachers' professional images. A professional image can be defined as the teachers' evaluations and opinions of the value and outlook of their occupation, including judgements on the teachers' prestige in society, the worth of the profession to society, the personal and behavioural characteristics of its members, as well as their occupational opportunities, and the achievement of the attributes of professionalisation.

8.3.1 The Case of RCS

Teachers' perceptions on the personal and behaviour characteristics of a good teacher seemed to vary according to how teachers reacted to the expectations for work performances, professional roles and responsibilities. For instance, Linjia seemed to be more influenced by the external environment of school curriculum reform in defining teachers' problem-solving skills as the key to success. As she said:

> I used to believe that knowledgeable teachers are successful teachers. While according to the school reform model, I think those who can solve multiple problems in students' lives are successful teachers. (Linjia, maths, female, 1 year of teaching experience)

She used the phrase "according to the requirements of the school reform model, I need to ..." as a way to explain the change in her understanding of teachers' professional roles and behaviours. Without the critical reflections on her own experiences and values, the teacher may fail to connect her perceptions and benefits with the changing environment, and hence remain silent about the tensions she might experience at work. When discussing her perception of performance-based appraisal and pay, Linjia mentioned its legitimacy by suggesting that "everyone will be more motivated". On the contrary, Ting linked her experiences of school bullying as a primary school student with her belief in social justice in education as a teacher. The consistency of her personal experiences with her professional values might also help Ting develop a stable professional identity in her daily practice.

> I might not look tired now, but once I walked into the classroom, I must get excited to inspire my students and be inspired by them. Otherwise, the class could exert adverse influences on students. For me, only the inspiring teachers can lead to really effective learning. (Ting, art, female, 1 year of teaching experience)
>
> I'm a teacher; I'm also a family member and life coach for my students because I need to advise them when they are in trouble. "Have a warm heart and smile," I say this to them every day. (Ting, art, female, 1 year of teaching experience)

Teachers also tended to hold negative views with regards to the attributes of professionalisation to their images, which might differ primarily due to the limitations of the school context. Teachers could draw their interests and disciplinary affiliation from their teacher education background. However, due to the high rate of teacher turnover in RCS, teachers have to remain flexible and face challenges when teaching unfamiliar subjects, which requires teachers to develop new skills and identities when they are assigned to teach different subjects. For example, although Meng is well aware of the significance of professional knowledge to his success as a teacher, his initial experience in transferring from history teaching to Chinese teaching was somewhat disappointing:

> I think one must receive basic training in classroom teaching to be a successful teacher. The teacher must be knowledgeable about his or her subject and have the capacity to deliver that knowledge to his or her students. I majored in History in college, but I was arranged to teach Chinese. (Wei, PE, male, 1 year of teaching experience)

The fast work pace left teachers very limited time for learning and improvement, which seemed to perpetuate teachers' low self-esteem. Linjia, for instance, considered RCS teachers as less capable of writing for educational journals and seemed unhopeful about belonging to a group of effective and creative teachers. Meanwhile, teachers' perceptions of their social prestige were mostly negative. Some teachers claimed state status as a determinant factor of their public image as legitimate teachers; the other teachers, by contrast, tended to label state teachers as unmotivated. Nevertheless, both sides tended to categorise teachers and their social status according to their employment relationship with the state. Therefore, as teachers without state employee status, the private school participant teachers' professional images seemed to be negative, although participant teachers could identify a strong sense of satisfaction and achievement when it came to the altruistic nature of their work.

8.3.2 The Case of AIS

Teachers from the international school are found to be more positive with regards to their professional images in that they actively engage with issues of their professional image in their daily work and the influences on their work and identity development. Teachers in AIS included a wide range of social and cultural factors in their professional lives and considered that certain social stereotypes about what teachers should be like would limit their sense of individuality in the workplace as well as in their personal daily lives.

> I feel there are stereotypes to how teachers should behave. Such social restrictions include fixed dressing codes and moderate social manners. I'm not allowed to be different. (Zhulin, English, female, 8 years of teaching experience)

Zhulin took a holistic view of TPI in that she believed a successful teacher needed to have certain personal charisma in every aspect of her professional lives, including daily communication, resilience and flexibility. In her own words, "this must come from inside of you". At the same time, Zhulin pointed out that teachers also often needed to negotiate the limitations imposed by social stereotypes and professional culture in practice. Cong shared the same concerns in her personal life that others could often easily recognise her behaviours and appearance as a teacher. "It's frustrating," she said. In contrast to teachers from RCS, teachers from AIS seemed to hold a higher professional status and tend to be more positive towards the impacts of school vision and culture.

> We hold higher expectations for education and have advanced educational ideas. [...] The school principal will share the broader view of international education from foreign countries. I find that very inspiring. (Zhulin, English, female, 8 years of teaching experience)

> I think I developed a strong identification with the school culture. I see the

change in myself, and that's very powerful. (Cong, maths, female, 20 years of teaching experience)

Like teachers in the charity school, AIS teachers' professional images involves high-performance expectations and certain levels of tensions with regards to teacher appraisal, pay and career pathways.

I would not say I like the atmosphere of competition [...]. However, I have to do this for better pay and a better life. [...] Perhaps the school could avoid significant gaps and make achievable targets for teachers, so we could see realising goals as possible. (Cong, maths, female, 20 years of teaching experience)

I hope to focus on teaching and have prospects of promotion. The school wanted me to take on more management roles, but I rejected this. (Baihe, Chinese, female, 7 years of teaching experience)

It is important to note here that Cong and Baihe are experienced teachers. Therefore, they could have more voice over the school management issues. In particular, Cong had worked as a school principal and seemed to be the most proactive member of the school. Not only did she support this research study by introducing teachers to me, but she also showed her strong interest in participating in this research. All the teachers talked about the challenges they faced at work, yet claimed they had made substantial investments in their continuous professional development at work. For instance, although Yu, the young Chinese teacher considered herself as a young teacher who had faced many challenges from the personal to the professional level, she felt she was resilient and had become particularly keen on improving her capacity in teaching and in carrying out her responsibilities for her students. As she said: "I would love to learn more to improve my practices and participate in more teaching contests in the future."

So far, I have shown the difference in professional images among participant teachers in the two private schools. Teachers in the international school retained a more positive attitude towards their professional images than those in the charity school. Such difference is only partially due to teachers' employment relationship with the state (bianzhi). The findings reveal the influences of other factors, such as school policies and teacher turnover, as well as teachers' workload and opportunities for professional development and career progress.

8.4 Narratives of Spirituality and Tangible Satisfaction

By reflecting upon the specific experiences of individual teachers, it is suggested that the non-religious but implicitly spiritual aspects are developed and connected to teachers' narrative identities in their work in different schools. In the Western cultural context, the word "spirituality" implies that individuals or a group of people can experience a transcendental dimension of human existence that is beyond the self. Such feelings might be being a part of something larger and more whole than oneself. Unlike the "vertical" Christian meaning of spirituality as the connection with God, the participant teachers' workplace spirituality in the Chinese context seemed to be more "horizontal", that is, strongly involved with community service, connections, compassion and a sense of achievement in their day-to-day work. Teachers used the expression of doing things from the "heart"[①] to describe the need to raise awareness of the desire within oneself in transitioning one's experiences.

8.4.1 The Case of RCS

For some teachers in the charity school, the process of teaching sub-orphan students and the reconstruction and reformulation of the story of who she or he is highlighted more profound transcendental features of life related to teachers' identities. Teachers' work contains a vibrant non-

---

① 用心做事

religious but implicit spiritual dimension connected to the teachers' specific identity as a member of the community. This implies that for some teachers, such as Ting and Meng, the transition will create an implicit spiritual concern related to identity reconstruction in addition to the challenges of pursuing a promotion, learning the subject knowledge and teaching methods, and constructing a new meaningful working life. In the case of Ting, for instance, the spiritual aspect is rooted in "loving the students", which is likewise anchored in some of the critical events taking place during her work in constructing her identity.

> I think [that sense of commitment] has not much to do with teacher training. I guess if one can't do it from the bottom of their heart, they would still keep themselves away from the mess. So, teachers must follow their hearts. Only in this way could the students follow your teaching. (Ting)

This implicit spiritual feature of teaching has occurred throughout Ting's narrative identity. Her childhood memory of the absence of care and support seemed to impact Ting's sense of identity in education profoundly. She lost her confidence and even a more profound meaning to life. Her close relationship with the three loving and extrovert college friends transcended her experiences, which further influenced her professional identity as a teacher in the school.

> Confucius said: "One should not impose on others what one does not desire oneself." This is simple. I had a bad experience, and I should stop the fault from continuing. I don't want my students to experience the same. Otherwise, it will cause psychological trauma, which is harder to heal than physical injuries.

The Confucian cultural mentality of "benevolent love"[①] seemed to be important in Ting's reflections. In Confucianism, benevolent love is the core

---

① 仁爱

value for people if they are to participate in human activities and if society is to be more harmonious. Ting's explanation mirrors the same cultural mentality when it comes to her position considering her love and care for students. Meng and Wei also pointed out that the sense of conscience led to their career decisions:

> I'm most likely to stay in this school [rather than transferring to another school]. I think I'm getting familiar with the school and the students. This is what my heart tells me, so I will follow my heart. (Meng)
> My conscience tells me to become a better teacher. I want to improve myself. So, I will not allow myself to be deprived of my virtue in the process. Otherwise, I'd rather leave the job without hesitation. (Wei)

In this sense, a teacher's work experiences transcended their selves beyond the conventional relational boundaries of daily lives. In comparison, the spiritual aspects of teachers' identity narratives that they created in this research study were related to the deeper awareness of a sense of purpose and integrity relating to identity constructions, in addition to the challenges of heavier workloads, difficult career progression and the lack of job stability.

8.4.2 The Case of AIS

For teachers in the international school, the process of career progress and professional lives are characterised by the tendency to pursue goodness in their practices and well-being. For Cong, previously a school principal in a local rural school, her decision to leave the rural school and the reconstruction process of who she was highlighted her pursuit of a better environment for career progression and her child's education through her work and professional learning. When it came to the perspectives for her current job, Cong tended to focus on what she called the "inner feeling" instead of others' opinions. As she later claimed:

> I have worked for nearly 20 years. I need to respect myself. I want to be more practical to help students' learning and development. Though the school managers keep encouraging me to achieve higher professional titles, I will just let nature take its course. I'm not particularly worried about it anymore.

Cong considered the changes to be unpredictable and closely related to her life courses and life attitude:

> I didn't expect such a change [in my attitude]. Perhaps it comes with my age. I was able to meet people of high titles and honours during these years. The titles and honours no longer impress me. I like and appreciate my colleagues who might lack such glories yet still do excellent jobs.

In contrast with the pursuit of excellence that motivated Cong to transfer to the international school, what she attempted to emphasize here is a sense of contentment of the "ordinary teachers" and the focus on "improving and enriching her experiences" in her everyday work. She then supported her viewpoint by pointing out the complexity of teachers' work and her position with regards to the standards of teacher professionalism:

> Professionalism is forever a goal. I can never make a statement on the level of professionalism because everything needs to be contextualised. In education, we need different methods and standards to help different children with different learning abilities every day and everywhere. Therefore, it's more important to consider professionalism as just a goal.

Pointing out the necessity of contextualisation in education, Cong seemed to be cautious in terms of using external criteria to judge a teacher's success. Such critical reflection could be built from her years of experience in teaching and school administration. The shift of her focus from meeting the external criteria to maintaining the sense of contentment that comes with practice, professional learning and supporting other teachers might also enhance her long-term well-being in her professional life. Cong reflected that such change had led her to become more tolerant and respected in the school, as well as in her family life. The young maths teacher Zhulin also left her job for a better work environment and career progress. Although she felt alienated at the beginning of her career in AIS due to her reluctance to ask for professional support, she gradually developed a sense of self-efficacy from feedbacks and practice. When it comes to her career goals, she hesitated to go with a clear plan, yet claimed that she would carry out her responsibilities and make "down-to-earth efforts" at work:

> I don't think I will make considerable contributions to the school. All I want to do is to make "down-to-earth efforts" at work. If there are opportunities, I would like to improve my competency. I need to be better. I need to attend more competitions.

An interesting finding here is that although there is a significant gap between Cong's and Yu's years of experiences in teaching, their narratives on work-related spirituality reflected very similar focuses on personal development in their everyday interactions and practices in the school. Baihe and Zhulin's narratives also indicated a sense of social embodiment in daily lives, mostly through their observation of other teachers and the tangible satisfaction gained from their interactions with students.

All the female participants claimed that they appreciated the intimacy they have with students. The male teachers' narratives, however, contained fewer stories about informal interactions with students. In the international school, teachers seemed to have a higher level of satisfaction with regards to their interactions with the students. All the four teachers described their relationship with students in the informal learning contexts as satisfactory and rewarding. The following quotation illustrates the emotional bonds developed:

> I asked her if she misses home, she said: "Sometimes I miss my mum, sometimes I miss you." Knowing that I'm essential for her makes me feel

happy. (Baihe, female Chinese teacher, AIS)

    I think I feel most happy through connecting with my students. Children of this age are delightful. They can bring a great deal of happiness to me. They hug me and kiss me. Sometimes, when they don't come to school, they will miss me. (Cong, female maths teacher, AIS)

The structure of school life could also exert influences on teachers' perceptions of their relationships with pupils. Both the private schools are boarding schools. Therefore, teachers spend more time taking care of students' school life. Some teachers claimed that they know the children better than their parents do, which gives them a sense of guardianship towards the students. It is worth noting that the teachers did not avoid talking about their struggles and conflicts when the wider range of considerations of students' behaviours and character development, parents' expectations as well as professional images were involved in teachers' experiences of their daily working life. As Baihe pointed out:

    Sometimes students have developed harmful habits at home. In the school, we teachers need to correct them. If the family does not change, our education would be the equation of 5+2=0. The two days of family life a week negate the efforts we made in the five school days. We can't make any difference. It is frustrating.

In the charity school, teachers said they needed to be aware of each student's special background and to avoid talking about parental love, which might cause harm for students who lacked such support. Teachers considered that building a rapport with students was the first basis for effective teaching in the school. For a group of teachers who did not receive training in special education, the process of rapport-building was often frustrating and disappointing. Two teachers had described their feeling of isolation and inability to communicate with students when they first started to teach in RCS (Linjia and Meng). Although teachers face tremendous challenges in coping with the orphan students' unique learning and emotional needs in RCS, they remained favourable towards their relationships with pupils. Teachers described their emotional closeness with the students as rewarding. Narrating their interactions with students seemed to help teachers reflect upon their professional values and the positive changes they made to reconstruct their relationship with the pupils. Such change often brings teachers a stronger sense of achievement and satisfaction. Linjia, for instance, tends to blame herself for being a "direct person with a quick temper" and an "authoritative teacher" in the classroom. Although she has not found a way to transform her relationship with her students, Linjia seemed to be less anxious to remember times when students showed understanding and respect to her in some informal learning contexts:

> Fortunately, some students could understand me and know that I do care about them. Sometimes they would surprise me with small things, and I'm easily touched by what they do. (Linjia, female, maths teacher, two years of teaching experience)

Teachers in both the charity school and the international school considered their commitment and attention to individual students, together with their close relationship with students, as the distinguishing features of their identities as PSTs.

In summary, to understand teachers' spirituality in different social and cultural contexts, the acknowledgement of different types of spirituality is necessary. The non-religious but implicit spiritual dimension in PSTs' identity narratives implies an openness to different cultural traditions and philosophies in promoting teachers' well-being and sense of satisfaction at work. This aspect of teacher identities may support teachers' ongoing adaptations in a changing work environment. It is advisable that teachers' professional development adopt methods from mindfulness and narrative psychology to provide alternative voices in teachers' identity narrative process.

8.5 Summary

The analysis in this section included four components of1 the eight PSTs' narratives that constituted their professional identities: 1) students' learning and development; 2) perspectives on the curriculum; 3) job involvement and professional image; and 4) sense of spirituality and satisfaction.

Teachers in the charity school tended to demonstrate a strong sense of agency in making changes and making efforts to support students' current learning and development, while the advanced international school teachers tended to have a stronger sense of membership and belongingness to a professional community. Teachers' narratives also showed different levels of integration of personal and professional goals and considerations. With the vast differences in school curriculum, the two groups of teachers had different focuses and levels of tension with regard to the curriculum. The charity school teachers seemed to take an evaluative position in addressing issues in the context of a coercive school-based curriculum reform; in contrast, participant teachers from the international school showed a lower level of tension and focused on professional learning and personal development. With both groups of teachers' positive perceptions of their professional involvement, the charity school teachers had a more negative professional image as PSTs. Cultural and moral norms also seemed to have strong influences on the charity school teachers' narratives of spirituality at work. Table 8-2 demonstrates the comparative characteristics of TRIs among teachers the two private schools.

Table 8-2 Comparative characteristics of TPIs (private school teachers)

	The charity school teachers	The international school teachers
Students' learning and development	Teachers' agency in change making	Teachers' sense of membership in a professional community
	Higher integration of personal histories and professional purpose	Lower integration of personal histories and professional purpose

Continued

	The charity school teachers	The international school teachers
Curriculum	Focus on its positive and adverse impact on students and professional lives	Focus on learning and personal improvement
	Higher tension	Lower tension
Job involvement and professional image	Positive job involvement and negative professional image	Positive job involvement and positive professional image
Spirituality and satisfactions	Cultural and moral norms	Personal development and social embodiment
	Importance of teacher-student relationships	Importance of teacher-student relationships

All the eight case studies of PSTs demonstrated their commitment to supporting students' academic and moral development and focus on students' learning and development needs. In the interviews, all the teachers addressed the significance of students' engagement in the classroom and positive parental involvement in children's education. Positive teacher-student interactions seemed to be one of the most significant contributing factors to those teachers' sense of achievement and satisfaction at work, although teachers' perceptions and engagement strategies with students' learning differed according to the different situations and educational needs of the students. All the participant teachers felt (or had felt) burdened by the heavy workloads in teaching and pastoral care for students in private schools. At the same time, seven teachers claimed that their professional practices strengthened as a result of the more competitive performance management policies in private schools. In this sense, teachers seemed to have constructed self-representations as PSTs. Teachers' narratives also reflected the positive influence of spirituality and embodiment in their daily interactions in constructing their sense of professional identity.

In summary, teachers shared the following characteristics of professional identities: (1) focusing on students' learning needs; (2) positive job involvement; (3) coping with a heavy workload; (4) self-representation as PSTs; (5) valuing teacher-student relationships for a stronger sense of satisfaction; and (6) embracing spirituality at work.

Chapter 9
Comparative Analysis: Exploring the Significance of Contexts

The process of comparative analysis employed in this thesis was presented in Chapter 4. In this chapter, I will extend the comparative elements of this research study by comparing themes across the cases of the eight SST and eight PST narratives in order to identify the common and contrasting characteristics of TPIs in the four different state and private schools. I will first summarise the comparative characteristics of teachers' professional identities in the private and state schools on the basis of the previous four chapters (Chapters 5-8). I will then present the main orientations of TPIs based on the two-dimensional matrix developed from the cross-case analysis. This section identifies four main orientations in TPI narratives: (1) flexibility; (2) regulation; (3) service; and (4) authority. The intersection of the four orientations is interpreted in terms of four types of identity strategies: (1) transcendence; (2) determination; (3) enhancement; and (4) control. At the end of this chapter, I will reconnect the conceptual findings with individual teacher cases. This will help to illuminate and better understand the patterns in teachers' narratives identified in this research study.

9.1 The Four Orientations of TPI Narratives

On the basis of the cross-case analysis, I suggest a two-dimensional matrix that demonstrates features in common with those of previous studies, but is distinct from earlier efforts in the following ways:

1. It provides concrete comparative features rather than a linear developmental stage.
2. It allows for the characterisation of TPIs relative to a comparative criterion rather than placing them within specific types. It characterises TPIs based on empirical evidence from multiple types of school contexts.

The matrix presents TPIs in terms of four overlapping circles across four quadrants (Figure 9-1). In this matrix, the constructed professional identities are characterised along these dimensions:

1. How do the teachers construct their professional identities? Do the teachers integrate their professional values and belongingness with their personal experiences and preference or/and institutional and organisational values?
2. How does the teacher position himself/herself in relation to others to negotiate the tensions around multiple structural changes and restrictions?

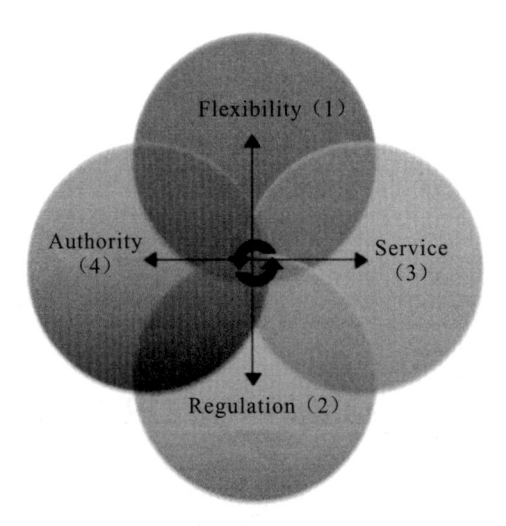

Figure 9-1 The orientations of teachers' professional identity narratives

9.1.1 The Vertical Axis: How do the Teachers Define Their Professional Identities?

The vertical axis represents how the teachers define their professional identities. At the top of this axis, teachers tend to retain flexibility and integrate multiple professional and personal roles in their narratives. This characteristic seems to involve a high level of tolerance to uncertainties and well-developed competencies to understand and adapt to changes. Examples of such characteristics include the unity of multiple sub-identities and a high level of teachers' trust in and collaborations with other members in the school contexts (Section 9.2 gives more detailed examples and descriptions). At the bottom of this scale, teachers tend to retain stable perceptions of sets of given social and cultural roles and responsibilities. Teachers' identities with such characteristics often involve strict tolerance and specifications. Teachers at this end of the axis also tended to feel strongly influenced by changes in their social status, career progression and institutional values. The two poles of the axis are:

1. *Flexibility* as an orientation in professional identity narratives reflects the teacher's awareness and capacity to switch between multiple roles in different situations. Therefore, teachers often develop a higher tolerance of the complexities, changes and conflicts in the workplace and show a stronger sense of trust and understanding to others in the workplaces.

2. *Regulation* as an orientation in professional identity narratives reflects the teacher's tendency to prioritise a set of social and professional roles, responsibilities and achievements in their professional narratives.

9.1.2 The Horizontal Axis: How does the Teacher Position Himself or Herself in Relation to Others?

The horizontal axis seeks to represent teachers' positioning in relation to others in their identity narratives. On the left side of this axis, teachers tended to focus on how to maintain or resume their professional authority in relation to others, in particular students' parents, the general public and the media. Examples of such identities could include teachers' claims of the importance of work ethics and a sense of integrity as professionals, and teachers' reflections on the existing (positive or negative) relationships with others in particular school contexts. On the right side of this axis, teachers tended to prioritise their responsibilities to provide an educational service to students and parents. In other words, these teachers' narratives often define their roles and responsibilities according to others' demands or needs. One example of such a characteristic is teachers' engagement with critical reflections on students' needs and engagement in personal development to cope with the challenges to achieve their professional goals.

1. *Service* as an orientation in professional identity narratives indicates the teachers' focus on navigating their ways to serve the public good through meeting students' and parents' educational needs. Teachers' coping strategies vary from critical engagements with others to linking professional goals to needs for further professional and personal development.

2. *Authority* as an orientation in professional identity narratives shows the teachers' focus on maintaining or resuming their professional authority and credibility in relation to others, in particular parents, the media and the education administration. Teachers' coping strategies include calling for the state's legal and structural support and addressing the institutional values.

I earlier discussed the four types based on the comparative analysis across 16 teacher cases. It is also important to note the overlaps among the four orientations embedded in individual teachers' narratives. This two-dimensional matrix suggests four situated TPIs. Table 9-1 summarises the characteristics of the typology of TPIs.

Table 9-1 The typology of teachers' professional identities

Teachers' approaches to multiple roles and identities	Teachers' positioning in relation to others	
	Service	Authority
Flexibility	**Quadrant 1: Transcendence** Different roles and sub-identities contribute to the development of each other (retrospectively) and connect the teahchers' personal expereinces, contexts and the professional goals to serve the public good. Teachers developed a sense of wholeness and integrity in teaching. *Sub-themes*: 1. Involving identities 2. Lifelong learning 3. Positive attitudes to continuing professional development (CPD) 4. Resilience and cross-boundaries	**Quadrant 2: Determination** Different roles and sub-identities coexist and contribute to awareness of need to change for equity and effectiveness in school education (prospectively). Teachers tend to address the significance of professional authority in achieving those goals. *Sub-themes*: Sense of membership Work ethics Specific CPD needs Representative
Self-regulation	**Quadrant 3: Enhancement** Alignments of multiple roles and sub-identities with structural rules and social expectations to recapture one's fitness and competences in unified professional images, status and culture that oriant oneself to meet the challenges in students' developments. *Sub-themes*: Need for community Resistance and/or representative	**Quadrant 4: Control** Struggles and ongoing attempts to aligh conflicting roles and sub-identities (tensions) to meet the need of professional authority and sense of achievements. *Sub-themes*: Role fragmentation Job progression Trust and relationships Internal conflicts and tensions

9.2 Towards a Typology of Situated TPIs

The proposed typology points to four main types of TPIs based on the 16 TPIs investigated in this thesis from a comparative perspective. In this section, I will describe these four types: (1) transcendence; (2) determination;

(3) enhancement; and (4) control. I will treat them as separate proposed types for discussion purposes and illustrate them using selected excerpts from different teachers' narratives. Finally, I will use these types as a basis for discussing hybrid professional identities through analysing specific examples of cases of the 16 teachers' narratives.

9.2.1 Transcendence

The word "transcendence" is often used in the literature to describe a kind of religious experience and a state of excelling or surpassing the limits of material experiences. As an emerging theme in this research study, this term is used here to describe the kind of teachers' narrative reflecting the state of being above the usual limits of one's previous experiences and current situations. The characteristics of TPI as transcendence is found in four teachers' narratives: Xiwen (A1); Qizhen (B1); Yu (C3); and Ting (D2). All of the four teachers positioned their experience of teaching in terms of active personal efforts and achievements. The narratives reflect a sense of transcendence that is both culturally conforming and individually focused for the four teachers. Table 9-2 summarises the background information about these four teachers.

Table 9-2　Teachers' backgrounds (transcendence group)

Teacher	School	Gender	Year of teaching	Subject	Education background
A1. Xiwen	Willow	Female	1 year	Chinese	MA
B1. Qizhen	Aspen	Female	20 years	Chinese	College diploma
C2. Ting	Redwood	Female	1 year	Find arts	BA
D4. Yu	Ash	Female	4 years	Chinese	BA

Flexibility and service are the two major orientations that characterise TPIs in transcendence. In terms of the teachers' personal understandings of their professional identities, these individual teachers' narratives demonstrated not only their awareness of their multiple roles, but their own capacities to adopt and create new roles in different situations, helping them to be more tolerant and reflective about changes and conflicts they experienced in teaching. These teachers' narratives also showed their feelings related to trust in and understanding of others in their daily interactions. The moral value of teaching as serving the public good is another common theme identified in these teachers' narratives. All four teachers in this group positioned themselves as "public servants" to parents and students and pointed out different coping strategies to link their professional goals with their personal development.

These teachers' narratives reflected their life as a fluctuating cycle of creation, destruction and transformation, with a sense of self as a constant and dynamic process of becoming. In this process, teachers began to connect their daily tasks in meeting assessment targets, behaviour management and curriculum objectives with a more creative and humanistic perspective on teaching. Being aware of the complications in teaching seemed to help these teachers to think deeply to respond appropriately and accurately to both the needs of the students and the curriculum reform. In the teachers' own words, "authenticity" in their personal experiences at work means teachers should not get lost in the curriculum reform as their self-understanding and sense of satisfaction are essential.

> I think each teacher has their own characteristics and they like to use different methods. I think a teacher needs to have his or her own teaching style. One must not follow others, doing whatever others are doing. I will try to become a teacher with my own personal characteristics. That's enough. (Qizhen)
> I hope one day I can make changes and be an innovator in education. I hope I can develop my own theory. (Xiwen)
> Every teacher has his or her own style. I'm the joyful kind of teacher for my students. In this way, I can make my students feel more energised. I like an engaging and active class. The school doesn't want to fix one learning model for everyone. I think every teacher is different. (Yu)

I think teaching is the same whereever you go. But I could always choose my own values and goals. Different people have different opinions. (Ting)

These four teachers' narratives were particularly characterised in four aspects, which I will explain in the following sections.

1. Evolving identities
2. Lifelong learning
3. Positive attitudes to CPD
4. Resilience and cross-boundaries

9.2.1.1 Evolving Identities

The word "evolve" derives from the Latin *evolvere* in the early 17th century, and in general means "to make more complex or develop". In this section, the four teachers were found to have experienced different stages of transition when they juggled a wide range of different responsibilities and requirements. In this process, these four teachers adopted a variety of strategies to adjust to the changing nature of their work and different demands from the students and schools. They were able to draw on multiple social and cultural notions to frame their professional identities, particularly with relation to teacher-student relationships and job progression, which both resisted and reaffirmed the given professional roles and professional pathways. Examples of these social and cultural notions included:

9.2.1.2 Teacher-student Relationship

Ting: "Do not do unto others what you would not like to do unto yourself."[①]

After quoting the well-known Confucius doctrine, Ting attempted to stress the importance of her own experiences in influencing her daily

---

① 己所不欲，勿施于人。

practices in teaching and interactions with students. She reflected upon and learned from her negative experiences with her primary school teachers and made it important in her job "not to create the same burden" for her own students.

> Qizhen: "A student will believe in teaching only when he gets close to his teacher."①

Qizhen explained her strategies in maintaining her positive relationship with her students. Although this sentence was originally said to encourage students, Qizhen quoted it to highlight her role as an instructor to organise school activities and create opportunities for students to express their feelings and thoughts and show their talent in front of the teachers and each other.

9.2.1.3 Expectations for Job Progression

> Yu: "Water flows to a lower place, a man (woman) goes to a higher position."②

Yu used this saying when she narrated the career choice that she made to leave the state rural school for the private international school. On the one hand, it showed the advantages of teaching in the private international school over the rural state school; on the other, it also expressed Yu's hope of working in a better environment, especially after she had achieved many teaching awards in the rural school.

> Xiwen: "Aim high, you may achieve the average; aim average, you may attain the low."③

Xiwen said she wanted to become a famous education theorist and to bring changes to the educational system and the culture in China. She em-

---

① 亲其师,信其道。
② 人往高处走,水往低处流。
③ 求其上者得其中,求其中者得其下。

ployed this quotation from both the *Analects* by Confucius and the *Art of War* by Sunzi to explain that she might not be able to achieve such an ambitious goal. Yet she still believed that keeping the aim high would help her work in the long term. And she could always learn something from this process.

In addition, these four teachers' narratives also reflected their competence to negotiate with others as well as changing organisational and societal contexts in constructing their professional identities. As such, teachers were developing and adopting more individual-oriented strategies to enable themselves to succeed and find satisfaction in teaching.

9.2.1.4 Lifelong Learning

The four teachers held views and perceptions that are more aligned with the vision of engaged lifelong learning. These teachers also tended to have developed broader views on their subject knowledge. This means that they did not perceive the subject as being bounded within the classroom assessment or school context; instead, they believed that it was also linked with lifelong skills such as critical thinking, communication and collaboration that support students' functioning in society.

The four teachers tended to place students' interests in the centre of their narratives of teaching. Their narratives of classroom teaching were also more attuned to the constructive pedagogical approach. In particular, these teachers notice that students' active participation is crucial to effective learning; they are also aware of the need to continuously develop their skills to elicit students' responses and facilitate their active engagement in analysing and questioning in classrooms. Xiwen (A1) shared and expressed these particular views during the interview:

> What we lack in our school now is the cultivation of students' independent thinking skills. Although we talked about it for a long time, it has not been realised. What I am facing is to try to change my role and inspire students' thoughts and motivate them to learn to solve problems. (Xiwen)

Despite the difficulties in dealing with the heavy workload and stress in managing classroom discipline, they are aware that they could learn and improve their pedagogical practices in the context of school reforms. For the SSTs (Xiwen and Qizhen), in particular, taking the role as facilitators in students' learning in group works was considered beneficial for students' learning. Although the teacher still has questions and issues in implementing the student-centered pedagogy, she was "open" to new ideas and to trying to adapt their practice to improve students' learning. For the PSTs, such as Yu and Ting, this aspect of teachers' narratives is closely linked with their positive attitudes towards professional development, which I will present in the following section.

9.2.1.5 Positive Attitudes to CPD

On the practical level, these four teachers tended to be more open to making changes, and committed to their professional development and to remain flexible so they could adopt new methods in their teaching. The teachers' narratives often reflected a broader concept of learning that connect the subject knowledge to lifelong learning and well-being for the learners' future success and happiness. Reviewing their past teaching, they could identify their limitations in understanding both the subject knowledge and requirement in implementing the curriculum reform. These teachers seemed to be receptive to the professional development arrangements in the school. They constantly pointed out the necessity of an open and humble attitudes towards personal limitations, commitment towards their professional development and willingness to find opportunities to learn new methods and engage with others in a broader community. In addition to such teachers' positive perceptions of their roles and responsibilities in terms of students' learning and their pedagogical practices, these teachers tended to be very active in aligning their identities to their own professional development in the context of educational reform. The four teachers emphasized the importance of reflecting their personal values and attitudes and beliefs about teaching to contribute to their students' development. They also demonstrated their confidence in their work and expressed the feeling of achievement in bringing positive changes to the students' future and the development of China's education system in general.

9.2.1.6 Resilience and Cross-boundaries

Teachers talked about the relational aspect of their work and the complex power dynamics with students, parents, the government and the media in the context of school reforms. The two SSTs (Xiwen and Qizhen) talked about the tension between parents and teachers. They pointed out the challenges to cope with parents' high demand but lack of engagement in pupils' learning, and further argued that the balance of power was the key to the success of schools to make changes. Teachers were capable of developing a series of strategies to negotiate the balance of power with parents. Xiwen and Qizhen constructed identities as active problem solvers and advocates for collaboration among different stakeholders in schools at the policy level. As for the two PSTs (Yu and Ting), a sense of vocation and personal satisfaction in teaching became an important element for making sense of their identities as teachers. The findings also indicate structural obstacles that were thought to undermine teachers' ability to place aspects of social justice and diversity in their instructions, which included: (1) the large numbers of students in classes; (2) conflicts and tensions with parents; (3) a lack of collaboration among stakeholders in schools; and (4) a lack of consensus and applicable guidelines on professional practice.

These four teachers seemed to differ in their position relative to the four orientations in the proposed matrix. Among the four teachers, Qizhen (B1, Chinese teacher, 20 years of teaching experience, female) was closest to the centre in the matrix. Although she considered serving students' needs as at the centre of her professionalism, Qizhen did not want to lose her sense of professional authority. She argued that teachers needed to maintain their professional authority by actively engaging with students and parents, to build connections and trust with each other, especially when the profession's absolute authority was often challenged and even attacked by the general public. At the same time,

Qizhen also developed a set of professional roles. For instance, she was more certain that classroom teaching should be the primary responsibility for teachers, and she spent a great amount of time helping young teachers to develop their professional and pedagogical skills. This was also supported by observation during the fieldwork.

Similarly, Xiwen also tended to connect the orientations of service and authority in her narrative. When she made changes in teaching as a response to parents' criticism and demands, Xiwen first needed to adjust her attitudes towards the parents—from considering them as "uneducated" to admitting that they "knew better about their children and how they learn". She argued that those criticisms and demands were helpful for her to understand others' needs, yet she retained the authority to make her own decisions. In her narrative, Xiwen also critically reflected on her previous experiences and expressed her willingness to make things different. Instead of putting herself in an oppositional position to others, Xiwen also called for collaboration between stakeholders in education to make positive changes possible for the children. In this sense, Xiwen maintained her flexibility and interests in new opportunities when it came to tensions and conflicts.

Yu and Ting are two teachers from the two different private schools. In comparison with the two SSTs, Yu and Ting's narratives were less involved with the discussion of teachers' authority; most of what they shared was focused on how they wanted to support students' learning as a way to be responsible for the schools and the students in undertaking their jobs. Therefore, their positioning seemed to align towards the orientation of service and move from the orientation of authority. Between these two teachers, Yu seemed to enjoy more possibilities for flexibility in her teaching than Ting. This could be mainly contributed to by changes of professional roles in different school contexts. To be more specific, the Redwood Charity School was going through a structural transition towards following the Dulangkou model, which attempted to change pedagogies and curriculum in a more systematic, yet intensified way.

9.2.2 Determination

Determination as one strategy in TPIs construction is characterised by the teachers' flexibility in dealing with change. The teachers in this group were often internally focused: they had a higher sense of autonomy in defining successful teaching, which was framed tacitly rather than explicitly. The theme of determination mainly emerged in the narratives of six teachers (A4,B3,C3,D1,D2,D3) as the process of developing the quality of courage and endurance in achieving one's professional goals and work ethics regardless of the difficulties and barriers in daily practices and career progressions. Like the transcendent identity process, determination indicated that the teachers were individually focused: the attention to individuals' actions and responsibilities contributed to these teachers' sense of professional identity. The background information about these six teachers is summarised in Table 9-3.

Table 9-3 Teachers' backgrounds (determination group)

Teacher	School	Gender	Year of teaching	Subject	Education background
A3. Yifan	Willow	Female	30 years	Maths	College diploma
B3. Zhe	Aspen	Male	3 years	Chinese	BA
C3. Meng	Redwood	Male	2 years	Maths	BA
D1. Zhulin	Ash	Female	8 year	English	BA
D2. Cong	Ash	Female	20 year	Maths	College diploma
D3. Baihe	Ash	Female	10 years	Maths	BA

Flexibility and authority are the two major orientations that characterise TPIs marked by determination. The five teachers in this category seemed well aware of the multiple roles they needed to take on in the school context and their narratives reflected their self-identities as teachers with authority. That is to say, all of the teachers, more or less, already assumed the necessity of giving authority to teachers, rather than framing their authority as a process of development and negotiation in different contexts (as could be found in the previous section on transcendence). As such, these teachers did not seem to engage with their previous experiences and personal stories to connect with their activities in schools. The participant teachers' self-images tended to be more aligned with each other. The common characteristics of the determination category are: 1) being reflective about one's professional practices; 2) keeping a positive attitude in the face of challenges; and 3) being open to learning to guide students through classroom teaching. These themes were common examples of the determination category, as they were perceived as helpful for the teachers to improve their professional skills and to retain moral and relational authority in teaching. These teachers' satisfaction seemed to come from the actualisation of their professional roles and responsibilities. Their multiple roles and sub-identities tended to be more unified and stable, and these teachers tended to enjoy a high level of trust and positive relationships with others.

9.2.2.1 Sense of Membership

These five teachers (A4, B3, C1, C2, C3) perceived themselves as belonging to a community and as creating a sense of unity within the school. Teachers' personal identities were more connected with the sense of membership in the community on top of the technical aspects of teaching. These teachers developed a strong sense of satisfaction in their working life, particularly through their involvement in activities and communications with colleagues and students. A distinguishing element of these teachers' narratives is the positive influences of school improvement, including the school vision (C1, C2, C3), leadership (C1, C2, C3), school facilities and the use of ICT (C1, A4), the school reputation (C1, C2, C3, B3) and curriculum changes (C1, C2, C3, A4), as well as the diverse and more advantaged students' family backgrounds (C1, C2, C3 B3) that contribute to their positive attitude towards their profession as well as their personal life. These five teachers presented an integrated sense of identity, thus demonstrating a strong sense of self-discipline and satisfaction through taking on different roles and responsibilities.

> I didn't do housework before I worked in this school; yet I will do some housework no matter how tired I am. I became more respectful to others and my family and became more understanding and tolerant. I don't know if this shows my tolerance or my lack of principles. (Cong)
>
> I think, to other colleagues, I'm very diligent and always want to achieve the best result. I think I'm a perfectionist, while others would say I'm a workaholic. [...] My work goes before anything else. If I can't finish my job, I wouldn't be at ease. I have many colleagues who are the same, because this is what the school requires of us. Our principal is a typical perfectionist. None of us could compete with him. (Baihe)

Teachers in this group often show their appreciation for the school culture where all those involved in influencing the lives of learners showed their respect and trust in each other in and beyond the learning community. They all expressed a sense of satisfaction with regards to the friendly collegial relationships in schools. However, these five teachers also faced the paradox of high-level commitment, a sense of belonging and the ever-increasing demands from the school and parents. As such, these teachers might face more challenges in developing strategies to maintain a sense of unity when situations become more complex and workloads get heavier. Balancing their ambition at work with a relaxing lifestyle seemed to be a major concern for these teachers.

9.2.2.2 Work Ethic

Teachers' belief in the benefits of hard work and diligence for improving their professional abilities and bringing in intrinsic values reflected the teachers' strong sense of work ethics. Often as a part of teachers' self-image and expectations, work ethic is closely linked to these teachers' understanding of their learning and professional progress. All the five teachers considered themselves hardworking and diligent in different contexts, a quality also expressed by others to them.

I don't settle until I'm sure I've done a good job. Some of my colleagues said I'm a very diligent and even a perfectionist or workaholic.(Ting)

I think I tend to set up high benchmarks for others and to myself. That's how others would see me as well. (Cong)

I'm trying to be good in every aspect really. I hope to be a capable teacher for the parents and the school. Therefore, if they ever need someone, they know I'm capable of helping. (Zhulin)

I'm not a very intelligent person. But I think I'm very diligent. I never ignore students' questions or mistakes. I guess diligence is my merit. [...] I think this is my job and I just need to love it and do it well. (Yifan)

I think every task in the school is important enough to be handled well. I think if the school gives me a job, I naturally need to do it well. I think a teacher needs to have the mindset. [...] I would not prioritise some tasks over others depending on my subjective judgement of what is more important. Rather I consider every aspect of my job as equally important. (Zhe)

A common theme in these five teachers' narratives is the attempt to carry out their responsibilities unquestioned and to do well in different aspects of their professional lives. These teachers also considered their work ethic as an inseparable part of their identities as hard-working employees. These tendencies were particularly evident among the female teachers (C1, C2, C3, A4). Ting, Cong, Zhulin and Yifan described their strong work ethic as their personal characteristic that may distinguish them from others, while Zhe (B3) tended to position himself in a more formal way, in which he expressed a way of doing one's job as how he thought it should be done. Nevertheless, these five teachers addressed their strong sense of work ethic as crucial in engaging with their job in schools.

9.2.2.3 Being More Specific with CPD Needs

Another common characteristic of these five teachers' narratives is that they seemed to be more specific when it came to their needs for CPD. This is a distinguishing feature from the last category, where teachers were more general and stressed the importance of their own engagement in development activities. These five teachers were very clear about what was and would be actually helpful to their professional development. Zhulin, for instance, considered learning about schools in other countries as most useful for her to reflect on her own experiences in Ash. Baihe also appreciated the observation of foreign teachers in Ash, as they helped her to learn about others' daily practice and to make specific adjustments at the micro level. After reflecting on her long-term career in teaching, Cong said she wanted to return to learning theories that could help her further contribute to the field of education. Yifan and Zhe believed that learning about the use of technology and classroom instruction would be helpful for them to make further progress in teaching.

9.2.2.4 Representative and Boundary-building

These five teachers also tended to be more representative of the professional group they found themselves belonging to. The three PSTs' narratives seemed to represent a "culture of care", whereas the two SSTs were more likely to represent themselves as belonging to a "culture of cadres".

> The difference between private schools and state schools was that we focus more on students' personalised learning. In the private school, everything matters, big or small. We need to know students' living habits and feelings. While in the state school, teachers could not do this because of the large group of students. Naturally, we would have different expectations for our students. (Baihe)
>
> [When I changed my job from a state school to Ash,] I didn't like to do the pastoral care. But now I think pastoral care is so important for students' moral and emotional development. It's not just about managing the students' behaviour; it's also about preparing them to live independently. (Cong)

What the three PSTs argued was that teachers needed to create a culture of care where students could feel more connected and supported, rather than managed, by the teachers in the private school. Teachers learned to change their positions after they had learned more about what was expected from

Chapter 9   Comparative Analysis: Exploring the Significance of Contexts

teachers. Similarly, the two SSTs seemed to retain a more institutionalised role as the "cadres", who needed to demonstrate certain leadership roles in the school contexts.

> I think I'm calmer and more engaged now. I'm heavily involved with editing the school magazine. The leader asked me to do it, so I thought I ought to do it well because I'm also a party member. I ought to embody the advancement of the Communist Party. (Zhe)
>
> I feel I'm a teacher everywhere and can't do things that are unethical or illegal. These even influence how I react to people and my relationship with neighbours and families. (Yifan)

The word "cadre" is originally a French word meaning "frame". The term is adopted by the communists and used in China as ganbu, a public official who is responsible for holding certain leadership and managerial positions. Although a ganbu may not always be a member of the Chinese Communist Party, it is more likely that someone who has attained an important position is a member of the party. Zhe came from a family that included a few governmental officials. According to him, he always wanted to become a cadre just like his other family members. He had experiences working as a college graduate cadre before becoming a teacher. Therefore, his identity as a party member became a part of his motivation in engaging with the school work. The phrase "the advancement of the Communist Party" first appeared in the 16th Party Congress Report in 2002 to stress the role and leadership of Communist cadres in Chinese society. Party members were encouraged to be role models and actively engage with local communities, so as to enhance the connections between the party and communities. Although Yifan did not explicitly emphasize her role as a Communist Party member, the image she portrayed of herself as a role model by "being a teacher everywhere she goes" was highly aligned with how Zhe considered himself as a Communist cadre.

The quadrant above demonstrates the comparative characteristics locating individual teachers in this category. Among the five teachers, Zhe

(B3, Chinese teacher, 3 years of teaching experience, male) was farthest from the centre of the matrix. In comparison with the other four teachers, Zhe tended to be more authority-oriented and less flexible than the rest of the group. On the one hand, he had more integrated and representative identities, which might be influenced by his family background and previous experience as a local cadre member. Zhe clearly described himself as a young and passionate teacher who was willing to take on different roles in the school context (i.e. editing the school magazine and receiving officials) according to the clearly defined professional stages. On the other hand, Zhe drew on institutional values and structural supports of teachers' roles, such as cultural heritage and occupational sacrifice as a narrative strategy, seemingly to help him cope with some of the tensions and changes for teachers to maintain their authority. Yifan (A4, maths teacher, 30 years of teaching experience, female) was an SST returning from her retirement. Yifan also tended to take an authoritative position in terms of her relationships with parents and students, yet she was more explicit about teachers' vulnerability and the difficulties she had faced in teaching in the past.

Zhulin (English teacher, 8 years of teaching experience, female) and Baihe (Math, Chinese, 10 years of teaching experience, female) were the least authoritative teachers in this category. They found themselves fitting into the school contexts and considered meeting students' needs as important to succeed in teaching. These two teachers were also flexible with adapting different roles in the school, which they considered important for students' informal learning at school. This was different from Zhe's positioning with regards to the non-classroom teaching work he was asked to carry out, although all the teachers reflected that they expanded their skills by taking on these non-classroom roles. The reason that Baihe was located as less flexible was that she certainly had a personal preference for focusing on classroom teaching, rather than other school activities. Cong (maths teacher, 20 years of teaching experience, female) assumed more authority in her narrative; perhaps most of this was due to her previous experiences in a leadership role in a rural school. She was capable of adopting a flexible approach to the differences between the two different schools and demonstrated an open attitude to changes in her relationship with students and parents. Cong also did not want to limit herself to being seen as a typical "female teacher"; as noted previously she pointed out that she was almost masculine in her determination and was iron-willed.

9.2.3 Enhancement

Enhancement is a strategy that teachers employ to make themselves feel good about being a teacher, particularly in situations of failure and when faced with threats to their self-esteem. In this research study, three teachers were very concerned about their work performances in schools, the decrease in their professional status and social relationships. The three teachers expressed a mixture of both positive and negative views on their relationships with others. They often accorded significant importance to job stability, which they regarded as their motive for remaining in teaching. These teachers tended to draw on institutional values, rather than school supports, to build their positive self-image. Peer comparisons were common among this group of teachers and the teachers also tended to use self-regulatory strategies to address their perceived weaknesses. Thus, the pattern of alignments of teachers' multiple roles and sub-identities with structural rules and social expectations emerged in the data analysis process. Teachers tended to recapture their fitness and competence in a unified professional image, status and culture. The background information for these three teachers is presented in Table 9-4.

Table 9-4 Teachers' backgrounds (self-enhancement group)

Teacher	School	Gender	Year of teaching	Subject	Education background
A4. Ruolan	Willow	Female	3 years	Chinese	BA
B4. Jianguo	Aspen	Male	5 years	Maths	BA
C4. Wei	Redwood	Male	1 year	PE	BA

9.2.3.1 Need for Communities

Communities and organisations often demonstrate how they engage with others in public in their work attitudes and practices by adopting or creating institutional values. In this research, teachers pointed out the lack of trust and mutual respect in the schools. Some teachers addressed the feeling of unhelpfulness when the value and attractiveness of teaching decreased among the public, in particular when the status given by the state is considered as being more important than their work itself. Likewise, teachers addressed the importance of including disadvantaged students in their classroom; they also tended to demonstrate their commitment and vision to engage learning experiences and outcomes and prepare students for a better future. Nevertheless, they often felt they do not "fit" in the social trend and are uncertain about possible policy and organisational changes. In the narratives, these three teachers highlighted the public values of their work for the students as well as for the society as a whole. They perceive themselves as important to create values for the public through their work and advocated that positive social environment would help them increase their sociability with the public and professional authorities in the classroom.

9.2.3.2 Resistance and Representative

It is important to note that such an indirect indication of teachers' identity enhancement could also be found in the observation of teachers' reactions to the researchers' presence and in their interactions with students in the classroom. The following fieldnote described one teacher's request for the researcher, which reflects teachers' identity enhancement to maintain authority in the classroom. While the researcher only agreed to present her student life to the grade-one students, the teacher tended to use the researcher's presence to legitimize corporal punishment as a "commonly used" method to discipline the students. The teacher invited me to give a public speech to his students and the following observations made me feel rather shocked:

Chapter 9 Comparative Analysis: Exploring the Significance of Contexts

[*Fieldnote*] I'm finally done with my story as a "successful learner" who went to Oxford. I was not prepared for this at all and I wished I didn't say anything that might give students any pressure after all. Students were quiet when I asked if they have any questions for me, so the teacher took the turn. "Teachers give corporal punishment in South Korea, right?" I was first shocked by his question, and my "scholar" role came up. "Yes. But it's not considered as a proper way of dealing with naughty students." What was really shocking to me happened: the teacher turned to the students (grade-one students) and said: "In many developed countries, like the UK, Japan or South Korea, corporal punishment is widely used. Teachers only use corporal punishments for the students' benefits."

In summary, authority and regulation were the two orientations that characterised the three teachers' narratives. Teachers tended to maintain and resume their professional authority in their narratives and the three teachers all addressed a fixed set of roles and responsibilities, rather than personal experiences and values to support their statements.

The quadrant demonstrates the comparative characteristics of the individual teachers in this category. Among the three teachers, Jianguo (B4, maths teacher, 5 years of teaching experience, male) was farthest from the centre of the matrix. In comparison with other two teachers, Jianguo was defensive and assumed a high level of authority in the way he responded to my questions. One of my observations was that Jianguo faced towards the door in front of us throughout the interview, looking like a soldier. He never looked me in the eye and seemed to resist engaging fully with the interview, despite his voluntary participation in this research study. Although I showed the consent form and tried to ask questions in different forms, he still maintained a distance from me as a researcher.

One way that Jianguo tended to assert his authority was through the way he presented himself in the interview. Most of his responses to the questions I asked were short. Three times during the interview, Jianguo refused to give specific examples of his personal experiences or observations to demonstrate these processes.

> I've worked in this school for five years until now. I don't have a particular story to tell. It's very plain.
> [...] I can't comment on that. I think I will just do the right thing.

The lack of trust in the researcher and later the misuse of the researcher's position with his students made the research process feel dehumanising to me. In a sense, Jianguo might actually have felt that his sense of identity was under constant threat; therefore, trying to limit and regulate what could be shared in the interview context might be his strategy to enhance his reputation and sustain his identity. In addition to this, the later misuse of the researcher's role to misrepresent corporal punishment in his classroom might indicate this teacher's need to enhance his authority in the classroom.

Wei (C4, PE and Chinese teacher, 1 year of teaching experience, male) was another case among the 16 teachers. Taking administrative and leadership roles and responsibilities at a very early stage of his career in a private school might require him to be very resilient to complexities in both teaching and working in general. Zhe's narrative was heavily engaged with philosophical concepts and theories, which also seemed to lack much connection with his actual experiences and practices. Zhe tended to be less closed with his narrative with regards to the openness and flexibility for his career plan and his respect and positive interactions with the researcher. In comparison, Ruolan (A2, three years of teaching experience, Chinese teacher, female) seemed more capable of (or willing to) elaborating on her experiences than the other two teachers in the group. She also incorporated the work of care in her narrative of being a professional teacher. In addition, she was also aware of the behavioural strategies (i.e. smiling in the mirror and giving positive words) she took when it came to negative thoughts and experiences of tension. The strategies might still be more restricting than empowering to her.

9.2.4 Control

This section focuses on a group of teachers whose TPIs were characterised by a sense of control, especially when teachers were experiencing a high level of tension and uncertainty described in their narratives. These three teachers (A2, B2, C1) viewed and talked about students' learning as bounded by external structures, such as the curriculum and examinations. Such teachers felt that they were forced to focus on the usability of subject knowledge learning in practical terms, such as students' performance in examinations or social functions. Their explanations also included sharing more life-applicable examples. Table 9-5 demonstrates the three teachers' backgrounds.

Table 9-5 Teachers' backgrounds (control group)

Teacher	School	Gender	Year of teaching	Subject	Education background
A2. Haoting	Willow	Male	10 years	Maths	College diploma
B2. Xinxin	Aspen	Female	3 years	Maths	BA
C1. Linjia	Redwood	Female	1 year	Maths	College diploma

9.2.4.1 Fragmentation

These three teachers might speak positively or negatively about school reform. However, despite being able to reflect on and claim the importance of such a practice, these three teachers often position themselves in the early stages of understanding the reform with a sense of uncertainty. Teachers' perceptions of their goals and their capacity to take up the practices consistently also seemed to vary due to different external conditions and situations. For instance, Haoting expressed his uncertainty due to the change in school leadership and management style:

> If we want the classroom reform to be successful, the school needs to keep with one model for a long term rather than being temporary or changing

too frequently [...] Otherwise, we would not achieve anything in the end.

According to Haoting, this policy was implemented three years ago but the school leader is not satisfied with the outcomes: "He thinks that teachers are not at ease letting students learn on their own, and still rely on lecturing in their teaching." Haoting explained that this was because teachers are under pressure to improve students' examination results and prove their performance in the ranking system for future job promotion. As he said: "The outcome could be better if they do not rank students and teachers. For the benefit of job promotion, teachers cannot ignore the scores, so still rely on lecturing in teaching."

The combination of perceived structural restraints and negative self-efficacy seemed to result in teachers in this category feeling frustration with a lack of career progression. As a whole, despite these teachers' comments on the positive influences of the constructive pedagogy and the idea of student-centredness, the findings suggested that the respondents often felt a bi-directional pressure— being pulled towards different sets of values, and beliefs or practices. The participant teachers often felt they needed to be prudent to fit some kind of future version of themselves. It was especially the case when these teachers tended to take into account a wider range of external factors, including school management, requirements in examinations, crowded classrooms and ineffective professional development training, etc. Although these teachers mentioned the importance of students' active learning, the consideration of external constraints seemed to have influenced their capacity to put into practice what they thought was ideal for students. This is indicative of the fragmentation of teachers' multiple identities, which seemed to further relate to teachers' low self-efficacy.

9.2.4.2 Low Trust Level and Negative Relations

These teachers reported persistent barriers in managing their relations with students' parents. They tended to be discouraged by the change in parent-teacher relations in schools, especially when the change did not align with their expectations for respect and collaboration. For these teachers, parents' disengagements from their children's education turned out to be one of the major challenges in teaching. This is not to say that parents and teachers did not engage with each other to promote students' learning and well-being. Instead, teachers noted that parents were too busy at work but they still tried to keep in regular contact with parents through mobile messages and WeChat groups, most of the time to inform parents about the homework for each day. What makes these teachers different is that they seemed to lack a sense of authority and feel insufficiently equipped to connect with and gain active support from others to realise their professional goals for children's development. This is in contrast to other teachers in the sample, who gave the impression at interview that they could more easily establish collaborations with other colleagues and parents and facilitate engagement by employing a range of communication strategies.

9.2.4.3 Job Progression

In comparison with other teachers in this study, those who belonged to this sub-group tended to be less capable of identifying the value and relevance of professional development to their practices and job progression. For example, Haoting and Xinxin, in particular, seemed to share experiences of ineffective professional training at different stages of their career. While observing Haoting's class, I realised that his PowerPoint presentation was very colourful and dynamic with little apples falling down from the tree to show the numbers. I was curious to know if Haoting made the presentation himself and if so, what did he mean by saying he needed more training on giving presentations. He then told me that he had found the high-quality presentation online, and he really liked it: "It has background music and so it's pretty good." Haoting's priority in professional development seemed to be not situated in the context of mathematics, but in his capacity to use various tools and skills (making PowerPoint files, playing music, drawing) in his teaching. In addition, Haoting said that he chose this job for security reasons. As a male teacher, he is also an important financial resource for his family. However, his said his wage was very low and he did not see much hope for job promotion, and thus Haoting appeared to struggle to maintain his commitment and investment in further professional development. As he said:

> I can see my career on one path, and I will basically be a teacher my entire life. My level is basically set and that means there's not much space for development. That's it.

Teachers who are located in this category seemed to be more willing to engage with professional development when they received sufficient encouragement and instructions. Real impact, contextualised goals and educational theories, as well as the sustainability of the implementation, are important for these teachers to be convinced to make changes to the classroom. Therefore, if teachers could receive their professional development in a way that is structured to meet their learning needs, as well as an appraisal system that motivates teachers in terms of job promotion, there would be more potential for teachers' learning to take place.

In summary, teachers whose identity narratives were characterised by control tended to feel confused and isolated, and experienced a lack of support in learning about and developing the curriculum. These teachers perceived the reform to promote constructivist pedagogy in both positive and negative lights, yet they felt that their lack of knowledge and support limited their capacity to implement the reform-based practices. They were not strongly committed to this pedagogical approach; rather, they tended to consider the pedagogical approach as simply "another trend" to follow. Moreover, these teachers did not seem to be devoted to professional development and appeared reluctant to change; they might also be inflexible in adapting to new technology and methods in teaching. They often felt unsupported and disempowered due to the lack of job progression and lacked knowledge about and resources for professional development. In terms of their social relationships, these teachers might not be receptive to the opinions of others and might feel insufficiently equipped to connect with others. Sometimes they saw themselves as legitimately entitled to deference and respect. Their interactions with others were based on reference to collectively expected values, interests and utility purposes, yet not necessarily on individualistic, materialistic or maximising bases. All combined, the multiple tensions created the feeling of suspense and control that may amplify the fluctuating effect experienced in existing multiple roles and sub-identities in response to changes.

9.3 Summary

In this section, I conducted a comparative analysis, in combination with diagrams, to identify teachers that were categorised in four different yet interrelated types of TPI: (1) transcendence; (2) determination; (3) enhancement; and (4) control.

The distribution of 16 teachers between authority and service (the horizontal axis) is generally equal. There were nine teachers who were more authority-oriented and seven teachers who were more service-oriented in their professional identity narratives. More teachers (10) were flexibility-oriented than regulation-oriented (6) (the vertical axis). This might indicate that overall TPIs across the state and private schools were more likely to differentiate in terms of teachers' individual strategies in specific contexts than the teachers' perceptions of their relationships with others in the school contexts. In the next section, I move on to the discussion of the distinguishing cultural values identified among the 16 teachers' narratives from China.

Chapter 10
Discussion and Conclusion

The findings of this research largely support the general conclusions of previous studies in the area of teacher knowledge, teacher emotions and reflection. Through an innovative methodology that combines narrative inquiry and cross-case analysis, and through drawing on the concept of narrative identity, professionalism and the empirical data from this research study, TPIs could be understood as not only assemblies of different sub-identities, but as processes of regenerating and creating narratives that integrate personal experiences, institutional values and professional discourses into an evolving story of the "teaching self" that provides the individual teacher with a sense of purpose, social status, expertise and belongingness.

10.1 Teacher Training and Education

The present research findings agreed with the general benefits of teacher training and education to contribute to the development of TPIs. Teachers in this research study demonstrated a generally positive attitude towards professional learning and a willingness to engage with further studies to adapt to further changes and challenges. This research is effective in responding to recent discussions on the potentially positive roles of tension and conflict in the development of TPIs in teacher training and educational settings. The limitations of such interpretations are that most of the discussion is based on the kind of systematic investigation in a particular teacher training project or education context.

Due to the exploratory nature of this small-scale research study, I did not focus on one or two particular training settings, which helped to clarify teachers' access to and general preferences for teacher training and education in different school contexts. Teachers' narratives allowed them to select the particular professional training experiences they found most helpful or inefficient in constructing their professional identities. In addition to the effective teacher training projects that involved teachers' reflection of their own practices and awareness of roles, the findings from this research study also suggest that teachers' awareness of their informal learning and the benefits of personal development in the school contexts could be a significant facet of their TPI development. This seems to further indicate that if the teacher training institute, universities or school-based training agencies could be the training vehicles for the development of TPIs, they too need to become flexible, as the teachers they are trying to engage have urgent needs for adaptability as a result of increasing complexity in the changing educational contexts. It is important to note here that teachers seemed to hold different attitudes towards a similar situation, which could be further categorised as positive tension and negative tension. The following are some examples:

1. Negative tension: Although the teachers disagreed with the focus on academic issues found in the Chinese educational system, they had to form an argument about the benefits of academic performance, yet complaining about the burden of curriculum and assessment. This seems to indicate a *negative tension* in which teachers reluctantly perform in certain ways due to the limitations of the external structure and the lack of teacher agency.

2. Positive tension: Some teachers tended to perceive the current limitations as resources for their reflection and a space for creativity and felt content with their imaginations about future changes of the system.

This difference might be influenced by various factors, including years of teaching experience, differences in the subjects (Chinese and maths), the kind of training they had or simply the quality of textbooks and the effectiveness of assessment themselves.

10.2　Professionalism and Policy Demands

The research findings suggest the "persistence of professionalism" in teachers' narratives in both state and private primary schools, which accords with earlier work (Hoyle and Wallace, 2014). Teachers' narratives also demonstrate the orientation of three pillars of teachers' professionalism: (1) peer networks; (2) professional knowledge base; and (3) autonomous decision making (Wang et al., 2014). On top of this, my research suggests that the state bianzhi status remains the main motivation for participants to remain in teaching: teachers perceived bianzhi as a guarantee of future job stability and legitimate professional status as state employees.

More research studies could be done to explore the potential contributions of teachers' subject knowledge in the construction of their professional identities. This is due to the situation that the process interview could very much depend on teachers' capacities to organise their language to perform a professional narrative. For instance, Chinese teachers might be more familiar with the literal meaning of identity and the dialogic self than maths teachers, so they might be more likely to become more engaged and demonstrate an integrated TPI than maths teachers. The English teacher, on the other hand, seemed to address the importance of leadership and the enjoyment of learning about education in foreign countries due to the link between language and cultural differences. In addition, school accountability and curriculum implementation were the other two influential dimensions of the educational policies. The approaches in implementing curriculum reform were often forceful and disengaging for teachers in the two state schools and the private charity school. The static job progression in the accountability system and the lack of professional autonomy often led to teachers' frustration and demoralising experiences. This is particularly the case for the participating SSTs in the mid-stage of their teaching career.

10.3　Community and Collaborations

All the teachers considered their collegial relationships as crucial for both their professional development and personal satisfaction. This finding generally agrees with other research studies in different country contexts on the influence of networks and professional communities from teachers' viewpoints (Graham, 2006; Lieberman, 2008). Most young teachers and mid-stage teachers found strong connections with colleagues in the context of professional collaborations and daily communication. Yet Wenger's (1998) CoP could be developed by including the casual aspect of teachers' school life and communication, through which teachers demonstrate care for each other and create a relaxing atmosphere for others to feel that they are accepted and emotionally supported. In this sense, teachers' "legitimate participation" might be enhanced not only by their access to certain professional and cultural capital in the formal setting, but also by an inclusive and friendly organisational culture shared by peers, managers and parents in the school.

10.4　Sense of Vocation and Personal Values

Another important part of the TPI literature argued that teachers' personal experience and emotions in their interactions with others on a day-to-day basis constitute an important part of their professional identities. A number of research studies have sought to integrate teachers' emotions in investigating TPIs, including Hargreaves (1998) and Day et al. (2007). As Hargreaves emphasised:

> Educational change initiatives do not just affect teachers' knowledge, skill and problem-solving capacity. They affect a whole web of significant and

meaningful relationships that make up the work of schools and that are at the very heart of the teaching process [...] Teachers make heavy emotional investments in these relationships. Their sense of success and satisfaction depends on them. (1998:838)

Some of the teachers' narratives seem to correspond to Nias' (1989) finding on the incorporation of the social identity as "a teacher" into individual teachers' self-images over time. In addition, teachers tended to stress the "core values" that they hope to bring through their work, regardless of the difference between state and private schools.

10.5 Revisiting the Concepts of "State" Versus "Private" Schools

This research, by developing a more developed typology of TPIs and the influencing factors and conditions, is intended to contribute to the debate about how teachers, school leaders, parents and local policy makers might better promote teachers' well-being and professionalism in primary education. Private schools have a long history in China. Current understandings of the role of private schools in the Chinese context needs to extend the current market-oriented approaches to private schools. Instead, an approach that is more in line with community-based understanding of private education seems to be more applicable. At the same time, the challenges in reforming the state schools are also worth noticing when SSTs also often face the pressure of parents demanding better education for their children yet who feel reluctant to engage with the school in a positive and guided way. Private schools are awarded freedom yet are highly reliant on the relationship with local government and a rigid system in protecting its roles to contribute to the public good in China's education system by celebrating diversity, addressing social mobility challenges, and promoting social and economic development and global citizenships.

At the level of practice, the contribution private schools could make to the development of TPIs is highly dependent on the collaboration between the local government and private school managers. With regards to teachers' professional development in both state and private schools, findings from this research are that teachers are no longer neatly bounded in a constrained community, nor do schools operate in a purely state-dominated educational system. For these reasons, teachers' and educators' abilities to challenge and negotiate the boundary between social and professional categories is worth encouraging. This research study also has helped to identify a series of values that could be further connected with the long-standing Chinese traditions of education and social development across two sectors through which teachers might feel engaged in educational reform. Teachers have argued that they need the space and support necessary to express their emerging and sometimes critical selves. The challenges lie in translating this call, in response to teachers' desire that other stakeholders in education treat them as respectable professionals, rather than the "educational labourers" or "second-class citizens".

10.6 Reflections on Trustworthiness and Quality in Narrative Studies

As has been discussed in Chapter 4, this research adopted a design for a qualitative study of teachers' narratives to explore TPIs in different school contexts in one province in China. While carrying out this research study, I pondered over questions of the quality of the study of teachers' narrated experiences. "How valid are narrative inquiry and the data analysis process? How do I know if the participants were telling truthful stories? What does it mean if the teachers make up stories?" I referred to influential texts in narrative inquiries and qualitative research methods in Chapter 4 and drew the conclusion that alternative terms to evaluate the quality of the qualitative research project need to be employed. Research validity should not be understood as a series of scientific rules for eliciting the "objective truth";

instead, it is a component of the research design and process that supports the credibility of the account of the description, interpretations or conclusions. A developmental approach was presented in Chapter 4 that included three connected parts: research design; data collection; and data analysis. As I went back and forth between different stages in developing this study, I found two analytical issues demand further details, namely verisimilitude and utility.

10.6.1 Verisimilitude

In research literature, verisimilitude was defined as "a criterion for a good literary study, in which the writing seems 'real' and 'alive'" for the audiences and can effectively guide the readers to the world of the study (Creswell, 2007:250). For this study to be trustworthy, it must achieve verisimilitude to allow others to experience what it is like to be the participant teachers in the similar situation and making decisions. To address this issue, techniques of member checking, and audience validation were used in this research.

10.6.2 Utility

The second issue that needed attention was how relevant and useful findings might be for members of the research community and teachers' professional communities. The list of criteria that Eisner (1998) developed might be useful to test this study's usefulness, namely (1) comprehension: could the research help understand a confusing situation? (2) anticipation: can the descriptions and interpretations provided go beyond the information given about them? And (3) guide and map: guide and map to provide directions and deepens current understandings of the research topic. The summary of my reflections on these three criteria will be included in the following section.

10.7 Summary of the Contribution to Knowledge, Strengths, Limitations and Recommendations for Further Studies

The primary contribution of this study comes from the cross-case analysis of SST and PST identity narratives in particular school contexts in Shandong, China. A wide range of influencing factors and narrative characteristics of TPIs were identified in four Chinese primary schools. In this research study, I also adopted a combination of narrative inquiry and cross-case design to explore the dynamic interactions between teachers' personal and professional identities. The matrix I developed is grounded on both a prior literature review and data analysis of teacher narratives and observations. It builds on and extends previous approaches to teacher identities by articulating key components based on this sample of 16 teachers.

Nevertheless, caution should be exercised when seeking to apply this matrix. The rationale for choosing 16 teachers embedded in their particular schools was that I could investigate TPIs from both state and private schools with the possibility of investigating the comparative dimensions of this research study. Although the findings have the potential to apply to other teacher cases in similar contexts, these findings were still only developed out of the analysis of a small number of teacher cases in four schools in one county in China due to the exploratory nature of the research and the limited time and resources. The matrix needs to be further tested and evaluated in different personal and professional situations. Notwithstanding these limitations, this research study has documented the complexity and dynamics of teachers' agency in their unique social and cultural contexts in China and developed original frameworks to help guide further research on TPIs based on teachers' narratives.

In conclusion, this study suggests that future research could further examine the applicability of the framework proposed here to other contexts. Through an in-depth analysis of teacher narratives, the findings may prove of value to teachers and teacher educators in both state and private schools in China's changing educational context and provide evidence on the kinds of support that may foster more positive TPIs. Indeed, this research also found the more diverse professional identities, with the boundary between "state" and "private" being dynamically blended in support of teachers' sense of identities and professional pursuits in increasingly complex settings.

References

Agar, M. H. (2008). *The professional stranger: An informal introduction to ethnography*. (2nd ed.). Emerald Group Publishing Limited.

Akkerman, S. F. & Meijer, P. C. (2011). A dialogical approach to conceptualizing teacher identity. *Teaching and Teacher Education*, 27(2), 208-319.

An, X. (2018). Teacher salaries and the shortage of high-quality teachers in China's rural primary and secondary schools. *Chinese Education & Society*, 51(2), 103-116.

Anderson, V. (2008). Communities of practice and part-time lecturers: Opportunities and challenges in higher education. In Kimble C., Hildreth P. & I. Bourdon (Eds.), *Communities of practice: Creating learning environments for educators* (Vol. 1, pp. 83-102). Information Age Publishing.

Apple, M. W. & Christian-Smith, L. (1991). *The politics of the textbook*. Routledge.

Ashley, D. L., et al. (2014). *The role and impact of private schools in developing countries: A rigorous review of the evidence*. Department for International Development.

Baert, P. (1995). *Social theory in the twentieth century*. Blackwell.

Ball, S. J. (1994). *Education reform: A critical and post-structural approach*. Open University Press.

Ball, S. J. (2003). *Educational studies, policy entrepreneurship and social theory*. In School effectiveness for whom? (pp. 76-89). Routledge.

Ball, S. J. & Goodson, I. F. (1985). Understanding teachers: Concepts and contexts. *Teachers' Lives and Careers*, 1, 1-26.

Ball, S. J., Goodson, I. & Maguire, M. (2007). *Education, globalisation and new times*. Routledge.

Barreto, I. (2010). Dynamic capabilities: A review of past research and an agenda for the future. *Journal of Management*, 36(1), 256-280.

Barry, C. A. (1998). Choosing qualitative data analysis software: Atlas. ti and Nudist compared. Sociological Research Online, 3(3). Retrieved from: http://www.socresonline.org.uk/3/3/4.html

Bassey, M. (1999). *Case study research in educational settings*. Open University Press.

Beauchamp, C. & Thomas, L. (2009). Understanding teacher identity: An overview of issues in the literature and implications for teacher education. *Cambridge Journal of Education*, 39(2), 175-189. doi: 10.1080/03057640902902252

Baumeister, R. F. (1998). The self. In D. T. Gilbert, S. T. Fiske & G. Lindzey (Eds.), *The handbook of social psychology* (4th ed., Vol. 1, pp. 680-740). McGraw-Hill.

Beck, U. (1992). *Risk society: Toward a new modernity*. Sage publications.

Beijaard, D., Meijer, P. & Verloop, N. (2004). Reconsidering research on teachers' professional identity. *Teaching and Teacher Education*, 20, 107-128.

Beijaard, D., Verloop, N. & Vermunt, J. D. (2000). Teachers' perceptions of professional identity: An exploratory study from a personal knowledge perspective. *Teaching and Teacher Education*, 16, 749-764.

Beltman, S., Mansfield, C. & Price, A. (2011). Thriving not just surviving: A review of research on teacher resilience. *Educational Research Review*, 6(3), 185-207.

Berger, J. L. & Kim, L. V. (2019). Teacher professional identity as multi-dimensional: Mapping its components and examining their associations with general pedagogical beliefs. *Educational Studies*, 45(2), 163-181.

Berger, P. L. & Luckmann, T. (1966). *The social construction of reality: A treatise in the sociology of knowledge*. Anchor Books.

Bloomberg, L. D. & Volpe, M. (2008). *Completing your qualitative dis-*

sertation: *A roadmap from beginning to end*. Sage publications.

Böhm, A. (2004). Theoretical coding: Text analysis in grounded theory. In U. Flick, E. von Kardorff & I. Steinke (Eds.), *A companion to qualitative research* (pp. 270-275). Sage publications.

Bray, D. (2005). *Social space and governance in urban China: The danwei system from origins to reform*. Stanford University Press.

Briggs, C. L. (2003). Interviewing, power/knowledge, and social inequality. In J.A. Holstein & J.F. Gubrium (eds.) *Inside Interviewing: New Lenses, New Concerns* (pp. 495-506). Sage publications.

British Educational Research Association. (2011). *Ethical guidelines for educational research* .[Publisher not identified as it is not provided]

Brislin, R. W. (1970). Back-translation for cross-cultural research. *Journal of Cross-Cultural Psychology*, 1(3), 185-216.

Britzman, D. (1993). Beyond rolling models: Gender and multicultural education. In S. K. Biklen & D. Pollard (Eds.), *Gender and education* (pp. 23-46). The University of Chicago Press.

Brodsgaard, K. E. (2002). Institutional reform and bianzhi system in China. *The China Quarterly*, 170, 361-386.

Brown, A. (1997). A dynamic model of occupational identity formation. University of Leeds. Retrieved from http://www.leeds.ac.uk/educol/documents/000000312.htm.

Brownell, S. E. & Tanner, K. D. (2012). Barriers to faculty pedagogical change: Lack of training, time, incentives, and ... tensions with professional identity? *Life Sciences Education*, 11(4), 339-346.

Bruner, J. (1987). Life as narrative. *Social Research*, 54(1), 11-32.

Bruner, J. (1991). The narrative construction of reality. *Critical Inquiry*, 18, 1-21.

Brunetti, G. J. (2006). Resilience under fire: Perspectives on the work of experienced inner city high school teachers in the United States. *Teaching and Teacher Education*, 22(7), 812-825.

Bryman, A. (2008). *Social research methods* (3rd ed.). Oxford University Press.

Bureau of Education of Nanqi (pseudonmym). (2013). The 12th five-year plan for education development.

Burn, C. (2007). Professional knowledge and identity in a contested discipline: Challenges for student teachers and teacher educators. *Oxford Review of Education*, 33(4), 445-467.

Cameron, J. E. (1999). Social identity and the pursuit of possible selves: Implications for the psychological well-being of university students. *Group Dynamics: Theory, Research, and Practice*, 3(3), 179-189.

Cassie, Q., Amy, T. & Nicole, B. C. (2013). The viability of portraiture for science education research: Learning from portraits of two science classrooms. *International Journal of Qualitative Studies in Education*, 28(1), 21-49.

Charmaz, K. (2006). *Constructing grounded theory*. Sage publications.

Chan, R. K. & Wang, Y. (2009). Controlled decentralization: Minban education reform in China. *Journal of Comparative Social Welfare*, 25(1), 27-36

Chen, T. (2003). Recommendations for creating and maintaining effective networked learning communities: A review of the literature. *International Journal of Instructional Media*, 30(1), 335-345.

Cheng, K. M. (1994). The changing legitimacy in a decentralizing system: The state and education development in China. *International Journal of Educational Development*, 14(3), 265-269.

Christensson, J. (2019). "This is where my inner history teacher appears": A methodological approach to analyzing student teachers' professional identity in interaction. *Classroom Discourse*, 10(2), 168-187.

Chua, B. L., Liu, W. & Chia, S. (2018). Teacher identity, professional practices, and inquiry (PPI) in teacher education. *Asia Pacific Journal of Education*, 38(4), 550-564.

Creswell, J. W. (2009). *Research design: Qualitative, quantitative, and mixed methods approaches* (3rd ed.). Sage publications.

Crotty, M. (2003). *The foundations of social research: Meaning and perspective in the research process*. Sage Publications.

Cohen, J. L. (2010). Getting recognised: Teachers negotiating professional identities as learners through talk. *Teaching and Teacher Education*, 26(3), 473-481.

Cohen, L., Manion, L. & Morrison, K. (2011). *Research methods in education* (7th ed.). Routledge.

Cohen, R. & Kennedy, P. (2007). *Global sociology* (2nd ed.). Palgrave Macmillan.

Coldron, J. & Smith, R. (1999). Active location in teachers' construction of their professional identities. *Journal of Curriculum Studies*, 31(6), 711-726.

Connelly, F. M. & Clandinin, D. J. (1987). On narrative method, biography and narrative unities in the study of teaching. *The Journal of Educational Thought (JET)/Revue De La Pensée Éducative*, 21(3), 130-139.

Connelly, F. M. & Clandinin, D. J. (1990). Stories of experience and narrative inquiry. *Educational Researcher*, 19(5), 2-14.

Connelly, F. M. & Clandinin, D. J. (2006). Narrative inquiry. In J. L. Green, G. Camilli & P. Elmore (Eds.), *Handbook of complementary methods in education research* (3rd ed., pp. 477-487). Erlbaum.

Cornelius, R. R. (1996). *The science of emotion: Research and tradition in the psychology of emotion*. Prentice-Hall.

Cooley, C. H. (1902). Looking-glass self. *The Production of Reality: Essays and Readings on Social Interaction*, 6, 126-128.

Cooper, K. & Olson, M. (1996). The multiple "I"s of teacher identity. In M. Kompf, W. R. Bond, D. Dworet & R. T. Boak (Eds.), *Changing research and practice: Teachers' professionalism, identities, and knowledge* (pp. 78-98). Falmer Press.

Crabtree, B. & Miller, W. (1999). A template approach to text analysis: Developing and using codebooks. In B. Crabtree & W. Miller (Eds.), Doing qualitative research (pp. 163-177). Sage Publications.

Creswell, J. W. (2007). *Qualitative Inquiry & Research Design* (2nd ed). Sage Publications.

Cross, M. & Elizabeth, N. (2015). On becoming and remaining a teacher: Rethinking strategies for developing teacher professional identity in South Africa. *Research Papers in Education*, 30(1), 95-113.

Crotty, M. (1998). *The foundations of social research: Meaning and perspective in the research process.* Sage publications.

Cui, Y. & Zhu, Y.(2014). *Curriculum reforms in China: History and the present day.* Revue internationale d'éducation de Sèvres.

Czerniawski, G. (2011). Emerging teachers-emerging identities: trust and accountability in the construction of newly qualified teachers in Norway, Germany, and England. *European Journal of Teacher Education*. 34(4), 431-447.

Dale, R. (2000). Globalization and education: Demonstrating a "common world education culture" or locating a "globally structured educational agenda"? *Educational Theory*, 50(4), 427-448.

Dang, T. K. A. (2013). Identity in activity: Examining teacher professional identity formation in the paired-placement of student teachers. *Teaching and Teacher Education*, 30, 47-59.

Darby, A. (2008). Teachers' emotions in the reconstruction of professional self-understanding. *Teaching and Teacher Education*, 24(5), 1160-1172.

Davey, N. (2013). *Unfinished worlds: Hermeneutics, aesthetics and Gadamer.* Edinburgh University Press Scholarship. Retrieved from: http://edinburgh.universitypressscholarship.com.

Daviet, B. (2016). Revisiting the principle of education as public good. *Education Research and Foresight: Working Papers.* UNESCO.

Day, C., Elliot, B. & Kington, A. (2005). Reform, standards and teacher identity: Challenges of sustaining commitment. *Teaching and Teacher Education*, 21(5), 563-577.

Day, C. & Kington, A. (2008). Identity, well-being, and effectiveness: The emotional contexts of teaching. *Pedagogy, Culture & Society*, 16(1), 7-23.

Day, C., et al. (2007). *Teachers matter: Connecting lives, work, and effectiveness.* Open University Press.

Day, C. & Sachs, J. (2004). Professionalism, performativity, and empowerment: Discourses in the politics, policies, and purposes of continuing professional development. In C. Day & J. Sachs (Eds.), *International handbook on the continuing professional development of teachers*. Open University Press.

Delpit, L. (1995). *Other people's children*. Houghton Mifflin Co.

Deng, P. (1997). *Private education in modern China*. Praeger.

Denzin, N. K. & Lincoln, Y. S. (2000). *Handbook of qualitative research*. Sage publications.

Deter, P. (2008). The professional acculturation of internationally educated teachers in Canada: Affordances, constraints, and the reconstruction of professional identity. Paper presented at the Sociocultural Perspectives on Teacher Education and Development Conference, University of Oxford.

Dikilitas, K. & Yayli, D. (2018). Teachers' professional identity development through action research. *ELT Journal*, 72(4), 415-424.

Dotger, B. H. (2010). "I had no idea": Developing dispositional awareness and sensitivity through a cross-professional pedagogy. *Teaching and Teacher Education*, 26, 805-812.

Dotger, B. H. & Smith, M. J. (2009)."Where's the Line?"— Negotiating Simulated Experiences to Define Teacher Identity. *The New Educator*, 5(2), 161-180.

Dow, A., Hattam, R., Reid, A., Shacklock, G. & Smyth, J. (2000). *Teachers' work in a globalizing economy*. Taylor & Francis.

Drucker, F. P. (1993). The rise of the knowledge society. *The Wilson Quarterly*, 17(2), 52-71.

Dvir, N. & Avissar, I. (2014). Constructing a critical professional identity among teacher candidates during service-learning. *Professional Development in Education*, 40(3), 389-415.

Easterby-Smith, M., Thorpe, R. & Lowe, A. (2003). *Management research: An introduction*. Sage publications.

Eisner, E. W. (1998). *The enlightened eye: Qualitative inquiry and the enhancement of educational practice*. Prentice Hall.

Ellemers, N., Spears, R. & Doosje, B. (2002). Self and social identity. *Annual review of psychology*, 53(1), 161-186.

Elliott, A. (2005). *Concepts of the self*. Polity Press.

Elliott, J. (2005). *Using narrative in social research: Qualitative and quantitative approaches*. Sage publications.

Erikson, E. H. (1968). *Identity, Youth and Crisis*. WW Norton & company.

Fang, Y. (2011). Pedagogy and curriculum reform in China—from the angle of one teacher's daily work. *Chinese Education & Society*, 44(6), 24-35.

Fearon, J. D. (1999). What is identity (as we now use the word). Unpublished manuscript, Stanford University, Stanford, Calif, 1-43.

Feng, C. (2003). Where does the teacher training for new curriculum go? *Basic Education Research*, 16(7-8), 9-15.

Fereday, J. & Muir-Cochrane, E. (2006). Demonstrating rigor using thematic analysis: A hybrid approach of inductive and deductive coding and theme development. *International Journal of Qualitative Methods*, 5(1), 80-92.

Flores, M. A. & Day, C. (2006). Contexts which shape and reshape new teachers' identities: A multi-perspective study. *Teaching and Teacher Education*, 22(2), 219-232.

Fu, G. & Clarke, A. (2019). Individual and collective agencies in China's curriculum reform: A case of physics teachers. *Journal of Research in Science Teaching*, 56, 45-63.

Fuller, C., Goodwyn, A. & Francis-Brophy, E. (2013). Advanced skills teachers: Professional identity and status. *Teachers and Teaching*, 19(4), 463-474.

Furlong, J. (2001). Reforming teacher education, re-forming teachers: Accountability, professionalism, and competence. In R. Phillips & J. Furlong (Eds.), *Education, reform and the state: Twenty five years of politics, policy, and practices* (pp. 118-135). Taylor & Francis.

Gadamer, H. (1979). *Truth and Method*. Sheed and Ward.

Gao, L. (1998). Cultural context of school science teaching and learning in the People's Republic of China. *Science Education*, 82, 1-13.

Gardner, P. (1995). Teacher training and changing professional identity in early twentieth-century England. *Journal of Education for Teaching*, 21 (2), 191-216.

Gee, J. P. (1985). The narrativization of experience in the oral style. *Journal of Education*, 167(1), 11.

Gee, J. P. (2001). Identity as an analytic lens for research in education. *Review of Research in Education*, 25, 99-125.

Germeijs, V., Luyckx, K., Notelaers, G., Goossens, L. & Verschueren, K. (2012). Choosing a major in higher education: Profiles of students' decision-making process. *Contemporary Educational Psychology*, 37, 229-239.

Gewirtz, S. (1997). Post-welfarism and the reconstruction of teachers' work in the UK. *Journal of Education Policy*, 12(4), 217-231. http://dx.doi.org/10.1080/0268093970120402.

Giddens, A. (1991). *Modernity and self-identity: Self and society in the late modern age*. Polity Press.

Glaser, B. G. (1978). *Theoretical sensitivity: Advances in the methodology of grounded theory*. Sociology Press.

Glaser, B. G. (1992). *Basics of grounded theory analysis: Emergence vs. forcing*. Sociology Press.

Golombek, P. R. (1998). A study of language teachers' personal practical knowledge. *TESOL Quarterly*, 32(3), 447-464.

Goodwyn, A. (2010). *The expert teacher of English*. Routledge.

Graham, B. (2006). Conditions for successful field experiences: Perceptions of cooperating teachers. *Teaching and teacher education*, 22(8), 1118-1129.

Graham, K. C. (1996). Running ahead: Enhancing teacher commitment. *Journal of Physical Education, Recreation & Dance*, 67(1), 45-47.

Grenz, S. (2005). Intersections of sex and power in research on prostitution: A female researcher interviewing male heterosexual clients. *Signs*, 30, 2091-1215.

Griffiths, V., Thompson, S. & Hryniewicz, L. (2010). Teacher educators: transition into higher education and developing research identities. In *Universities' Council for the Education of Teachers Conference*.

Gu, M. (2006). Reflections on the reform of teacher education. *Teacher Education Research*, 18(6), 3-6.

Gu, Q. (2007). *Teacher development: Knowledge and context*. Continuum.

Gu, Q. & Day, C. (2007). Teachers' resilience: A necessary condition for effectiveness. *Teaching and Teacher Education*, 23(8), 1302-1316.

Gu, Q. & Li, Q. (2015). Sustaining resilience in times of change: stories from Chinese teachers. In Q. Gu (Ed.), *The work and lives of teachers in China* (pp. 179-196). Routledge.

Guan, Q. & Meng, W. (2007). China's new national curriculum reform: Innovation, challenges, and strategies. *Frontiers of Education in China*, 2(4), 579-604.

Gubrium, J. F. & Holstein, J. A. (2003). *Inside interviewing: New lenses, new concerns*. Sage Publications.

Guest, G., MacQueen, K. M. & Namey, E. E. (2012). *Applied thematic analysis*. Sage publications.

Guo, L. (2012). New curriculum reform in China and its impact on teachers. *Canadian and International Education / Education Canadienne et Internationale*, 41(2), 87-105.

Hackmann, D. G. (2002). Using portraiture in educational leadership research. *International Journal of Leadership in Education: Theory and Practice*, 5(1), 51-60.

Hammersley, M. & Atkinson, P. (1995). *Ethnography: Principles in practice* (2nd ed.). Routledge.

Han, X. (2012). Big moves to improve the quality of teacher education in China. *On the Horizon*, 20(4), 324-335.

Han, X. & Paine, L. (2010). Teaching mathematics as deliberate practice through public lessons. *Elementary School Journal*, 110(4), 519-541.

Hargreaves, A. (1978). The significance of classroom coping strategies. In L. Barton & R. Meighan (Eds.), *Sociological interpretations of schooling and classrooms: A re-appraisal* (pp. xx-xx). Nafferton Books.[Note: Replace "xx-xx" with the actual page numbers]

Hargreaves, A. (2000). Mixed emotions: Teachers' perceptions of their interactions with students. *Teaching and Teacher Education*, 16(8), 811-826.

Hargreaves, A. (2003). *Teaching in the knowledge society: Education in the age of insecurity*. Teacher College Press.

Hargreaves, A. (2005a). The emotions of teaching and educational change. In A. Hargreaves (Ed.), *International handbook of educational change* (pp. 278-295). Kluwer Academic Publishers.

Hargreaves, A. (2005b). Educational change takes ages: Life, career and generational factors in teachers' emotional responses to educational changes. *Teaching and Teacher Education*, 21, 967-983.

Hargreaves, A. & Goodson, I. (2002). Teachers' professional lives: Aspirations and actualities. In I. Goodson & A. Hargreaves (Eds.), *Teachers' professional lives* (pp. 9-35). Falmer Press.

Harris, A. (2003). Behind the classroom door: The challenge of organisational and pedagogical change. *Journal of Educational Change*, 4(4), 369-382.

Hekman, S. (1984). Action as a text: Gadamer's hermeneutics and the social scientific analysis of action. *Journal for the Theory of Social Behavior*, 14(3), 333-354.

Helsby, G. (2000). *Changing teachers' work and culture*. Open University Press.

Hennink, M. (2008). Language and communication in cross-cultural research. In P. Liamputtong (Ed.), *Doing cross-cultural research: Methodological and ethical perspectives* (pp. 21-33). Springer.

Hiebert, J., Stigler, J. W., Jacobs, J. K., Givvin, K. B., Garnier, H., Smith, M. & Gallimore, R. (2005). Math teaching in the United States today (and tomorrow): Results from the TIMSS 1999 video study. *Educational Evaluation and Policy Analysis*, 27, 111-132.

Hoban, G. (2007). Consideration for designing coherent teacher education programs. In J. Butcher & L. McDonald (Eds.), *Making a difference: Challenges for teachers, teaching, and teacher education* (pp. 173-187). Sense Publishers.

Holland, D., Lachicotte, W. Jr., Skinner, D. & Cain, C. (1998). *Identity and agency in cultural worlds*. Harvard University Press.

Holland, D. & Lachicotte, W. (2007). Vygotsky, Mead, and new sociocultural studies of identity. In H. Daniels, M. Cole & J.V. Wertsch (Eds.), *The Vygotsky reader* (pp. 101-135). Cambridge University Press.

Holstein, J.A. & Gubrium, J.F. (1995). *The active interview*, Sage publications.

Hooley, N. (2007). Establishing professional identity: Narrative as curriculum for pre-service teacher education. *Australian Journal of Teacher Education*, 32(1), 49-60.

Hord, S. (1997). *Professional learning communities: What are they and why are they important?* Southwest Educational Development Laboratory (SEDL).

Hoyle, E. (1980). Professionalization and deprofessionalization in education. In E. Hoyle & J. Megarry (Eds.), *World yearbook of education* 1980 (pp. 42-57). Kogan Page.

Hoyle, E. & Wallace, M. (2014). Organisational studies in an era of educational reform. *Journal of Educational Administration and History*, 46(3), 244-269.

Inhetveen, E. (2012). Translation challenges: Qualitative interviewing in a multi-lingual field. *Qualitative Sociology Review*, 8(2), 28-45.

Izadinia, M. (2012). A review of research on student teachers' professional identity. *British Educational Research Journal*, 39(4), 694-713.

Izadinia, M. (2015). A closer look at the role of mentor teachers in shaping preservice teachers' professional identity. *Teaching and Teacher Education*, 52, 1-10.

Kayi-Aydar, H. (2019). A language teacher's agency in the development of her professional identities: A narrative case study. *Journal of Latinos and Education*, 18(1), 4-18.

Kelchtermans, G. (1993). Getting the story, understanding the lives: From career stories to teachers' professional development. *Teaching and Teacher Education*, 9(5-6), 443-456.

Kelchtermans, G. (1996). Teacher vulnerability: Understanding its moral and political roots. *Cambridge Journal of Education*, 26(3), 307-323.

Kelchtermans, G. & Vandenberghe, R. (1994). Teachers' professional development: A biographical perspective. *Journal of Curriculum Studies*, 26(1), 45-62.

Kemper, E., Stringfield, S. & Teddlie, C. (2003). Mixed methods sampling strategies in social science research. In A. Tashakkori & C. Teddlie (Eds.), *Handbook of Mixed Methods in Social and Behavioral Research* (pp. 273-296). Sage publications.

Kennedy, A. (2005). Models of continuing professional development: A framework for analysis. *Journal of In-Service Education*, 31(2), 235-250.

Kenny, A., Finneran, M. & Mitchell, E. (2015). Becoming an educator in and through the arts: Forming and informing emerging teachers' professional identity. *Teaching and Teacher Education*, 49(1), 159-167.

Kerlinger, F. N. (1970). *Foundations of Behavioral Research*. Holt, Rinehart and Winston.

Kerlinger, F. N. (1973). *Review of research in education*. F. E. Peacock.

Kimmel, A. (1988). *Ethics and Values in Applied Social Research*. Sage publications.

Korthagen, F. A. J., Kessels, J., Koster, B., Lagerwerf, B. & Wubbels, T. (2001). *Linking Practice and Theory: The Pedagogy of Realistic Teacher Education*. Lawrence Erlbaum Associates.

Korthagen, F. & Vasalos, A. (2005). Levels in reflection: Core reflection as a means to enhance professional growth. *Teachers and Teaching: Theory and Practice*, 11(1), 47-71.

Knowles, G. J. (1992). Models for understanding pre-service and beginning teachers' biographies: Illustrations from case studies. In I. F. Goodson (Ed.), *Studying teachers' lives* (*pp*.99-152). Teachers College Press

Kvale, S. (1996). *InterViews-An Introduction to Qualitative Research Interviewing*. Sage publications.

Kvale, S. (2009). *Interviews: Learning the Craft of Qualitative Research*

Interviewing (2nd ed.). Sage publications.

Kyriacou, C. & Kobori, M. (1998). Motivation to learn and teach English in Slovenia. *Educational Studies*, 24, 345-351.

Kyriacou, C. & Coulthard, M. (2000). Undergraduates' views of teaching as a career choice. *Journal of Education for Teaching*, 26(2), 117-126.

Lagemann, E. C. (2000). *An Elusive Science: The Troubling History of Education Research*. University of Chicago Press.

Lai, M. (2010). Teacher development under curriculum reform: A case study of a secondary school in the Chinese Mainland. *International Review of Education*, 56(5-6), 613-631.

Lai, K. C., Chan, K. W., Ko, K. W. & So, K. S. (2005). Teaching as a career: A perspective from Hong Kong senior secondary students. *Journal of Education for Teaching*, 31(3), 153-168.

Lamote, C. & Engels, N. (2010). The development of student teachers' professional identity. *European Journal of Teacher Education*, 33(1), 3-18.

Lamont, M. (1992). *Money, Morals, and Manners: The Culture of the French and American Upper-Middle Class*. University of Chicago Press.

Lamont, M. & Molnár, V. (2002). The study of boundaries in the social sciences. *Annual Review of Sociology*, 28, 167-195.

Langdridge, D. (2007). *Phenomenological psychology: Theory, research, and methods*. Pearson Education.

Lasky, S. (2005). A sociocultural approach to understanding teacher identity, agency, and professional vulnerability in a context of secondary school reform. *Teaching and Teacher Education*, 21(8), 899-916.

Lawrence-Lightfoot, S. & Davis, J. (1997). *The art and science of portraiture*. Jossey-Bass.

Lawson, A. (2014). Learner identities in the context of undergraduates: A case study. *Educational research*, 56(3), 343-356.

Lave, J. & Wenger, E. (1991). *Situated learning: Legitimate peripheral participation*. Cambridge University Press.

Le, X. B. & Lao, K. S. (2004). 中国民办教师问题研究[*Researching the*

problem of minban *teachers in China*]. Beijing Normal University Press.

Lee, R. M. (1993). *Doing research on sensitive topics*. Sage Publications.

Lee, J. C. K. & Song, H. (2018). Primary education. In J. Morgan, Q. Gu & F. Li (Eds.), *Handbook of education in China* (pp. 52-66). Edward Elgar Publishing.

Lee, J. C. K., Yin, H. B., Zhang, Z. H. & Jin, Y. L. (2011). Teacher empowerment and receptivity in curriculum reform in China. *Chinese Education & Society*, 44(4), 64-81.

LeTendre, G., Baker, D., Akiba, M., Goesling, B. & Wiseman, A. (2001). Teachers' work: Institutional isomorphism and cultural variation in the U.S., Germany, and Japan. *Educational Researcher*, 30(6), 3-15.

Lewin, K., Xu, H., Little, A. & Zheng, J. (1994). *Educational innovation in China: Tracing the impact of the 1985 reforms*. Longman Group.

Li, D. J. (1996). 政府、地方社区与乡村教师——靖远县及23县比较研究 [*Government, local community and rural teachers: A comparative study of Jingyuan county and other 23 counties*]. Peking University.

Li, H. (1993). 中国单位现象与城市社区的整合机制 [*China's* danwei *phenomenon and the mechanisms of conformity in urban communities*]. Sociology Research. Retrieved from http://wenku.baidu.com/view/439745d1240c844769eaeef0.html.

Li, Q. & Ni, Y. (2011). Impact of curriculum reform: Evidence of change in classroom practice in Mainland China. *International Journal of Educational Research*, 50, 71-86.

Li, Q. & Ni, Y. (2012). Debates on the basic education curriculum reform and teachers' challenges in China. *Chinese Education & Society*, 45(4), 9-21.

Lieberman, A. (2008). Teacher learning: The key to educational reform. *Journal of Teacher Education*, 59(3), 226-234.

Lieblich, A., Tuval-Mashiach, R. & Zilber, T. (1998). *Narrative research: Reading, analysis, and interpretation*. Sage Publications.

Lin, J., Wang, N., Sun, J. & Yu, F. (2005). Trust, ownership, and autonomy: Challenges facing private higher education in China. *The China*

Quarterly, 183, 61-81.

Lincoln, Y. S. & Guba, E. G. (1985). *Naturalistic inquiry*. Sage Publications.

Liu, H. (2012). Teaching in the shadow: Exploration into teachers' professional identities in private tutoring institutes in China. Unpublished master's thesis, University of Oxford.

Liu, J. & Kang, C. (2011). Reflection in action: Ongoing K-12 curriculum reform in China. InJ. Ryan (Ed.), *Education reform in China: Changing concepts, contexts and practices* (pp.21-40). Routledge.

Liu, S. & Onwuegbuzie, A. J. (2014). Teachers' motivations for entering the teaching profession and their job satisfaction: A cross-cultural comparison of China and other countries. *Learning Environments Research*, 17, 75-94.

Liu, S. & Teddlie, C. (2003). The ongoing development of teacher evaluation and curriculum reform in the People's Republic of China. *Journal of Personnel Evaluation in Education*, 17(3), 243-261.

Liu, S. & Zhao, D. (2013). Teacher evaluation in China: Latest trends and future directions. *Educational Assessment, Evaluation and Accountability*, 25(3), 231-250.

Livingston, K. (2016). Developing teachers' and teacher educators' professional identity in changing contexts. *European Journal of Teacher Education*, 39(4), 401-402.

Lozano, L., Fiorentini, D. & Villarreal, M. (2018). The development of a mathematics teacher's professional identity during her first year teaching. *Journal of Mathematics Teacher Education*, 21(3), 287-315.

Luehmann, A. L. (2008). Using blogging in support of teacher professional identity development: A case study. *The Journal of the Learning Sciences*, 17(3), 287-337.

Ly, T. T. & Nhai, T. T. (2013). Mediating teacher professional identity: The emergence of humanness and ethical identity. *International Journal of Training Research*, 11(3), 199-212.

Ma, X. (2015). Cultural features of the Shandong dialect: A discussion with

Professor Ogi Hirofumi. *International Research of Yamaguchi Prefectural University*, 27(4), 51-82.

Ma, L. & Long, L. (1999). 中国农村教育问题研究[*Study of education in rural China*]. Fujian Education Press.

Manuel, J. & Hughes, J. (2006). It has always been my dream: Exploring pre-service teachers' reasons for choosing to teach. *Teacher Development*, 10(1), 5-24.

Maxwell, J. A. & Loomis, D. M. (2003). Mixed method design: An alternative approach. In A. Tashakkori & C. Teddlie (Eds.), *Handbook of mixed methods in social and behavioral research* (pp. 241-272). Sage Publications.

Maxwell, J. A. (2010). Validity: How might you be wrong? In W. Luttrell (Ed.), *Qualitative educational research: Readings in reflexive methodology and transformative practice* (pp. 279-287). Routledge.

McEachern, K. P. & Horton, J. L. (2016). Developing a research identity: Promoting a research mindset among faculty and students. *The Educational Forum*. 80(4), 444-456, Routledge.

McDonald, J. & Star, C. (2006). Designing the future of learning through a community of practice of teachers of first year courses at an Australian university. In *Proceedings of the 1st International LAMS Conference: Designing the Future of Learning* (pp. 65-76). LAMS Foundation.

McLaughlin, M. W. & Talbert, J. (2006). *Building school-based teacher learning communities: Professional strategies to improve student achievement*. Teachers College Press.

Mead, G. H. (1934). *Mind, self and society*. University of Chicago Press.

Mei, H. (2007). 民办学校中小学教师生存状态调查研究[*Investigation of minban primary and secondary school teachers' living conditions*]. Unpublished master's thesis. Sichuan Normal University.

Menter, I. (2008). Tradition, culture, and identity in the reform of teachers' work in Scotland and England: Some methodological considerations. *Pedagogy, Culture & Society*, 16(1), 57-69. https://doi.org/10.1080/14681360701877768.

Menter, I. (*2010*). Teachers: Formation, training, and identity: A literature review. *Creativity, Culture, and Education*.

Mertens, D. (2005). *Research and evaluation in education and psychology: Integrating diversity with quantitative, qualitative, and mixed methods* (2nd ed.). Sage Publications.

Mertkan, S. & Bayrakli, H. (2018). Re-inventing researcher identity: When the individual interacts with the contextual power dynamics. *Higher Education Research & Development*, 37(2), 316-327.

Mishler, E. G. (1986). The analysis of interview-narratives. In T. R. Sarbin (Ed.), *Narrative psychology: The storied nature of human conduct* (pp. 233-255). Praeger Publishers/Greenwood Publishing Group.

Miller, T. & Bell, L. (2002). Consenting to what? Issues of access, gate-keeping and 'informed' consent. In M. Mauthner, M. Birch, J. Jessop & T. Miller (Eds.), *Ethics in qualitative research* (pp. 10-24). Sage Publications.

Mills, C. W. (1959). *The sociological imagination*. Oxford University Press.

Miles, M. B. & Huberman, A. M. (1994). *Qualitative Data Analysis: An Expanded Sourcebook*. Sage publications.

Milner, H. R. (2013). *Policy reforms and de-professionalization of teaching*. National Education Policy Centre. Retrieved on August 5, 2015, from http://greatlakescenter.org/docs/Policy_Briefs/Milner_Deprof.pdf.

Ministry of Education of People's Republic of China. (2013). 中国教育发展概况 [*Government report on educational reform and development*]. Retrieved from http://www.moe.gov.cn/jyb_sjzl/moe_364/moe_902/moe_1002/tnull_9381.html.

Ministry of Education of People's Republic of China.(2017). 2016 年全国教育事业发展统计公报 [*2016 National statistical bulletin on education development*].Retrieved from http://www.moe.gov.cn/jyb_sjzl/sjzl_fztjgb/201707/t20170710_309042.html.

Ministry of Justice of the People's Republic of China. (2018). 中华人民共和国民办教育促进法（修订草案）[Regulations on the implementations of Minban education promotion law in the People's Republic of China (Draft revision)]. Retrieved from http://www.moj.gov.cn/government_public/content/2018-08/10/tzwj_38281.html.

Moate, J. & Ruohotie-Lyhty, M. (2014). Identity, agency and community: Reconsidering the pedagogic responsibilitiesof teacher education. *British Journal of Educational Studies*, 62(3), 249-264.

Mok, K. H. (1997). Marketization and quasi-marketization: Educational development in post-Mao China. *International Review of Education*, 43(5-6), 547-567.

Mok, K. H. (2009). The growing importance of the privateness in education: Challenges for higher education governance in China. In T. W. B. Terance & D. E. N. Deane (Eds.), *Higher education in Asia/Pacific: Quality and the public good* (pp. 15-29). Palgrave Macmillan.

Moore, M. & Hofman, J. E. (1988). Professional identity in institutions of higher learning in Israel. *Higher Education*, 17(1), 69-79.

Moreau, M. P. (2014). Becoming a secondary school teacher in England and France: Contextualising career "choice". *Compare: A Journal of Comparative and International Education*, 45(3), 401-423.

Morgan, B. (2004) Teacher identity as pedagogy: towards a field-internal conceptualisation in bilingual and second language education. *International Journal of Bilingual Education and Bilingualism*, 7(2-3), 172-188.

Morrison, C. M. (2013). Teacher identity in the early career phase: Trajectories that explain and influence development. *Australian Journal of Teacher Education*, 38(4), 91-107.

Morse, J. M. (1994). Designing funded qualitative research. In N. K. Denzin & Y. S. Lincoln (Eds.), *Handbook of qualitative research* (pp. 220-235). Sage Publications.

Munro, P. (1998). *Subject to fiction: Women teachers' life history narratives and the cultural politics of resistance*. Open University Press.

Newman, S., Niemeyer, B., Seddon, T. & Devcos, A. (2014). Understanding educational work: Exploring the analytic borderlands around the labour that enables learning. *Globalisation, Societies and Education*, 12(3), 321-335.

Nias, J. (1989). *Primary teacher talking: A study of teaching as work*. Routledge.

Nida, E. A. (1982). *Translating meaning*. English Language Institute.

Nida, E. A. (1984). Approaches to translating in the Western world. *Foreign Language Teaching and Research*, (2), 13.

Nixon, J., Martin, J., McKeown, P. & Ranson, S. (1997). Toward a learning profession: Changing codes of occupational practice within the new management of education. *British Journal of Sociology of Education*, 18(1), 5-28.

Oancea, A. (2011, November 20). *Ethics in educational research: Philosophical perspectives* [Lecture handout]. Strategy of Educational Research Lecture, Oxford University.

OECD (2011). *Education at a Glance 2011: OECD indicators*, OECD publishing. Retrieved from: http://dx.doi.org/10.1787/eag-2011-en.

Onwuegbuzie, A. J. & Johnson, R. B. (2006). The validity issues in mixed research. *Research in the Schools*, 13(1), 48-63.

Onwuegbuzie, A. J. & Leech, N. L. (2007). Sampling designs in qualitative research: Making the sampling process more public. *The Qualitative Report*, 12(2), 238-254.

Orde, H.V. *(2016). Perspectives on identity: An overview of identity concepts from psychoanalysis, sociology and psychology. Tevevizion*, 1-9. Retrived from: https://izi.br.de/english/publication/televizion/29_2016_E/vom_Orde-Perspectives_on_identity.pdf.

Oswald, M., Johnson, B. & Howard, S. (2003). Quantifying and evaluating resilience-promoting factors: Teachers' beliefs and perceived roles. *Research in Education*, 70, 50-64.

Oxley, D. (2001). *Organising schools into small learning communities*. NASSP Bulletin, 85(625), 5-16.

Oyserman, D., Bybee, D. & Terry, K. (2003). Gendered Racial Identity and Involvement with School. *Self and Identity*, 2(4), 307-324.

Packer, M. J. (1991). Interpreting stories, interpreting lives: Narrative and action in moral development research. *New Directions for Child Develop-*

ment, 54, 63-82.

Paine, L. & Ma, L. (1993). Teachers working together: A dialogue on organisational and cultural perspectives of Chinese teachers. *International Journal of Educational Research*, 19(8), 675-697.

Paine, L. Y. N. N. & Fang, Y. P. (2007). Dilemmas in reforming China's teaching: Assuring "quality" in professional development. *Reforming teaching globally*, 17, 21-53.

Patterson, M. E. & Williams, D. R. (2002). Collecting and analyzing qualitative data: Hermeneutic principles, methods, and case examples. *Advances in Tourism Application Series*, 9, 127.

Patton, M. Q. (2002). *Qualitative research and evaluation methods* (3rd ed.). Sage Publications.

Patton, M. Q. (1990). *Qualitative evaluation and research methods* (2nd ed.). Sage Publications.

Pepper, S. (1996). *Radicalism and education reform in 20th-century China*. Cambridge University Press.

Perryman, J. (2006). Panoptic performativity and school inspection regimes: Disciplinary mechanisms and life under special measures. *Journal of Education Policy*, 21(2), 147-161.

Pescarmona, I. (2017). Reflexivity-in-action: How complex instruction can work for equity in the classroom. *Journal of Education for Teaching*, 43(3), 328-337. https://doi.org/10.1080/02607476.2017.1321673.

Pillen, M. T., Den Brok, P. J. & Beijaard, D. (2013). Profile and change in beginning teachers' professional identity tensions. *Teaching and Teacher Education*, 34, 86-97. https://doi.org/10.1016/j.tate.2013.04.003.

Polkinghorne, D. (1983). *Methodology for the human sciences: Systems of inquiry*. State University of New York Press.

Polkinghorne, D. (1988). *Narrative knowing and the human sciences*. State University of New York Press.

Polkinghorne, D. E. (2007). Validity issues in narrative research. *Qualitative Inquiry*, 13(4), 471-486. https://doi.org/10.1177/1077800406297670.

Prior, L. (2003). *Using documents in social research*. Sage publications

Publications.

Punch, K. (1998). *Introduction to social research: Quantitative and qualitative approaches*. Sage Publications.

Qian, H. Y. & Walker, A. (2013). How principals promote and understand teacher development under curriculum reform in China. *Asia-Pacific Journal of Teacher Education*, 41(3), 304-315. https://doi.org/10.1080/1359866X.2013.809056

Ranson, S. (2007). Public accountability in the age of neo-liberal governance. In *The Routledge Falmer reader in education policy and politics* (pp. 208-229). Routledge.

Río, P. & Álvarez, A. (2007). Inside and outside the zone of proximal development: An ecofunctional reading of Vygotsky. In H. Daniels, M. Cole & J. V. Wertsch (Eds.), *The Cambridge companion to Vygotsky* (pp. 276-303). Cambridge University Press.

Roberts, L. (2000). Shifting identities: An investigation into student and novice teachers' evolving professional identity. *Journal of Education for Teaching*, 26(2), 185-186. https://doi.org/10.1080/02607470050024748

Robertson, S. L. & Verger, A. (2012). *Public private partnerships in education: New actors and modes of governance in a globalizing world*. Edward Elgar Publishing.

Robson, C. (2002). *Real world research: A resource for social scientists and practitioner-researchers* (2nd ed.). Blackwell Publishing.

Ryan, G. W. & Bernard, H. R. (2003). Techniques to identify themes. *Field Methods*, 15, 85-109. https://doi.org/10.1177/1525822X02239569

Sachs, J. (2003). *The activist teaching profession*. Open University Press.

Sachs, J. (2005). Teacher education and the development of professional identity: Learning to be a teacher. In P. Denicolo & M. Kompf (Eds.), *Connecting policy and practice: Challenges for teaching and learning in schools and universities* (pp. 3-15). Routledge.

Sammons, P., Day, C., Kington, A., Gu, Q., Stobart, G. & Smees, R. (2007). Exploring variations in teachers' work, lives and their effects on pupils: Key findings and implications from a longitudinal mixed-method study. *British Educational Research Journal*, 33(5), 681-701. https://doi.org/10.1080/01411920701582264.

Sargent, T.(2011). "New curriculum reform implementation and the transfor-mation of educational beliefs, practices, and structures in gansu province."*Chinese Education and Society*, 44(6), 49-74.

Sargent, T. (2012). Belief as the prerequisite to action: Curriculum reform and the transformation of teaching conceptions in rural China. In H. B. Yin & J. C. K. Lee (Eds.), *Curriculum reform in China* (pp. 123-140). Nova Science Publishers, Inc.

Sassen, S. (2000). Spatialities and temporalities of the global: Elements for a theorization. *Public Culture*, 12, 215-232. https://doi.org/10.1215/08992363-12-1-215.

Sautman, B. (1991). Politicization, hyperpoliticization, and depoliticization of Chinese education. *Comparative Education Review*, 35(4), 669-689.

Scartezini, R. A. & Carles, M. (2018). The development of university teachers' professional identity: A dialogical study. *Research Papers in Education*, 33(1), 42-58. https://doi.org/10.1080/02671522.2016.1225792.

Schwandt, T. A. (2000). Three epistemological stances for qualitative inquiry: Interpretivism, hermeneutics, and social constructivism. In N. K. Denzin & Y. S. Lincoln (Eds.), *Handbook of Qualitative Research* (2nd ed., pp. 189-213). Sage Publications.

Sennett, R. (1998). *The corrosion of character: The personal consequences of work in the new capitalism*. W. W. Norton & Company.

Shandong Provincial Education Department. (2015). Notice on solving the problem related to overcrowded classrooms in urban areas. Retrieved from http://www.sdedu.gov.cn/sdjy/_zcwj/706379/index.html.

Shanghai Education Science Research Institute. (2004). Approaches and policies for the development of private education in China. Retrieved from http://www.sdei.com/a/zhengcefagui/2004/1027/11.html.

Skerrett, A. (2008). Biography, identity, and inquiry: The making of teacher, teacher educator, and researcher, *Studying Teacher Education*, 4(2), 143-156.

Smyth, J., Dow, A., Hattam, R., Reid, A. & Shacklock, G. (2000). *Teachers' work in a globalizing economy*. Falmer Press.

Soloman, J. & Tresman, S. (1999). A model for continued professional development: Knowledge, belief, and action. *Journal of In-Service Education*, 25(2), 307-318. https://doi.org/10.1080/13674589900200076.

Song, Y. (2012). Poverty reduction in China: The contribution of popularizing primary education. *China & World Economy*, 20(1), 105-122. https://doi.org/10.1111/j.1749-124X.2012.01284.x.

Stanford, B. H. (2001). Reflections of resilient, persevering urban teachers. *Teacher Education Quarterly*, 28, 75-87.

Steele, C. M. (1997). A threat in the air: How stereotypes shape intellectual identity and performance. *American Psychologist*, 52(6), 613-629.

Strauss, A. & Corbin, J. (1990). *Basics of qualitative research: Techniques and procedures for developing grounded theory* (2nd ed.). Sage Publications.

Su, Z., Hawkins, J. N., Huang, T. & Zhao, Z. (2001). Choices and commitment: A comparison of teacher candidates' profiles and perspectives in China and the United States. *International Review of Education*, 47(6), 611-635. https://doi.org/10.1023/A:1012790025798.

Sutherland, L. & Markauskaite, L. (2012). Examining the role of authenticity in supporting the development of professional identity: An example from teacher education. *Higher Education*, 64(6), 747-766. https://doi.org/10.1007/s10734-012-9516-3.

Sutton, M. & Levinson, B. A. U. (2001). *Policy as practice: Toward a comparative sociocultural analysis of educational policy*. Ablex Publishing.

Tashakkori, A. & Teddlie, C. (1998). *Mixed methodology: Combining qualitative and quantitative approaches*. Sage Publications.

Taylor, C. (1971). Interpretation and the science of man. *The Review of Metaphysics*, 25(1), 3-51.

Taylor, C. (1994). *Multiculturalism and the politics of recognition*. Princeton University Press.

Taylor, L. A. (2017). How teachers become teacher researchers: Narratives as a tool for teacher identity construction. *Teaching and Teacher Education*, 61, 16-25. https://doi.org/10.1016/j.tate.2016.10.001.

Terwee, S. J. S. (1990). *Hermeneutics in psychology and psychoanalysis*. Springer.

The State Council of the People's Republic of China. (2017). 国务院关于鼓励社会力量兴办教育促进民办教育健康发展的若干意见[*Several opinions of The State Council on Encouraging Social Forces in Education and Promoting the Healthy Development of Minban Education*]. Retrieved from https://www.gov.cn/zhengce/content/2017-01/18/content_5160828.htm.

Thi Tran, L. & Thi Nguyen, N. (2013). Mediating teacher professional identity: The emergence of humanness and ethical identity. *International Journal of Training Research*, 11(3), 199-212.

Thomas, G. (2011). *The meaning of theory*. British Education Research Association Online Resource. Retrieved from http://www.bera.ac.uk.

Thomas, S. (2005). The construction of teacher identities in educational policy documents: A critical discourse analysis. *Melbourne Studies in Education*, 46 (2), 25-44.

Thomson, S. (1997). Adaptive sampling in behavioral surveys. In L. Harrison & A. Hughes (Eds.), *The validity of self-reported drug use: Improving the accuracy of survey estimates* (NIDA Research Monograph 167, pp. 296-319). Rockville, MD: National Institute on Drug Abuse.

Tsang, W. K. (2004). Teachers' personal practical knowledge and interactive decisions. *Language Teaching Research*, 8(2), 163-198. https://doi.org/10.1191/1362168804lr134oa.

Tsui, A. B. M. (2007). Complexities of identity formation: A narrative inquiry of an EFL teacher. *TESOL Quarterly*, 41(4), 657-680.

Tuckman, B. W. (1972). *Conducting educational research*. Holt, Rinehart and Winston.

Turner, L. & Tobbell, J. (2018). Learner identity and transition: An ethnographic exploration of undergraduate trajectories. *Journal of Further and Higher Education*, 42(5), 708-720.

Urrieta, L., Jr. & Noblit, W. G. (2018). *Cultural constructions of *identity*: *Meta-ethnography and theory*. Oxford University Press.

Varghese, M. M. (2000). *Bilingual teachers-in-the-making*: *Advocates, classroom teachers, and transients*. University of Pennsylvania.

Varghese, M., Morgan, B., Johnston, B. & Johnson, K. A. (2005). Theorizing language teacher identity: Three perspectives and beyond. *Journal of Language, Identity, and Education*, 4(1), 21-44.

Vescio, V., Ross, D. & Adams, A. (2008). A review of research on the impact of professional learning communities on teaching practice and student learning. *Teaching and Teacher Education*, 24(1), 80-91.

Vogt, W. P. (1999). *Dictionary of statistics and methodology*: *A nontechnical guide for the social sciences*. London: Sage publications.

Vygotsky, L. S. (1978). *Mind in society*: *The development of higher psychological processes*. Harvard University Press.

Walford, G. (1989). *Private schools in ten countries*: *Policy and practice*. Routledge.

Wang, F. Y. (2018). An expert EFL reading teacher's readers club: Reader identity and teacher professional development. *European Journal of Teacher Education*, 41(4), 517-528.

Wang, X. (2005). 中国民办教师始末[*Historical perspective of China's minban teachers*]. Zhejiang University.

Wang, Y. (2013). *Managing institutions*: *The survival of* minban *schools in the Chinese Mainland*. Cambridge Scholars Publishing.

Wang, L. (2014). *The road to privatization of higher education in China*: *A new cultural revolution?* Springer.

Wang, L., Lai, M. & Lo, L. N. K. (2014). Teacher professionalism under the recent reform of performance pay in China. *Prospects*, 44, 429-443.

Wang, F. Y. (2018). An expert EFL reading teacher's readers club: reader identity and teacher professional development. *European Journal of Teacher Education*, 41(4), 517-528.

Watt, H. M. G. & Richardson, P. W. (2007). Motivational factors influencing teaching as a career choice: Development and validation of the FIT-choice scale. *The Journal of Experimental Education*, 75(3), 167-202.

Webb, R., Vulliamy, G., Sarjar, A., Kimonen, E. & Nevalainen, R. (2004). A comparative analysis of primary teacher professionalism in England and Finland. *Comparative Education*, 40(1), 83-107.

Wedel, J. R., Chore, C., Feldman, G. & Lathrop, S. (2005). Toward an anthropology of public policy. *The ANNALS of the American Academy of Political and Social Science*, 600(30), 30-51.

Wellington, J. (2015). *Educational research: Contemporary issues and practical approaches*. Bloomsbury.

Wen, D. (2008). *The legitimacy crisis and reconstruction of converted schools*. Retrieved from http://www.cnsaes.org/homepage/saesmag/jyfzyj/2008/7/gj080706.htm.

Wen, W. (2009). *The formulation of China's education policy from 1978 to 2007*. University of Oxford.

Wenger, E. (1998). *Communities of practice: Learning, meaning, and identity*. Cambridge University Press.

Wenger, E. (2000). Communities of practice and social learning systems. *Organization*, 7(2), 225-246.

White, H. (1980). The value of narrativity in the representation of reality. *Critical Inquiry*, 7(1), 5-27.

Williams, A. (2003). Informal learning in the workplace: A case study of new teachers. *Educational Studies*, 29(2), 207-220.

Whitty, G., Power, S. & Halpin, D. (1998). *Devolution and choice in education: The school, the state and the market*. Open University Press.

Whitty, G. & Power, S. (2000). Marketization and privatization in mass education systems. *International Journal of Educational Development*, 20, 93-107.

Winter, G. (2000). A comparative discussion of the notion of validity in qualitative and quantitative research. *The Qualitative Report*, 4(3). Retrieved on October 16, 2014, from http://www.nova.edu/ssss/QR/QR4-3/winter.html.

Wood, P. (1979). *The divided school*. Routledge.

Woods, P. (1986). *Inside schools: Ethnography in educational research*. RoutledgeFalmer.

Woods, P. (1995). *Creative teachers in primary schools*. Open University Press.

Woods, P. & Carlyle, D. (2002). Teacher identities under stress: The emotions of separation and renewal. *International studies in Sociology of Education*, 12(2), 169-190.

Wu, H. (2012). *Private education in China-current conditions, issues and future prospects* [Lecture handout]. Seminar held on November 29, at China Centre, Oxford University.

Wu, X. (2011). *"I am only a migrant worker!" — A critical ethnographic study of private high school teachers*. Zhejiang Normal University.

Xu, G. & Ge, Y. (2003). *Implications of the Minban Education Promotion Law*. Retrieved from http://www.chinaelections.org/article/504/17325.html.

Yan, C. (2015). "We can't change much unless the exams change": Teachers' dilemmas in the curriculum reform in China. *Improving Schools*, 18(1), 5-19.

Yan, F. & Lin, X. (2004). *Minban education in China: Background and current situation*. Retrieved from http://www.tc.columbia.edu/centers/coce/pdf_files/b5.pdf.

Yan, Y. T. (2006). 国家与教师身份 [*The state and teacher identity*]. PhD Thesis, North East Normal University.

Yanow, D. (2000). *Conducting interpretive policy analysis*. Sage publications.

Yang, D. (2006). 中国教育的转型与发展 [*The transformation and development of China's education*]. Social Science Literature Publishing.

Yardley, L. (2000). Dilemmas in qualitative health research. *Psychology & Health*, 15(2), 215-228. https://doi.org/10.1080/08870440008400302

Yeager, D., Bundick, M. & Johnson, R. (2012). The role of future work goal motives in adolescent identity development: A longitudinal mixed-methods investigation. *Contemporary Educational Psychology*, 37, 206-217.

Yin, H. B. & Lee, J. C. K. (2011). Teachers' emotions and professional identity in curriculum reform: A Chinese perspective. *Journal of Educational Change*, 12(1), 25-46.

Yin, H. B. & Lee, J. C. K. (2012). Be passionate, but be rational as well: Emotional rules for Chinese teachers' work. *Teaching and Teacher Education*, 28(1), 56-65.

Yin, H. B., Lee, J. C. K. & Law, E. H. F. (2012). Emotion as a lens to understand teacher development in curriculum reform. In H. B. Yin & J. C. K. Lee (Eds.), *Curriculum reform in China* (pp. 1-10). Nova Science Publishers, Inc.

Zboralski, K. & Germunden, H. G. (2005). The impact of communities of practice. In E. Coakes & S. Clarke (Eds.), *Encyclopedia of communities of practice in information and knowledge management* (pp. 6-11). Information Science Reference.

Zembylas, M. (2003). Emotions and teacher identity: A poststructural perspective. *Teachers and Teaching*, 9(3), 213-238.

Zembylas, M. (2005). Discursive practices, genealogies, and emotional rules: A poststructuralist view on emotion and identity in teaching. *Teaching and Teacher Education*, 21(8), 935-948.

Zhang, W., Hu, X. & Pope, M. (2002). The evolution of career guidance and counseling in the People's Republic of China. *Career Development Quarterly*, 50(3), 226-236.

Zhong, Q. Q. (2006). Curriculum reform in China: Challenge and reflections. *Frontiers of Education in China*, 1(3), 370-382.

Zhou, J. (2014). Teacher education changes in China: 1974—2014. *Journal of Education for Teaching*, 40(5), 507-523.

Zhou, K., et al. (2016). Exploratory analysis of Chinese preservice PE teacher professional identity structure. *Research Quarterly for Exercise and Sport*, 87(2), 33-34.

Zhou & Tan. (2010). 教师流动问题研究 [*Research on the problem of teacher flow*]. Doctoral dissertation, Huazhong Technology University.

Zhu, H. (2005). The mismatch of concepts and behavior. *Continuing Education*, 17(1), 22-23.